International

International Marketing

L S WALSH

SECOND EDITION

THE M & E HANDBOOK SERIES

Pitman Publishing
128 Long Acre, London WC2E 9AN

A Division of Longman Group UK Limited

First published 1978
Second edition 1981
Reprinted 1983, 1986, 1987, 1988, 1989, 1990
Reprinted in this format 1991 (twice)

© Macdonald & Evans Ltd 1978, 1981

A CIP catalogue record for this book is available from the British Library.

ISBN 0 7121 1021 6

All rights reserved; no part of this publication may be reproduced, stored in a retrieval system, or transmitted in any form or by any other means, electronic, mechanical, photocopying, recording, or otherwise without either the prior written permission of the Publishers or a licence permitting restricted copying in the United Kingdom issued by the Copyright Licensing Agency, 90 Tottenham Court Road, London W1P 9HE. This book may not be lent, resold, hired out or otherwise disposed of by way of trade in any form of binding or cover other than that in which it is published, without the prior consent of the Publishers.

Founding Editor: P. W. D. Redmond

Printed and bound in Singapore

Preface

This book is concerned with international marketing, i.e. with those aspects of marketing management that are of special importance in an international context. The problems of marketing both across and within national boundaries are discussed; in other words, the book covers the whole field of international marketing, from indirect and direct export to the marketing operations of the multinational company.

As far as possible the book covers *only* international marketing: it avoids the more general aspects of marketing management, except for a brief explanatory introduction to those chapters where otherwise the reader unfamiliar with marketing theory might find himself at a disadvantage. *International Marketing* is thus likely to be of greatest interest to the domestic marketing executive taking over international responsibilities for the first time or to the student who already has a grasp of basic marketing principles.

Part I of the book presents the essential principles of international marketing, condensed into the form of study notes for ease of reference and comprehension. There has been no diversion into international trade theory on the one hand, or into the mechanics of exporting, e.g. transportation, documentation, insurance, etc., on the other. This is not because these subjects have no relevance to the international marketer, but because in these areas he is already well served by a number of excellent textbooks.

Part II examines briefly, by way of illustrating the general principles of international marketing set out in Part I, the problems of marketing in six specific countries which are all currently of real interest to the international marketer and likely to remain so for some time to come.

Part III consists of three brief case studies. Two of these are conventional in format and are intended principally as a basis for class discussion. The third case study gives a stage-by-stage account of the research and strategic planning undertaken by a major U.K. manufacturing group before entry into the West German market. The reader is given the opportunity to prepare his own solutions to the problems encountered at each stage before comparing them with the decisions actually taken by the company.

Paradoxically, any book concerned with international marketing must have a national orientation if it is to deal in more than generalisations; even the multinational company has a home base. This book is written quite deliberately from the point of view of the *U.K.-based* international marketer. For similar reasons it adopts, as a rule, the outlook of a manufacturing company, though much of the book will also be of relevance to service industries. Finally, it has aimed, whenever possible, at a practical and decision-making, rather than a merely descriptive, approach.

It is hoped, therefore, that *International Marketing* will prove of interest to the hard-pressed U.K. marketing executive with little time to read the more voluminous (and almost all American) works on the subject. As regards students, it is written primarily for the mature student undertaking his first formal course in marketing at a polytechnic or college of technology. Perhaps, too, the university student may find it of value as a supplement or introduction to the still limited range of U.K. textbooks available in this specialised area.

International Marketing draws extensively on the author's experience as an export manager, and, subsequently, as an international marketing consultant. But experience alone is never enough. A debt is owed, and is here acknowledged, to a variety of textbooks (most of which are mentioned in the bibliography or in the list of acknowledgments) and, inevitably of course, to a whole range of the invaluable publications of the British Overseas Trade Board.

The author would like to express his appreciation of the reception accorded to the first edition of this book and, in particular, of its inclusion in the recommended reading lists of the Diploma examinations of the Institute of Marketing and for the examinations of the C.A.M. Foundation and the Institute of Export. The examples used to illustrate the principles of international marketing seem to have been particularly welcomed and, where space has permitted, the opportunity has been taken to include one or two more such examples. A number of minor matters have been revised and updated. Regrettably, in the light of recent events, it has been thought best to omit the chapter on Iran.

July, 1981   L.S.W.

Acknowledgments

The author would like to record his sincere thanks to the authors and publishers listed below who so readily gave permission for the publication in *International Marketing* of extracts from their work.

He would also like to express his particular gratitude to those authorising the publication of the case studies, all of whom devoted much time and thought to consideration of the early drafts and made many valuable suggestions for their improvement.

Examples on the pages given below are quoted, with permission, from the publications mentioned. (Examples given in the text but not listed below are original to the author.)

Pages 4 and 5: Walsh, L. S., in *Modern Marketing Thought* (eds. Miracle and Albaum), Collier Macmillan, 1975.

Pages 14, 99 (second example), 102, 140 (all) and 154: I.T.I. Research, *Concentration on Key Markets: A Development Plan for Exports* [the Betro Report], Betro Trust Committee of the Royal Society of Arts, 1977.

Pages 24 and 25 (1): Cranch, G., "Research Resources Outside Europe: India", International Marketing Research Supplement, *Market Research Society Newsletter* No. 120, p. xxii, March, 1976.

Page 25 (2): Dunn, S. Watson, in *Handbook of Marketing Research* (ed. Ferber), McGraw-Hill, 1974.

Page 38: Piper, Julia, "Black Gold in the Nigerian Market Place", *Marketing*, p. 40, January, 1978.

Page 43: Robinson, R. D., "The Challenge of the Underdeveloped National Market", *Journal of Marketing*, p. 21, Vol. XXV, No. 6, October, 1961.

Page 61: "£25 Million Deal for Herbert", *The Sunday Times Business News*, p. 57, 18th December, 1977.

Page 75 (second and third examples): *Industrial Cooperation in Eastern Europe*, East European Trade Council, 1972.

Pages 110 (first example), 111 (second and third examples), and 112: Weigand, Robert E., "International Trade without Money", *Harvard Business Review*, p. 28, November/December, 1977.

Pages 110 (second example) and 111 (first example): Paulden, S., "How Barter Trading Works", *Marketing*, p. 39, April, 1977.

Page 118: Mason, H. R., Miller, R. R. and Weigel, D. R., *The Economics of International Business*, John Wiley and Sons, 1975.

Pages 121 and 124 (second example): Ash, B., *Tiger in Your Tank*, Cassell, 1969.

Page 124 (first example): Mauser, Ferdinand F., "Losing Something in Translation", *Harvard Business Review*, p. 14, July/August, 1977.

Page 134: Nuttall, Gwen, "Exporters Need Never Feel Out in the Cold", *The Sunday Times Business News*, p. 57, 6th November, 1977.

Page 143: Dixon, M., Jobs Column, *The Financial Times*, p. 14, 24th November, 1977.

Page 176: Poole, J., "Ins and Outs of Japan's Silent Trading War", *The Sunday Times Business News*, p. 62, 12th February, 1978.

Definitions quoted with permission from other publications are as follows.
Marketing (page 1): *Marketing*.
Multinational company (page 5): James C. Baker, in *Marketing in a Changing World* (ed. Morin), American Marketing Association, 1969.
Market research (page 15), *trade mark* (page 44), *brand* (page 44), *advertising* (page 120), *sales promotion* (page 129), and *public relations* (page 129): Alexander, Ralph S., et al., *Marketing Definitions: A Glossary of Marketing Terms*, American Marketing Association, 1960.

Figures and text have been reproduced with permission as follows.
Figure 4: *Market Research Society Newsletter*, No. 142, 1978, and the advertisers mentioned.
Figure 7: Wadinambiaratchi, G., in *The Marketing Channel* (ed. Mallen), John Wiley and Sons, 1975.
Figure 12: adapted from *Retail Distribution in Japan*, British Overseas Trade Board, 1975.
Chapter XVI, **22**, (a)–(m): *Businessman's Guide to the Foreign Investment Review Act*, Government of Canada Foreign Investment Review Agency, 1975.

Where so indicated, questions have been reproduced with permission from recent examination papers of the Institute of Marketing, the Institute of Export and the C.A.M. Foundation. Quotations from *Concentration on Key Markets: A Development Plan for Exports*, Betro Trust Committee of the Royal Society of Arts, 1974, have been included in other questions as indicated. The quotation in Examination Question 5 of Chapter I (Appendix IV, page 236) is taken with permission from Kotler, Philip, *Marketing Management: Analysis, Planning and Control*, 2nd edition, Prentice-Hall, 1972.

The three case studies are published with permission as follows.

Chapter XXVI: Sr. Gilberto Huber, President, and the board of directors of Editôra de Guias (LTB) S.A., Rio de Janeiro.

Chapter XXVII: Mr. John Soper, Letraset International Ltd., London.

Chapter XXVIII: Mr. W. A. Hunter, Director of Corporate Communications, and Mr. Norman Burden, formerly Director of Group Marketing, CompAir Ltd., Slough, Berks.

Contents

Preface v
List of Illustrations xv
List of Tables xvi

Part One: PRINCIPLES OF INTERNATIONAL MARKETING

I *The International Marketing Concept* 1
   Marketing; International marketing

II *Strategic Decisions in International Marketing* 7
   Introduction; The international marketing decision; The market selection decision

III *International Market Research* 15
   Introduction; International research strategy; Desk research; Field research; Organising for international market research

IV *International Product Decisions I: Product Policy* 33
   Introduction; Product modification; New product development; Product elimination

V *International Product Decisions II: Packaging, Labelling, Servicing and Trade Marks* 41
   Packaging; Labelling; Servicing; Trade Marks

VI *International Distribution Decisions I: Alternative Channels* 47
   Introduction; Channels between nations; Channels within nations

VII *International Distribution Decisions II: Indirect Export* — 54
   Export houses; U.K. buying offices; Co-operative export marketing

VIII *International Distribution Decisions III: Direct export* — 62
   Sales direct to customer; International trading companies abroad; Agencies; Distributors and stockists; Branch offices; Marketing subsidiary abroad

IX *International Distribution Decisions IV: Joint Ventures* — 70
   Licensing; Franchising; Industrial co-operation agreements; Contract manufacture; Management contract

X *International Distribution Decisions V: Manufacture Abroad* — 79
   The initial investment decision; Location of investment; Assembly operations; Joint ventures; Acquisition of a company abroad

XI *International Distribution Decisions VI: Foreign-Market Channel Design and Management* — 90
   Channel design; Channel management

XII *International Pricing Decisions I: Pricing Strategies* — 97

XIII *International Pricing Decisions II: Export Pricing* — 102
   The export quotation; Marginal-cost pricing; Devaluation; Barter trading

XIV *International Pricing Decisions III: Foreign-Market Pricing Decisions* — 115
   Government influences on pricing; International transfer pricing

XV	*International Communications I:* *Media Advertising* Introduction; Standardisation The advertising message; Advertising media; Advertising agency selection	120
XVI	*International Communications II:* *Sales Promotion and Public Relations* Introduction; Sales promotion in general; Exhibitions; Store promotions; Public relations	129
XVII	*International Communications III:* *International Sales Management* Introduction; The travelling sales force; The export salesman abroad; The national sales force	138
XVIII	*International Communications IV:* *Agency Sales* Agency search; Agency selection; The agency agreement; Agency motivation	146
XIX	*Organising For International Marketing* Introduction; The export department; The international division; Multinational organisation	156

PART TWO: MARKETING IN SELECTED COUNTRIES

XX	*Marketing in Brazil*	169
XXI	*Marketing in Japan*	175
XXII	*Marketing in Nigeria*	181
XXIII	*Marketing in the U.S.A.*	185
XXIV	*Marketing in the U.S.S.R.*	189
XXV	*Marketing in the Federal Republic of Germany*	194

Part Three: CASE STUDIES

XXVI	*Editôra de Guias (LTB) S.A.: A Brazilian Sales Force*	199
XXVII	*Letraset in N. America; A Contrast in Distribution Strategies* Letraset Ltd.; Letraset Canada Ltd.; Letraset in the U.S.A.	205
XXVIII	*CompAir Ltd.: Entry into the West German Market*	214

Appendixes
I Bibliography 229
II Addresses of Organisations Mentioned in the Text 231
III Examination Technique 233
IV Examination Questions 236
Index 249

List of Illustrations

1.	International marketing: the five major decisions	8
2.	Geographical market segmentation on a global scale	13
3.	International research strategy: a stage-by-stage approach	18
4.	Omnibus surveys abroad	19
5.	Distribution channels between nations (direct and indirect export)	50
6.	Distribution channels between nations (manufacture abroad)	51
7.	Typical wholesale–retail distribution patterns	91
8.	Marketing organisation structures	158
9.	Development of export function as export sales increase	160
10.	The international division: functional and regional organisation	162
11.	Multinational company organisation	167
12.	Typical wholesale–retail distribution system in Japan	177
13.	The Letraset dry transfer process	206
14.	CompAir's product lines	216 and 217
15.	CompAir Ltd. research terms of reference	219
16.	CompAir Ltd. research design	222

List of Tables

I	Systematic desk research: guides to information sources in the U.S.A.	22
II	International market research: agency selection	28 and 29
III	B.O.T.B. assistance for market research abroad	30
IV	Alternative international product modification strategies	34
V	Comparison of typical characteristics of U.K. export houses	55
VI	Some central purchasing agencies and groups covering department and variety stores in France	63
VII	CompAir's competitors	223

PART ONE

THE PRINCIPLES OF INTERNATIONAL MARKETING

CHAPTER I

The International Marketing Concept

MARKETING

1. Definition of marketing. As marketing has developed as a technique, numerous definitions have been offered. Today there are several different, authoritative and entirely acceptable definitions. The U.K. Institute of Marketing defines marketing as: "the management process responsible for identifying, anticipating and satisfying customer requirements profitably".

2. The essentials of marketing. Whatever the formal definition, it is generally accepted that true marketing requires, on the part of the supplying organisation:

(*a*) a genuine attention to customers' needs and wants (usually a specific target segment is selected);
(*b*) satisfaction of those needs and wants *at a profit*;
(*c*) orientation of the whole organisation towards the customer-satisfaction process.

3. The marketing mix. Marketing includes such business activities as:

(*a*) *the planning and development of products* that customers require, with appropriate packaging and support services, e.g. repair facilities;
(*b*) *the distribution of those products* through appropriate channels, e.g. wholesalers, retailers, etc., which will provide the services required by the customers;
(*c*) *the establishment of prices* which offer both value to the customers and a satisfactory profit for the supplier;
(*d*) *promotion of the products*, including advertising, sales promotion, public relations and personal selling.

These four activities (often referred to as product, place, price and promotion) constitute the *marketing mix*. They include, in summary, all the elements of marketing decision-making under the supplier's control, i.e. *controllables*.

4. The marketing environment. The marketer must also take into account environmental factors over which he has no control, i.e. *uncontrollables*, but which will significantly affect the degree of success he achieves. These environmental factors include:

(*a*) *economic development;*
(*b*) *technological development;*
(*c*) *social and cultural influences;*
(*d*) *political and legal decisions;*
(*e*) *business practices and institutions;*
(*f*) *competitive activity.*

The task of marketing management is to formulate and implement the marketing mix which will enable the organisation to adapt to its environment in such a way that its profit and other objectives are achieved as nearly as possible.

INTERNATIONAL MARKETING

5. The international marketing environment. The task of international marketing management is, similarly, to adapt the marketing mix to the environment, but in this case the environment is vastly changed. Although environmental differences may readily be discerned *within* any one nation, those differences *between* nations are, as a rule, far more marked.

(*a*) *Economic development.* There is, of course, a striking disparity in levels of economic development between nations, from subsistence economies still dependent on primitive agriculture, through nations relying largely on raw-material exports (Chile) and industrialising nations (Brazil), to the industrialised economies of North America and Western Europe.

(*b*) *Technological development.* Each country has developed to a different technological level. The marketer is concerned not merely with high-level technology but with the whole range of technology, right down to manpower skills.

(*c*) *Social and cultural influences.* Adaptation to social and cultural differences between nations is a major concern of the international marketer, particularly in advertising and promotion.

(d) *Political and legal decisions.* Some governments may be hostile to imports, or even to foreign investment; other countries may actively encourage investment from abroad. These attitudes may change suddenly in politically unstable countries; expropriation is to be feared. Price controls or exchange restrictions may be imposed.

(e) *Business practices and institutions.* As regards business practices, reference need only be made to the fundamentally opposed views held in the U.S.A. (*see* XXIII) and Soviet Russia (*see* XXIV). As regards institutions the field is wide, but banks may be taken as an example: in some Western European countries banks play a much more direct and influential role in business than, say, in the U.K.

(f) *Competitive activity.* The international marketer may face different competitors in different countries. In some, local competition may be well entrenched, perhaps enjoying governmental (or customer) discrimination in its favour.

6. International aspects of marketing. The environmental differences summarised above, significant though they are, do not imply any fundamental change in marketing as a technique. There still remains a basic similarity of human motivation and economic practice throughout the world. The *principles* of marketing are of universal application.

International environmental differences, however, do require a change of emphasis. Certain aspects of marketing that are largely irrelevant in a purely national context, such as barter trading (*see* XIII, **14**) achieve real importance. Other aspects of marketing require, in international trade, a far more detailed knowledge than might be necessary within any one nation, e.g. licensing (*see* IX, **2**), joint ventures (*see* IX and X, **15**) and the use of agents in the selling function (*see* XVIII).

It is with these special international aspects of marketing, and as far as possible with these aspects only, that this book is concerned.

7. Definition of international marketing. Although "international marketing" is a common enough expression among marketers, there is no generally accepted formal definition. It is perhaps best regarded as a shorthand expression for the special international aspects of marketing already discussed (*see* **6**).

An appropriate formal definition of international marketing however, might be:

(*a*) the marketing of goods and services across national frontiers; *and*

(*b*) the marketing operations of an organisation that sells and/or produces within a given country when:

(*i*) that organisation is part of, or associated with, an enterprise which also operates in other countries; *and*

(*ii*) there is some degree of influence on or control of that organisation's marketing activities from outside the country in which it sells and/or produces.

It is in this sense that the expression international marketing is used throughout this book, i.e. covering the whole gamut of international marketing operations, from indirect export on the one hand to the marketing operations of multinational companies (*see* **9**) on the other.

8. The international marketing approach. Another view is that international marketing is simply an attitude of mind, the approach of a company with a truly global outlook, seeking its profit impartially around the world, "home" market included, on a planned and systematic basis. The following passage illustrates this point of view.

EXAMPLES: (1) International marketing offers a difference in basic philosophy: it starts with world markets, including the U.K., and aims to maximise profits from these markets. It takes a global and profit-oriented view. It will still be concerned—vitally concerned—with export marketing, but it will be actively seeking wider profit opportunities. How many successful *exporting* companies could make more money by investment in productive capacity overseas? How many have considered the advantages of third-country manufacture, combining low labour costs with access to otherwise protected markets? How many, if capital costs are a problem, have considered local contract manufacture, or have actively sought local partners in a joint venture? How many have taken into account the benefits from international transfer pricing? How often do companies seriously consider component assembly abroad in low-labour-cost areas? How often does the make-or-buy decision take into account components from abroad? How many quite small companies are neglecting opportunities of obtaining profitable licences for their research or even simple design skills? How many such companies, having sold one or two such licences, almost by chance, fail to seek further licences on a systematic basis? How many more have sold such licences without adequate market research, leaping at the chance of a short-term gain, only to find their licensee taking the lion's share of the profits? How many exporting companies regularly take advantage of the established distribution facilities of overseas manufacturers, but never even attempt to sell abroad the use of their own similarly established distribution network, a capital asset often of immense value to a would-be importer? How many companies import compatible but non-competitive products on their own account to make full use of their domestic distribution network?

(2) Another definition of international marketing is that it is the marketing function of multinational companies. Those mammoth prestigious corporations which, it is whispered with awe, wield more power than many a sovereign state. With no obvious national identity, and a polyglot executive staff, such companies sell their products in any or all of the world's markets, manufacture in perhaps a dozen or more countries where costs are lowest, make their profits in those countries where tax rates are most advantageous, and hold these profits in tax sanctuaries, or where interest rates are highest. The mistake many smaller companies make is to assume that the concept is of relevance only to these multinational giants, and that it has no advantages to offer to the vast majority of companies of more modest size.

9. The multinational company. The term multinational company is loosely used and has been variously defined.

As a minimum, a multinational company would have a manufacturing investment (or service operation) in at least one foreign country, and would also have adopted a global outlook, making its production, marketing and other decisions in the light of the options open to it anywhere in the world.

Many, however, would regard such a company as merely *international*. For them the term *multinational* implies, in addition, international operations of some significance (as is suggested by Example 2 above, which gives perhaps the popular view). For the purposes of this book the definition offered by James C. Baker is adopted.

The multinational corporation is defined as a company:

(*a*) which has a direct investment base in several countries; and

(b) which generally derives from 20 per cent to 50 per cent or more of its net profits from foreign operations; and
(c) whose management makes policy decisions based on the alternatives available anywhere in the world.

10. Transnational companies. Multinational companies are usually organised around a national headquarters, from which international control is exercised—they still have a national identity, even though their subsidiaries may not always care to allow that identity to obtrude in the markets they serve. Some authorities distinguish the *transnational* company, a multinational in which both ownership and control are also dispersed internationally: there is no principal domicile and no one central source of power. Examples are Royal Dutch–Shell and Unilever.

PROGRESS TEST 1

1. What is marketing? **(1)**
2. What are the three essential characteristics of a market-oriented organisation? **(2)**
3. What is meant by the "marketing mix"? **(3)**
4. What is meant by the "marketing environment"? **(4)**
5. How does the international marketing environment differ from the domestic marketing environment? **(5)**
6. What is international marketing? **(7)**
7. How would you define the term "multinational company"? **(9)**
8. What is a transnational company? **(10)**

CHAPTER II

Strategic Decisions in International Marketing

INTRODUCTION

1. The major international marketing decisions. When a company contemplates marketing abroad, or expanding existing international marketing activity, management faces five major decisions:

(a) *the international marketing decision*, i.e. the initial and fundamental decision on whether or not to market (or expand) abroad;

(b) *the market selection decision*, i.e. determination of which market(s) to enter;

(c) *the market entry decision*, i.e. determination of the most appropriate methods of entry into those markets, e.g. exporting, licensing, manufacture abroad;

(d) *the marketing mix decision*, i.e. planning and implementing a marketing mix appropriate to the market environment;

(e) *the organisation decision*, i.e. determining the appropriate organisation structures.

All these decisions must be taken on an informed basis, and some of the required information will arise from market research and forecasting procedures.

These five major decisions are shown diagrammatically in Fig. 1. Together with market research, they represent the international aspects of marketing covered in Part I of this book.

It will be realised that the first three decisions, (a)–(c), are interdependent. For instance, the various methods of market entry open to a company in respect of a given country, and the amount of investment and risk each implies, will influence the company's decision on whether or not to enter that market. Similarly, the possibility of entering a potentially highly profitable market will influence a company's decision on whether to market abroad at all. However, for the sake of simplicity, each decision is separately considered.

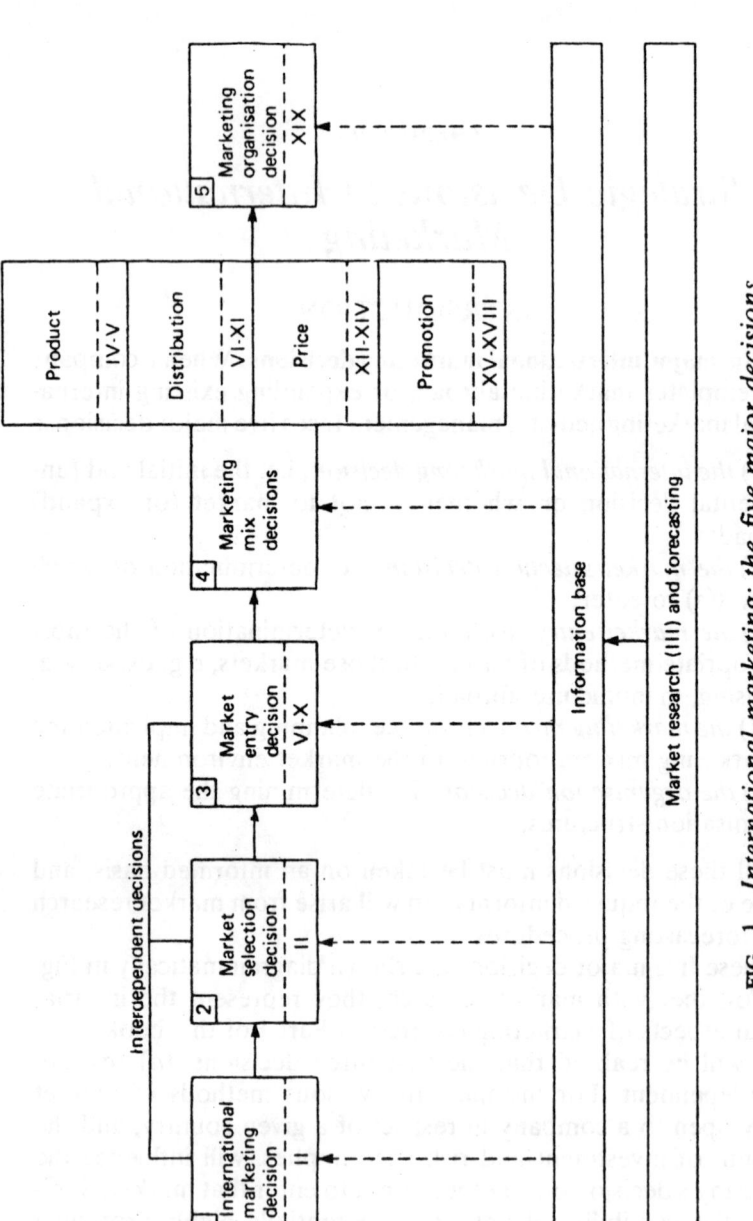

FIG. 1 *International marketing: the five major decisions*
(Roman numerals refer to chapter numbers.)

II. STRATEGIC DECISIONS IN INTERNATIONAL MARKETING 9

2. Market forecasting. Forecasting future market potential is inevitably more difficult internationally than in the domestic market. The forecaster will be less well acquainted with the economic, political and cultural background or with the current business climate, and the impact of local competition will be particularly difficult to assess. To the extent, therefore, that forecasting is based on judgmental factors, the international marketer must be prepared to allow a greater margin for error—and there is little he can do to remedy the situation.

Further, to the extent that the forecast relies on quantitative techniques (and given that the special problems of international data collection are considered under the heading of market research), international forecasting becomes simply the manipulation of data within the home company. It offers no distinctive international characteristics or techniques.

Forecasting is therefore not considered further in this book.

THE INTERNATIONAL MARKETING DECISION

3. The importance of planning. Some companies drift into international marketing, often as a result of an approach from potential customers or would-be agents; an organisation and a coherent policy then gradually develop from the stimulus of events. Often the results are by no means unsatisfactory, but they are usually sub-optimal; occasionally the early drifting gives rise to expensive complications in the future (*see* **XXVII**).

The international marketer should plan logically, step by step, with one eye on the current situation and the other on the possible future implications of his actions.

4. General considerations. Many arguments are put forward in favour of "going international", and to most of them it is not difficult to find a counter-argument.

(*a*) *Arguments in favour of international marketing.*
(*i*) Profit margins are often higher abroad; while, even if *margins* are lower, *total* sales, and *total* profit in absolute terms should increase.
(*ii*) Sales volume may increase to a level offering significant reductions in cost per unit.
(*iii*) The product life cycle is extended as the product is introduced into new markets.

(*iv*) Seasonal fluctuations in demand may be evened out by sales in the southern hemisphere.

(*v*) At worst, exporting offers opportunities for marginal-cost pricing (*see* XIII, **6**) in times of low domestic demand.

(*vi*) Internationalism spreads the risks inherent in any business, e.g. tax changes in the domestic market become less significant.

(*vii*) Obsolescent products can be sold off overseas without detriment to the home market.

(*viii*) A global, rather than a national, image gives prestige.

(*ix*) It is in the national interest to export.

(*x*) Research and development costs may be amortised over a larger turnover.

(*xi*) Growth may be easier, especially where domestic demand has reached saturation point or where a company is approaching a monopoly position (*see* XIV, **5**).

(*xii*) Foreign competition is a yardstick by which to measure efficiency—it keeps a company fighting fit.

(*b*) *Arguments against international marketing.*

(*i*) Profits are at the mercy of the exchange rate (for exporters) or political whim (for investment overseas).

(*ii*) The product modifications required for successful marketing abroad may be such that the hoped-for economies of scale are not achieved.

(*iii*) If the product is nearing the end of its life cycle, it may be preferable to devote resources to developing new products, rather than endeavouring to export obsolescent products.

(*iv*) Exact reverse seasonal patterns are not easy to find and markets that do offer such seasonal patterns may not be the most attractive in other respects.

(*v*) Anti-dumping duties (*see* XIII, **8**) are being imposed rather more promptly than was formerly the case, so that marginal-cost pricing becomes increasingly difficult.

(*vi*) Internationalism also brings risks of its own, often far greater than any encountered in the domestic market (e.g. expropriation).

(*vii*) Whether or not an international image brings prestige, prestige in itself is of no value unless it leads to increased profit.

(*viii*) Whatever the *national* need for exports, it is not necessarily in the *company's* interest to export; while it may be doubted whether exporting at a loss is in anyone's interest.

II. STRATEGIC DECISIONS IN INTERNATIONAL MARKETING

5. The essential justification for international marketing.

(*a*) *Opportunities*. The general considerations outlined above are only a background to the international marketing decision. Logically, that decision must be based on the opportunities open to the company abroad. These opportunities *must* be greater than those available in the home market (if only to compensate for the extra uncertainty and risk of trading abroad), either:

(*i*) because they are in themselves specially attractive in terms of likely profit; or

(*ii*) because there is a general lack of opportunity in the home market.

(*b*) *Resources*. The international marketer must also consider whether his company has the managerial, financial and other resources necessary to market abroad. A small company may be much better advised to limit itself at most to indirect exporting (*see* VII). Further consideration should be given to international operations only if opportunities appear favourable *and* the company has the resources to take advantage of them.

THE MARKET SELECTION DECISION

6. Differentiated, undifferentiated and concentrated marketing. Three alternative strategies are open to any marketer.

(*a*) *Undifferentiated marketing*. With a strategy of undifferentiated marketing a company offers a standard product and endeavours to attract the largest possible number of buyers with a standard marketing programme. It hopes in this way to minimise both its production and its marketing costs.

(*b*) *Differentiated marketing*. With a strategy of differentiated marketing a company segments its market. It still operates in all or several segments of the market but modifies both products and marketing programmes to achieve maximum customer appeal within each segment. This naturally increases both production and marketing costs, but the company hopes to more than recover its additional expenditure as a result of increased market response.

(*c*) *Concentrated marketing*. With a strategy of concentrated marketing a company devotes its whole marketing effort to one market segment, or to a very few segments, i.e. the segment(s) it believes will prove most profitable, and designs its products and marketing programme accordingly. The aim is maximum exploitation of a very limited market area, and the strategy is likely to appeal most, of course, to companies with limited resources.

Segmentation may be based on a variety of market or customer characteristics (geographic, demographic, buyer behaviour, etc.). Geographic segmentation is naturally of special importance to international marketing strategy, and this is illustrated in Fig. 2.

7. Undifferentiated marketing. In an international context undifferentiated marketing implies one standard marketing mix world-wide (*see* Fig. 2(*a*)). Only a very limited number of companies can offer the appropriate product lines, or have the necessary resources, to attempt genuine exploitation of world markets on this basis, though such companies can be found.

> EXAMPLE: Coca Cola is a standard beverage, bottled to strict standards of conformity by local distributors, whose advertising campaigns are planned in advance at the company's American headquarters.

8. Differentiated marketing. Differentiated marketing on a world scale implies that a company has identified very different market needs in various parts of the world and is endeavouring to gear its marketing mix to the needs of each market. This is a mammoth task which is rarely practicable unless it is associated with a high degree of company decentralisation (*see* Fig. 2(*b*)).

9. Concentrated marketing. The two preceding strategies imply that a company endeavours to exploit the world market, or much of it. A strategy of concentration would aim at thorough exploitation of a very limited number of markets, those few that offer the greatest profit opportunity (*see* Fig. 2(*c*)).

10. Choice of strategy. The decision as to which strategy to adopt is for every individual company to take. As a general rule, however, it can be stated that, *internationally, most companies would do well to adopt a strategy of concentration on a limited number of key markets.* The field is too wide, and most companies' resources are too limited, to permit of any other approach.

It may also be reasonably asserted that too few companies adopt such a strategy of concentration. Particularly in the field of exports, many companies cover too many markets: they are really engaged in haphazard export selling rather than a planned and profit-maximising marketing operation. Certainly, in the case of British exporters, this view is supported by the Betro report

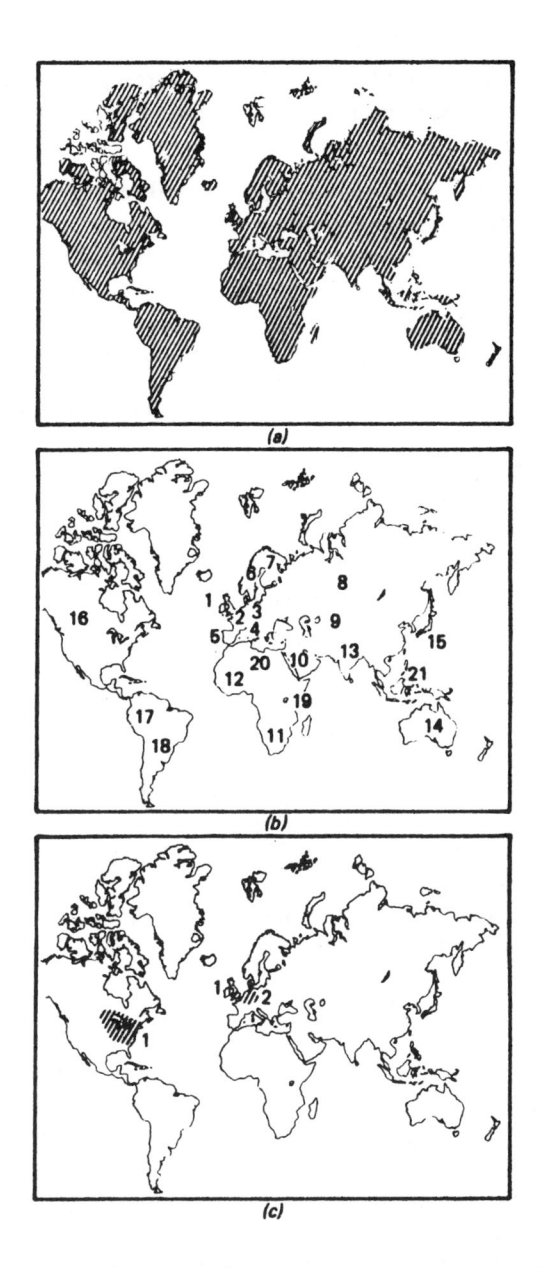

FIG. 2 *Geographical market segmentation on a global scale*

(*a*) Undifferentiated marketing. One standard marketing mix worldwide. (*b*) Differentiated marketing. Each number indicates a different marketing mix. (*c*) Concentrated marketing. Each number indicates a different marketing mix.

Concentration on Key Markets, which covered companies responsible for some 25 per cent of total U.K. exports of manufactures. It concluded that:

> EXAMPLE: Many British companies sell to too many markets. Most of the companies interviewed—large and small—are over-extended and are trying to do too much (in relation to the manpower and other resources available). They would be better off if they concentrated on fewer countries but more intensively.... Virtually all companies would benefit from identifying the five or six best markets and preparing special annual marketing plans for a particularly concentrated drive.

11. Selection of key markets. It is, of course, essential that a company adopting a strategy of concentrated marketing should select, out of all the markets open to it, the market(s) offering the highest profit potential. Thus the company will need to estimate for a number of possible markets:

(*a*) the current and future size of the market;
(*b*) its own market share;
(*c*) its own relevant current and likely future manufacturing costs.

On this basis it can calculate its likely return.

As described, the process is simple enough—deceptively so, for it is no mean task in any *one* market and will often involve heavy expenditure on market research.

The following chapter suggests how that research task might be most economically undertaken (*see* III, **5–14**).

PROGRESS TEST 2

1. What are the five major decisions facing the management of a company that is planning to market its products abroad for the first time? **(1)**
2. What general arguments can you adduce for and against a company's involvement in exporting? **(4, 5)**
3. What is meant by "undifferentiated marketing", "differentiated marketing" and "concentrated marketing"? **(6)**
4. How should a company select its markets abroad? **(11)**

CHAPTER III
International Market Research

INTRODUCTION

1. Market research. Market research has been defined as "the systematic gathering, recording, analysis and interpretation of data on problems relating to the market for, and the marketing of, goods and services".

2. Desk research and field research. "Data gathering" may be considered under two headings: desk research and field research.

(*a*) *Desk research* (also known as secondary or bibliographical research) involves the location and examination of available (usually published) data of relevance to the research project.

(*b*) *Field research* (also known as primary or original research) involves obtaining information from informants by means of interviews, questionnaires, etc. As a method of information collection it is inevitably many times more expensive than the comparatively simple desk research.

3. Consumer research and industrial research.

(*a*) Consumer research is market research directed to individuals (i.e. the ultimate consumers or potential consumers of the goods or services).

(*b*) Industrial research is market research directed to organisations (e.g. companies, government departments). There are significant differences in technique between the two categories.

This chapter covers generally both consumer and industrial research, mentioning technique differences only when they are of particular relevance to international research.

4. Market research projects. Most market research projects will follow a logical sequence:

(*a*) definition of the market problem (or opportunity);
(*b*) decision on whether or not market research can assist in the solution of the problem;

(c) if so, careful definition of the objectives and scope of the research;
(d) preparation of detailed terms of reference;
(e) information collection;
(f) information analysis and interpretation;
(g) research report and conclusions;
(h) marketing decision.

Most of these stages will vary little, whether the research is undertaken at home or abroad. Information collection, however, does require a significantly different approach internationally, in relation to both desk research and field research.

After an initial discussion of international research strategy, this chapter covers the international aspects of desk and field research.

INTERNATIONAL RESEARCH STRATEGY

5. Marketing strategies. Few companies are in a position to adopt a strategy of undifferentiated or differentiated marketing on a world-wide scale (*see* II, **6**); most companies will prefer a concentrated marketing strategy, selecting a limited number of markets for thorough exploitation. Under these circumstances it is vital that they should select, out of all the markets open to them, those few that offer the highest profit potential.

The selection of these most profitable markets cannot be arbitrary or haphazard. It must result logically from a factual appraisal of all markets open to the company. Such an appraisal is likely to rely heavily on market research.

A full programme of research in all world markets would, however, prove hopelessly uneconomic. What is required is some systematic procedure which:

(a) is based principally on the relatively inexpensive desk research (most of which can be satisfactorily undertaken within the U.K.);
(b) initially covers all potential markets;
(c) then eliminates in successive stages the less suitable markets; and
(d) ranks the remaining markets in some reasonable order of priority.

The vastly more expensive field research can then be under-

III. INTERNATIONAL MARKET RESEARCH 17

taken in these few priority markets before a decision is made to enter one or more markets.

6. Research procedure. Such a systematic procedure is illustrated in Fig. 3. The research stages are explained in greater detail below (*see* 7–13).

7. Accessibility. The first step is to list all markets that might conceivably offer potential. These markets are then assessed as to their degree of accessibility in terms of tariff and non-tariff barriers. This step is usually straightforward. Information on tariffs and non-tariff barriers can be obtained from the Overseas Tariffs and Regulations Section, Export Data Branch of the Department of Trade and (if the barriers are technical regulations) from T.H.E. (Technical Help to Exporters). This first stage alone will usually eliminate a large number of markets entirely. Other markets will remain to be considered only in relation to some form of local manufacture, assembly, or licensing (*see* IX and X).

8. Profitability. At this stage the minimum requirement is a knowledge of local market prices for comparison with the manufacturer's landed cost. Price details may well be unobtainable in the U.K. but can often be readily obtained by correspondence. In the case of certain products, however, as with some industrial goods, reliable price information may prove difficult to obtain. It may then be preferable to defer price consideration until market sizes have been examined (thus almost certainly leaving fewer markets to consider from a price viewpoint).

9. Market size. A broad approximation of market size and potential is adequate at this stage. In the case of consumer goods this can often be reasonably assessed from published statistics covering population, per capita income, private consumption expenditure, etc. Statistics will also usually be available for broad categories of industrial goods (steel products, cement, etc.).

For many industrial goods, however, even an approximate estimate of the size of the market can present a difficult problem. Some ingenuity will often be required in arriving at an estimate of market size on the basis of available statistics. In some cases the problem will only be resolved by original research.

10. Desk research abroad. Up to this point, research will have been confined to the U.K. It will usually pay, however, to undertake further desk research in the now limited number of markets

```
◄── NUMBER OF MARKETS UNDER CONSIDERATION ──►
```

7	Consider market accessibility (desk research)
8	Consider profitability (desk research)
9	Consider market size (desk research)

It will sometimes be preferable to take stages **8** and **9** in reverse order

DESK RESEARCH IN U.K.

10	Desk research abroad
11	Field research (omnibus survey)
12	Initial field research
13	Main field research

DESK AND FIELD RESEARCH ABROAD

Marketing plan

Market entry

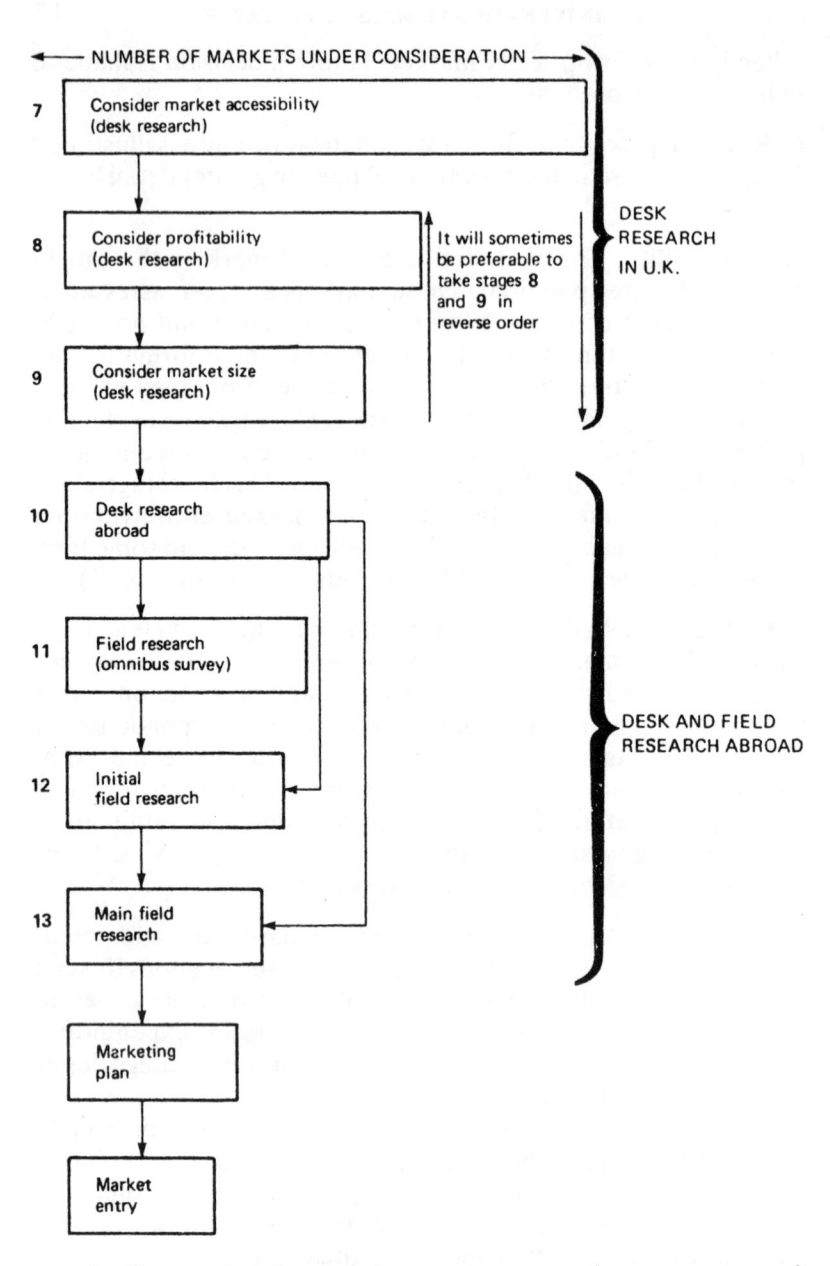

FIG. 3 *International research strategy: a stage-by-stage approach aimed at selection of the markets of greatest potential at the lowest possible research cost*

(**7–13** refer to the text.)

III. INTERNATIONAL MARKET RESEARCH

still under consideration before embarking on expensive field research.

11. Omnibus surveys. Even now it may be undesirable to commission a major programme of field research. In particular, the consumer researcher requiring only limited data on one or two points crucial to the market-entry decision *may* find it will pay to take advantage of an omnibus survey (i.e. a survey undertaken at regular intervals on behalf of several clients, each of whom commissions a limited number of questions). Figure 4, taken from one issue of the Market Research Society's *Newsletter*, gives an indication of the nature and scope of the omnibus surveys.

12. Initial field research. For similar reasons an initial and limited programme of field research *may* be authorised in certain markets, again covering key points only.

FLEXIBUS
A multi-national omnibus service throughout Europe, the Americas, Australia, South Africa, the Far East. Sample details: all adult/household/housewife samples available in most countries. Sample sizes: from 500 upwards per country. Frequent fieldwork dates. Contact Ruth Pitcher/Gabi Coatsworth 01-903 8511. Telex: 923755.
RESEARCH SERVICES LTD
Station House, Harrow Road
Wembley, Middx HA9 6DE

EUROPEAN OMNIBUS

sample details all 9 EEC countries + Sweden, Denmark, Finland, Norway, Switzerland, Austria and Spain *field dates* weekly or fortnightly *rates* on application *contact* Gordon Heald 01-794 0461
GALLUP INTERNATIONAL RESEARCH INSTITUTES INC
202 Finchley Road, London NW3 6BL

MIDDLE EAST OMNIBUS

sample details 3,000 interviews (18+), random location in Iran, Lebanon, Kuwait, Saudi Arabia. Participants can subscribe to one or several countries *field dates* twice per annum *rates* on application *contact* George V Vassiliou.
MEMRB—MIDDLE EAST MARKETING RESEARCH BUREAU LTD PO Box 2098, Nicosia, Cyprus Tel 45413 Cables VASMARKET Telex 2488

SRG—MALAYSIA
Survey Research Malaysia conduct quarterly surveys of 1,000 housewives, offering omnibus facilities, with nationwide probability sample. Also available, at different intervals, are omnibus surveys of individuals. Extensive syndicated data available for over 60 products, some stretching back for 10 years. Call Euan Blauvelt 01-437 8555
SURVEY RESEARCH GROUP LTD
European Office, 27 Lexington Street, London W1R 3HQ

FIG. 4 *Omnibus surveys abroad (taken from advertisements in the Market Research Society's Newsletter, No. 142)*

13. Main field research. The main field research programme will thus be undertaken only in a limited number of markets, those offering the greatest chance of success. Such research may result in the elimination of yet further markets, but, where the research results are in favour of market entry, it must also provide sufficient information for the preparation of a marketing plan and subsequent entry into the market.

14. Applicability of the systematic approach. The systematic research procedure outlined above is, of course, particularly relevant to a company moving into international markets for the first time. It will readily be realised, however, that it is also of value to a company:

(*a*) contemplating expansion of its international operations;
(*b*) undertaking a periodic review of its existing markets.

The success of the approach depends, however, on thorough and competent desk research, which is considered below.

DESK RESEARCH

15. Desk research in the U.K. The research procedure outlined above (*see* 7–13) has emphasised a truism of all market research: desk research must be exhaustively undertaken before expensive field research is commissioned. Such exhaustive desk research is especially important in the international field, simply by reason of the sheer volume of data, let alone its relative unfamiliarity.

It is no part of the aim of this book to provide lists of documents that may or may not prove of value in any particular case. Rather is it the intention to suggest a systematic approach that can be adopted by all. Such an approach is outlined below.

(*a*) Examine all information available from internal company records and company personnel.

(*b*) Obtain competitors' catalogues (which will often provide not merely product, but also market, information).

(*c*) Consult specialist libraries. Two libraries of vital importance to the international researcher are the Department of Industry Statistics and Market Intelligence Library and the City Business Library, London.

(*d*) Consult the Department of Trade and relevant foreign embassies. The U.S. Embassy library can be particularly useful, while the U.S. Department of Commerce commissions market

III. INTERNATIONAL MARKET RESEARCH

research, publishing reports which are available in the U.K.

(*e*) Contact the major international organisations such as the United Nations, which often produce statistical information available from no other source.

(*f*) Consult relevant indexing and abstracting services.

(*g*) Consult systematically the various *guides to information sources*, i.e. directories or similar publications which, though offering no market information themselves, act as signposts to other reference works or organisations which may be able to provide that information. As a minimum, these guides should cover:

   (*i*) government and other official statistics;
   (*ii*) trade directories;
   (*iii*) trade associations;
   (*iv*) trade and technical magazines;
   (*v*) market survey reports previously published. There is, of course, no point in undertaking a market survey that has already been carried out by someone else.

Such information guides should be identified for any industrialised country in which research is undertaken, e.g. Table I gives an example covering the U.S.A. It is not always possible to adopt the same approach in the case of developing countries and the researcher may have to rely on more general data from the international sources already mentioned. For some developing countries, however, the Department of Trade has prepared booklets covering major statistical sources likely to be of interest to the U.K. company, e.g. *Sources of Statistics and Market Information 5–Ecuador.*

16. Desk research abroad. Desk research abroad should follow a similarly systematic approach, but a personal call on the national statistical office(s) will usually prove worthwhile. The addresses of these offices are given in the Department of Industry booklet *National Statistical Offices of Overseas Countries.*

In addition, once field research has begun, industrial research interviewers should make a point of asking informants specifically for details of any relevant published information.

17. Problems of international statistics. The procedure outlined above should enable the researcher to find his way through what would otherwise be a statistical morass. Nevertheless, the

Table I. Systematic desk research: guides to information sources in the U.S.A.

Information Sources	Guides to Information Sources	Publishers
U.S. Government statistics	*Statistical Abstract of the U.S.*	Bureau of the Census
	Bureau of the Census Catalog	Bureau of the Census
	Statistical Services of the U.S. Government	Bureau of the Budget
	American Statistics Index	Congressional Information Service
	Monthly Catalog of U.S. Government Publications	Government Printing Office
Directories	*Guide to American Directories*	McGraw-Hill, New York
Trade etc., associations	*Directory of National Trade and Professional Associations in the U.S.A.*	Potomac Books, Washington
Trade and technical magazines	*Standard Rate and Data*	Standard Rate and Data Service, Skokie, Illinois
	Directory of Newspapers and Periodicals	N. W. Ayer, Philadelphia
Published market research surveys	*Advertising Age*, market data issue	Advertising Publications, Chicago
	U.S. and Canadian Marketing Surveys and Services	C.H. Kline & Co., Fairfield, New Jersey
	International Directory of Published Market Research	British Overseas Trade Board, London
Indexing and abstracting service	*F. and S. Index of Corporations and Industries*	Predicasts Inc., Cleveland, Ohio

III. INTERNATIONAL MARKET RESEARCH

researcher should be continually on his guard; secondary data in many markets suffers from a number of serious shortcomings.

(*a*) Data on specific products or product groups, that one might normally expect to be available in the U.K., will often not be produced, especially in developing countries.

(*b*) Available data are often years out of date.

(*c*) The data are often of suspect reliability, especially if they originated from some tax-based function such as value-added tax.

(*d*) Despite continuing efforts at standardisation of statistical classifications, data are often not comparable between one country and another.

18. Using international statistics. For the reasons given in **17** the international researcher, before relying on any secondary data, should consider:

(*a*) exactly what products are included in the statistical classification;

(*b*) who originally collected the data, for what purpose, and whether there might be any motive for misrepresentation;

(*c*) from whom the data were collected, and whether *respondents* might have any reason for misrepresentation;

(*d*) how the data were collected, and how reliable the methodology might have been;

(*e*) how consistent the data are with other local or international statistics, and whether any serious inconsistencies can be satisfactorily explained.

FIELD RESEARCH

19. The nature of field research problems. The problems of international field research stem largely from the linguistic, social, cultural and environmental differences between nations. The nature and extent of these problems will vary significantly from one country to another, but generally become far more pronounced in developing, rather than in industrialised, countries. In the U.S.A., for instance, the U.K. researcher may feel himself very much at home, while in some developing countries he may require all his ingenuity to overcome local difficulties and produce a reasonably reliable report. (For research in Eastern bloc nations, *see* **XXIV, 7**.)

The problems and the suggested (necessarily generalised) solutions discussed below should be regarded as applying mainly to developing countries.

20. Sampling. In many developing countries it is simply not possible to draw a reliable probability sample. Often, demographic statistics are quite inadequate, street maps are not available or are out of date, or houses may not be numbered. Dwellings may be occupied by several family units.

In these circumstances, the international researcher will often have to rely on convenience sampling, with all the risks of inaccuracy that that implies.

> EXAMPLE: Sampling (in India) is considered very seriously, random walks, selection from voting lists and sophisticated stratification being fully examined. But commercial research usually covers only the top tranches of the population and ingenious selection procedures to locate them are used. One consumer durable study . . . was based on a random selection of private telephone subscribers.

21. Questionnaires. Every questionnaire demands the most careful phrasing if unintentionally misleading answers are to be avoided. In international research, translation of the questionnaire is often essential, providing yet more scope for misunderstanding.

Ideally, the questionnaire will be drawn up by a trained researcher who is both a native of the country in which the research is to be undertaken and fluent in the language of the research sponsor, though this ideal cannot always be achieved. In any case, translation alone is not sufficient; in order to achieve cross-cultural comparability, substantial changes are often required in the wording of the questionnaire.

22. Telephone interviewing. In a few countries, notably the U.S.A., the telephone penetration rate per household is such that telephone surveys are feasible even for consumer research.

In contrast, in many developing countries, the number of telephones is so limited, delays in installation are so long, and the cost of both installation and rental is so high, that, even in industrial research, reliance on the telephone may be called into question.

23. Personal interviewing. In the U.K. the personal interview, expensive though it is, is overwhelmingly the preferred method in consumer research, and is heavily relied on in industrial research.

It will now be clear that the personal interview is even more necessary in many countries if reliable data are to be obtained. Unfortunately, however, in many developing countries, the personal interview presents special problems, for two main reasons:

(*a*) recruitment of interviewers is difficult and in some cultures it is impossible to recruit female interviewers at all;

(*b*) the refusal rate is often significantly higher, since:

(*i*) male interviewers seem to have greater difficulty in obtaining the co-operation of female informants;

(*ii*) in some cultures a woman may be interviewed only in the presence of her husband (or, sometimes, an acquaintance);

(*iii*) there is sometimes a general mistrust of strangers;

(*iv*) suspicions may arise of a political motivation on the part of the interviewers;

(*v*) rather more topics than in the U.K. tend to be socially embarrassing to discuss;

(*vi*) in industrial research, businessmen are often accustomed to keeping to an absolute minimum any disclosure of information to government, employees and shareholders, let alone market researchers.

EXAMPLES: (1) Interviewers include many men, unemployed graduates and moonlighters. The Indian mother is not yet emancipated from the kitchen or deference to the male. Housewife interviewing, therefore, is frequently possible only between 07.30 and 09.30 and between 18.00 and 19.30, when the husband is at home. There is currently a government drive against tax evasion. Matters of salary or expenditure or possession of more expensive items therefore present problems. It puts an increased burden on confidentiality and willingness to be interviewed. A random sample may have a 30 per cent or more refusal rate.

(2) In a survey in the Middle East, one male respondent who fell within the sample turned out to be a government official who was highly suspicious of the survey, particularly so when he heard it had American sponsorship. However, he did not complain about the interview until it was completed and the interviewer was about to leave. He then threatened to have her arrested. She reported this to the native supervisor who telephoned the respondent immediately to assure him the survey had government approval and he (the supervisor) offered to

come to the respondent's house to discuss the survey in person. This pacified the irate respondent.

24. Successful research in developing countries. As mentioned above, adaptability and ingenuity are essential for research in developing countries, but it is possible to lay down general guidelines. It will usually pay to:

(*a*) rely entirely on the personal interview;

(*b*) in consumer research, rely heavily on the group interview;

(*c*) ensure good communications with respondents by an even-greater-than-usual reliance on display cards, illustrations and samples;

(*d*) provide more than usually thorough training and briefing for interviewing staff;

(*e*) arrange for company research staff to participate in experimental interviews;

(*f*) give closer and more direct interviewer supervision;

(*g*) place greater emphasis on the issuing of credentials to interviewing staff, including photographs;

(*h*) anticipate any politically sensitive questions, rewording or deleting whenever possible;

(*i*) where there is any possibility of the imputation of political motives, however unjustified, clear the research programme in advance with the appropriate authorities.

ORGANISING FOR INTERNATIONAL MARKET RESEARCH

25. Agency or in-house research. The international marketer considering a research project abroad must decide whether to undertake the research in-house or to commission a research agency.

(*a*) *Circumstances favouring agency research.* The use of a research agency is likely to be preferred when:

(*i*) the research is quantitative consumer research, requiring an established field-interview force abroad;

(*ii*) the research is of a highly specialised nature, as, for instance, with motivation research;

(*iii*) the company has little or no previous experience of the market;

(*iv*) communications difficulties, linguistic or cultural, are anticipated;

(v) the company has limited market research resources, or its resources are already fully loaded;

(vi) there is a clear need for an independent and objective assessment of the market, as may be the case, for instance, when a joint venture is contemplated.

(b) *Circumstances favouring in-house research.* A company is more likely to undertake its own research when:

(i) the research is industrial, and requires a limited number of interviews;

(ii) the company has significant experience in the market, or considers that the market potential is such as to make it worthwhile acquiring such experience;

(iii) communications difficulties may arise between the company and the research agency, as, for instance, with a high-technology product;

(iv) the company has available trained researchers with appropriate linguistic competence and overseas experience;

(v) suitably competent research agencies are not to be found in the market.

As a general rule, however, it might be said that most companies undertaking original research abroad will need to make extensive use of research agencies.

26. Selecting the appropriate type of agency for international research. The U.K. marketer may select one of five categories of research agency:

(a) a national research agency located within the country in which the research is to be undertaken;

(b) a U.K. agency which is part of a group under the same corporate ownership;

(c) a U.K. agency operating abroad through associates *not* under the same corporate ownership;

(d) a U.K. agency sub-contracting on the client's behalf to agencies abroad, but remaining responsible for centralised control and co-ordination, and for overall research results;

(e) a U.K. agency having research staff competent to undertake the research themselves.

Criteria for the selection of the appropriate type of agency are set out in Table II.

27. Selection of the individual agency. The international marketer is offered a wide choice of agencies in Western Europe, North

Table II. International market research: agency selection

Type of research agency	Agency selection and evaluation	Briefing, supervision and co-ordination	Communication problems (language)
National research agency located within the country in which the research is to be undertaken.	Need to visit and evaluate several agencies. Time-consuming, expensive and more difficult than the evaluation of U.K. agencies.	Personal briefing from the U.K. is highly desirable. This and subsequent supervision are highly expensive in management time, travelling and subsistence costs, etc.	None between agency and informants. May be problems between agency and client.
U.K. agency which is part of a group under the same corporate ownership.	Once the U.K. agency is selected the choice of local agencies is automatically determined.	Client briefs only U.K. agency, but agency will still need to brief its local subsidiaries. This may be expected to be a simpler operation, however, by virtue of the group's continuing relationship.	None between agency and informants, or between agency and client.
U.K. agency operating abroad through associates *not* under the same corporate ownership.	As above.	Client briefs only U.K. agency. Ease of briefing agencies abroad depends very much on closeness of association. *Client should investigate this aspect carefully before commissioning project.*	None between agency and informants, or between agency and client. Problems and misunderstandings might arise between U.K. agency and local agency.
U.K. agency sub-contracting on the client's behalf to agencies abroad, but remaining responsible for centralised control and co-ordination and for overall research results.	Client relieved of problems of selection and evaluation of agencies abroad.	Client briefs only U.K. agency. Agency, however, faces significant problems in briefing and supervision for which client ultimately must expect to pay.	As above.
U.K. agency with research staff themselves competent to undertake the research abroad.	Evaluation of agency personnel is facilitated, but this alternative is usually open only when a locally-based interviewing force is not required, e.g. in industrial market research or certain specialised types of consumer research.	Briefing, supervision and de-briefing present no problems whatever.	None between agency and client. Serious problems could arise between agency and informants. Client should investigate carefully linguistic competence of agency staff.

Table II. (continued). International market research: agency selection

Type of research agency	Special market knowledge	Standard of competence that might be expected	Cost comparisons
National research agency located within the country in which the research is to be undertaken.	Good.	Must be assessed for each individual agency. But it is possible to select the agency most appropriate to the type of research required.	Not likely to offer any savings in costs as compared with other alternatives. (Agency fees abroad tend to be higher than in the U.K.)
U.K. agency which is part of a group under the same corporate ownership.	Good.	A major and successful group *ipso facto* offers some guarantee of competence, as do standardised training procedures. But groups often have a weak link in the chain. *Client should investigate competence of local company*, even if only at second hand.	Group company will still have to charge the appropriate local rates. U.K. agency supervision likely to be rather more expensive than direct client supervision.
U.K. agency operating abroad through associates *not* under the same corporate ownership.	Good.	Will vary very significantly from one country to another. *A general standard of competence is not to be expected*, and client has no opportunity of selecting the best agency for his purpose.	As above.
U.K. agency sub-contracting on the client's behalf to agencies abroad, but remaining responsible for centralised control and co-ordination and for overall research results.	Good.	The agency most appropriate to the type of research required can be selected, by an experienced research agency.	U.K. agency is an additional cost. But it is possible to achieve cost savings by shopping around, though local rates will still have to be paid.
U.K. agency with research staff themselves competent to undertake the research abroad.	Could be inadequate. Problems could arise from researcher's ignorance of market background and culture. *Client should investigate this aspect before commissioning project.*	Client can shop around in the U.K. for the most suitable agency, and can normally expect a high standard of competence.	The generally lower level of U.K. agency fees may offer significant savings in research costs.

America, Japan and Australia, covering all research specialisations. In these areas, his problem will be one merely of selecting the agency most appropriate to the research task.

In most of Asia, and in Africa, the choice of agencies is more restricted, though research agencies can be found in the more economically developed countries. In addition to research specialists, research services may be offered by advertising agencies, management consultants and certain international accountancy organisations.

Appropriate research organisations may be located from:

(a) *The International Directory of Market Research Organisations* (Market Research Society, London);

(b) *Bradford's Directory of Marketing Research Agencies and Management Consultants in the U.S. and the World* (Ernest Bradford, Middleburg, Virginia);

(c) *International Directory of Marketing Research Houses and Services* (American Marketing Association, Chicago).

28. Financial assistance for market research abroad. The B.O.T.B. will, in approved cases, pay a substantial part of the cost of export market research undertaken by U.K. companies, as shown in Table III. The research will normally be carried out by research agencies, though support may also be given towards the purchase of multi-client studies or to research undertaken overseas by a company's own U.K.-based market research staff.

Table III. B.O.T.B. assistance for market research abroad.

Applicants for assistance	Levels of assistance (%)
Individual companies	33⅓
Groups of two or more unconnected firms participating in joint research	50
Trade associations	66⅔

Support for agency projects is based on the total fees and expenses charged. For projects undertaken in-house, support is normally 50 per cent of overseas travel and subsistence costs necessarily incurred in the course of the research, but the B.O.T.B. must be satisfied that the applicant's research ability is comparable with that of professional agencies. A company with no qualified research staff, but wishing to establish a research

III. INTERNATIONAL MARKET RESEARCH

department, may receive financial support during the first year of operation of the new development.

The final research report is inspected by the B.O.T.B. to ensure that work has been carried out to the required professional standards. It is, however, returned immediately to the applicant and remains entirely confidential (except in the case of trade association research reports, which are confidential to association members for an initial agreed period but are then offered for general sale).

Priority in awarding grants is given according to the merits of a particular project, but the factors considered in assessing the awards include:

(a) the applicant's previous experience in market research (newcomers to export research are encouraged);

(b) the probable effect on U.K. exports;

(c) the share of the market already held by British companies;

(d) the suitability and qualifications of those carrying out the research, whether agency or in-house staff;

(e) the research objectives, method, and cost.

29. Market Entry Guarantee Scheme. If market entry is decided upon, further assistance may be available from the B.O.T.B. under the Market Entry Guarantee Scheme. This scheme is aimed at assisting small- to medium-size manufacturing companies (or merchants acting as a sales organisation under contract to manufacturers) in the development of a new export market.

In approved cases, and at the discretion of the B.O.T.B., the scheme will contribute 50 per cent of the eligible costs of the market venture in return for a levy on sales receipts which is intended to recover the contributions plus a commercial rate of return on the investment. If, however, by the end of an agreed period, sales have not materialised as expected, no further levies are required and the loss is shared between the scheme and the exporter. The exporter pays the scheme an annual premium to cover this guarantee against 50 per cent of the loss.

Eligible costs consist of overheads which are written off as incurred, i.e. not capital investment. They include:

(a) overseas office accommodation, including rental, insurance, maintenance, cost of services, property taxes, cars, etc.;

(b) overseas staff costs, including salaries, employment taxes, travel and other expenses (other than entertainment), recruitment and relocation costs;

(c) training of overseas staff;

(d) sales promotion, including advertising, publicity and sales literature;

(e) stockholding, including showroom and warehouse costs, but excluding product transport, stock financing and interest charges, deterioration, etc.;

(f) legal costs associated with the establishment of the operation; external audits; fees for patents, licences, and trade marks, and for product testing to local standards.

The exporter must prepare proposals for a "well planned sales attack based on a substantial examination of the market". An isolated publicity campaign or market visit will not be eligible. The scheme's contribution for any one venture may not exceed £100,000 but must be a minimum of £20,000.

PROGRESS TEST 3

1. What is market research? **(1)**
2. What is meant by "desk research" and "field research"? **(2)**
3. What systematic research strategy can you suggest with a view to selecting the international markets of greatest potential at the lowest possible research cost? **(7–13)**
4. What is an omnibus survey? **(11)**
5. What systematic desk research procedure can you suggest to keep desk research costs to the absolute minimum? **(15)**
6. What special precautions might an international researcher take before relying on secondary data from abroad? **(18)**
7. What difficulties are encountered in field research abroad which would not be encountered in the U.K.? **(19–23)**
8. What factors might a company take into consideration before deciding whether to conduct its own research abroad or use the services of a research agency? **(25)**
9. What financial assistance is available from the B.O.T.B. towards the cost of export marketing research, and under what conditions? **(28)**
10. What financial assistance is available to exporters under the B.O.T.B.'s Market Entry Guarantee Scheme? **(29)**

CHAPTER IV

International Product Decisions I: Product Policy

INTRODUCTION

1. Product. From a marketing viewpoint, a product is the total utility, or satisfactions, that a buyer receives as a result of a lease or purchase. It consists of:

(*a*) *the tangible product*, i.e. the goods *or service* offered to the buyer;

(*b*) *the services that accompany the product*, e.g. packaging, labelling, pre-sale and after-sale service, and the confidence derived from the trade mark or brand name;

(*c*) *the benefits the buyer expects to receive* from his purchase.

2. Product policy. Product policy consists essentially of:

(*a*) the modification of existing products with a view to:
 (*i*) improving product performance in current markets;
 (*ii*) extending into new markets;
(*b*) the planned development and introduction of new products;
(*c*) the planned elimination of failing products.

Product policy is fundamental to the whole marketing mix. Promotion of an unacceptable product, for instance, may give rise to initial purchases but it will not achieve the all-important repeat purchases. All three aspects of product policy are of critical importance in domestic marketing.

3. International product policy. Internationally, buyers' needs, and the benefits they perceive as a result of their purchases, will often vary significantly according to the level of economic development and the social and cultural environment. Because of this, the most important aspect of international product policy is undoubtedly that of adaptation of existing products to widely differing world markets. This chapter therefore concentrates on product modification, though it also considers briefly new product development and product elimination in an international context.

Other aspects of product policy of major significance to the international marketer (packaging, labelling, servicing, brand names) are considered in V.

PRODUCT MODIFICATION

4. Product modification strategies. It is generally accepted that international product modification should be considered in conjunction with communications (*see* XV, **1**) strategy. On this basis the four alternative modification strategies illustrated in Table IV may be distinguished.

Table IV. Alternative international product modification strategies

	Product unchanged	*Product modified*
Communications unchanged	Standardisation, world-wide, of product and communications	Modification of product only
Communications modified	Modification of communications only	Both product and communications modified

Each of these strategies is considered below:

(*a*) *Standardisation of product and communications.* This strategy means simply introducing the product in the same form and with the same communications as in the domestic market. It is perhaps the obvious strategy for the occasional or haphazard exporter, and is sometimes adopted by major international companies. Its obvious appeal is minimisation of production and marketing costs.

> EXAMPLE: PepsiCo sells exactly the same product in every country in which it operates, relying on the same advertising and the same promotional themes as in the U.S.A.

The approach is not feasible, however, for all products.

> EXAMPLE: Campbell tried to sell its U.S. tomato soup formulation in the U.K., only to discover, after heavy losses, that its

taste was unacceptable. The Briton prefers a less bland flavour than the American.

(b) *Modification of communications only.* This strategy can be adopted when one and the same product fulfils a different need or function in different markets. It is *not*, it should be emphasised, a strategy aimed at persuading all markets to accept a standardised product regardless of product acceptability in the market place.

EXAMPLE: Bicycles are used as a basic means of adult transport in many countries. In the more advanced economies they are more frequently used for recreational purposes or by children.

(c) *Modification of product only.* This strategy is applicable when the product serves the same purpose in all markets but conditions of use vary.

EXAMPLE: Esso (Exxon) necessarily adapts its petrol formulations to the varying climatic conditions around the world, but standardised its communications appeal in its "Put a Tiger in your Tank" campaign, with considerable success.

(d) *Modification of both product and communications.* This strategy is clearly the most costly in terms of both manufacturing and marketing costs, but is sometimes essential to proper exploitation of the market.

EXAMPLE: A U.S. manufacturer of price-marking systems produced a new design of labelling gun in high-grade plastic which was significantly stronger than the metal gun previously marketed. The reduced cost of the new gun meant that replacement was now cheaper than repair. In the U.S.A. this advantage was emphasised in advertising and promotion, the gun being promoted initially as a throw-away item. In W. Germany, however, where customers clearly had a preference for the (imagined) extra quality and robustness of the metal gun, the throw-away message produced an adverse reaction. It was decided to chromium-plate the new gun, to avoid the inferior image of plastic, and to emphasise in the promotional message the strength and quality of the new design.

5. The product modification decision. A criticism often levelled at the exporter is that he fails to modify his product to meet special market needs, thus losing valuable export sales. Enough has probably been said by now to suggest that such criticisms are often ill-founded. Marketing is concerned (*see* 1, 2) with the satisfaction of consumer needs *at a profit*. The international marketer will make a logical decision, comparing:

(*a*) likely improvements in sales turnover and price levels, on the one hand;

(*b*) with, on the other hand, the additional costs of product modification.

The decision is not an easy one, and no general rules can be laid down, but some of the factors to be considered in arriving at the product modification decision are given below (*see* 6, 7).

6. Factors encouraging standardisation. The following factors will all tend to influence the international marketer towards product standardisation.

(*a*) *Production economies of scale.* Where, as may be the case with an exporting company, the product is manufactured in one plant, long production runs can offer significant economies. These become less attractive, of course, as production is extended into different countries.

(*b*) *Development costs.* A standardised product permits amortisation of development costs over a larger turnover.

(*c*) *Stock costs.* Standardisation reduces stock costs. Additional products give rise to additional records and stock audits. Each product must be carried at a level that reflects normal demand plus a safety margin to cover unexpected upsurges in demand; as a result the minimum safe stock level for several different products exceeds that applicable to one standard product.

(*d*) *Components.* In multinational production, some plants rely on components from the parent plant.

(*e*) *Technological content.* Although cultural and other environmental differences often necessitate changes in consumer products, industrial processes usually will not change from one country to another, so that many industrial products can be standardised.

(*f*) *Consumer mobility.* Standardisation is essential to consumer acceptance where products are of particular relevance to travellers or tourists, e.g. Hilton hotels, Kodak film, Nestlé baby foods.

(*g*) *Market homogeneity.* For some products a world market is available without product modification, e.g. the youth market for jeans, records, etc.

For economies resulting from standardisation of communications, *see* XV, **5**.

7. Factors encouraging modification. The following factors will tend to influence the international marketer towards product differentiation.

(*a*) Consumer tastes, especially in foodstuffs.

(*b*) Inadequate consumer purchasing power, which may necessitate a lower price and a corresponding reduction in quality.

(*c*) The general level of technical skills, which may necessitate product simplification.

(*d*) Poor maintenance standards (often a problem in developing countries) which may indicate either improvements in product reliability or, again, product simplification.

(*e*) Local labour costs, which may suggest a need for a higher (or lower) degree of automation.

8. Mandatory product modifications. So far, the discussion has assumed that the international marketer has discretion in the matter of product modification. In some cases, of course, he has no choice; either he modifies the product or he abandons the market.

(*a*) *Legal requirements.* Minimum or special product standards are often imposed by law.

(*b*) *Tariffs.* Tariff levels may be such that local manufacture or assembly and local purchase of components are essential, in which case standardisation may not be possible.

(*c*) *Nationalism.* Governments may require that an increasing proportion of components should be of local manufacture, with results similar to (*b*) above.

(*d*) *Technical.* Certain technical changes, e.g. in voltage, or in calibration of measuring instruments, are clearly essential, though they are often of minor importance.

(*e*) *Taxation.* Government taxation policy may leave the international marketer with little choice, e.g. car tax related to engine size.

(*f*) *Climate.* Sometimes climatic conditions require a product modification, e.g. the composition of car tyres varies according to the extremes of climate.

NEW PRODUCT DEVELOPMENT

9. The new product development process. New product development is a continual preoccupation of the marketing-oriented company. Most of the procedures are of general application, however, and are not considered here.

The international marketer, however, has potentially an immense advantage in the important first stage of the innovation process: idea generation. New product ideas originate from many sources, e.g. the research and development laboratory, customer requests or complaints, etc., but one highly important source is ideas already generated, and perhaps already successfully developed, in other parts of the world.

It is not enough to accept that this advantage exists. The international marketer must ensure that an organisational machinery is developed to harvest and collate all ideas from wherever he has a presence. For the exporter, this may mean no more than briefing and encouraging distributors, agents and company sales staff; for the multinational company it can constitute a major management function. In either case, the investment in management time is likely to pay off handsomely.

This is not to say, of course, that a new product successful in one market will necessarily be successful in another; normal screening and business analysis are still essential.

10. New inventions for specific markets. One strategy open to the international marketer, akin to product modification, is, of course, the development of entirely new products to open up new markets. This is an approach which, it is suggested, is particularly relevant to developing nations, which have tended to adopt the products of industrialised nations, which are by no means always suitable to the local scene. As a general rule, market potential in most developing nations is unlikely to justify the commercial development of entirely new products, though examples of such products can be found.

> EXAMPLE: Emcol International has developed a product called Instant Road Repair which repairs any size of pothole in tarmacadam, asphalt or concrete with a minimum of equipment. The material is a special formula of liquids and graded aggregate which is tipped from a container into the pothole, then banged flat with a shovel and traffic can proceed over the repair immediately. Thus a lorry loaded with containers of the

product and some men with shovels can repair a broken road in around three minutes. This is particularly useful for road repairs in Nigeria, where access may be a problem and the labour is unskilled.

PRODUCT ELIMINATION

11. Need for product elimination. Many obsolescent or marginal products linger on in the range until their lack of profitability becomes too obvious to ignore. Long before this they represent a costly burden which cannot be adequately demonstrated by any financial accounting system. Such products, for instance:

(*a*) involve expensive short-run production as demand declines or becomes sporadic;

(*b*) take up an excessive amount of management and salesman time;

(*c*) give an image of an unprogressive and technologically backward company;

(*d*) delay the search for new products (management continue to hope that the poor product performance is temporary, or that the marketing is inadequate).

12. Product elimination procedure. For these reasons companies should establish some form of product elimination procedure (often a product review committee) to periodically review the range and phase out unwanted products. Before abandonment, of course, the committee would consider not merely current product profitability but also such factors as:

(*a*) the likely effect on sales and profits of product rejuvenation, in the light of future market potential;

(*b*) the likely advantages of a change in the product marketing strategy;

(*c*) alternative product opportunities open to the company;

(*d*) the extent to which the product assists in the sale of other products in the range.

13. International product elimination. In essence, the review and elimination procedures remain much the same in an international context, though the scale of the problem is often much greater (an international company may have more products, or modifications of products, to consider, and many more markets). Product abandonment procedures are of yet greater importance.

In addition, the international marketer may need to consider product elimination from two different angles: on the assumption of one production source only (the exporter's viewpoint) and several production sources (the multinational viewpoint).

(a) *The exporter's view.* An exporting company should take into account market potential in all its markets. Although the product may not be over-profitable in the domestic market, it could be in the growth stage of its life-cycle in other markets with different per capita incomes or purchase influences.

(b) *The multinational view.* If the product is produced in several different markets, then a far greater range of supply and market combinations must be taken into account before a product is eliminated. This could lead to reduced standardisation of the international product range, which some companies are reluctant to consider. Increased diversity is to be welcomed, however, if it increases total profits.

14. International alternatives to product elimination. The international marketer is fortunate in that rather more alternatives are open to him, as a rule, than to his domestic counterpart. He is sometimes in a position to give up involvement in manufacture but to continue to derive some profit from the sale of services associated with the product, e.g. from licensing, franchising, contract manufacture or management contracting (*see* IX, **2, 9, 14** and **17**). Such a course should be considered for instance, when it is production costs or small-scale production, rather than market potential, that are the cause of the product's decline.

PROGRESS TEST 4

1. What alternative product modification and communications strategies are open to the international marketer? **(4)**
2. What circumstances might favour a policy of international product standardisation? **(6)**
3. What factors might militate against international uniformity of a company's product range? **(7, 8)**
4. What advantage does the international marketer have over his domestic counterpart in the development of new products? **(9)**
5. What modifications to a product elimination policy might be required when a company is involved in international operations? **(13, 14)**

CHAPTER V

International Product Decisions II: Packaging, Labelling, Servicing and Trade Marks

PACKAGING

1. Standardisation. As is the case with the tangible product, packaging is subject to pressures tending towards standardisation on the one hand, and, on the other hand, towards adaptation to special market needs. The decision is rarely so critical in profit terms as the product standardisation decision, but it nevertheless deserves careful thought. In arriving at the decision both the protectional and the promotional aspects of packaging should be considered.

2. Protectional aspects of packaging. Protectional aspects include:

(*a*) climatic conditions in the market place, and in transit to the market place;
(*b*) the handling the product is likely to receive;
(*c*) the amount of time the product is likely to spend within the distribution chain, bearing in mind that the distribution chain may include many more intermediaries than at home;
(*d*) consumer usage rate and consequent storage time.

3. Promotional aspects of packaging. Promotional aspects include:

(*a*) package size, e.g. a high level of car ownership and a developed hypermarket/supermarket retail system will indicate larger packs, while in developing countries a very low per capita income may suggest individual packs—razor blades, chewing gum and even cigarettes may be sold individually;
(*b*) the cost of the package, e.g. the standard package may be over-elaborate, adding significantly and unnecessarily to the price of the contents;
(*c*) local preferences in terms of colour of material, e.g. white is associated with mourning in the Far East;

(*d*) legal requirements, e.g. Venezuela does not permit on-pack promotional gifts;

(*e*) recognition, e.g. tourist items, such as Kodak film, should be immediately recognisable to all nationalities and therefore require a standard package;

(*f*) literacy, e.g. a low level of literacy may require greater emphasis on pictorial design.

LABELLING

4. Labelling and government regulations. The international marketer must adhere in every country to local labelling regulations. These vary widely, but typically they require an indication of the manufacturer, country of origin, weight, description of contents, nature of ingredients, etc.

Details of labelling regulations for specific products and countries can be obtained from the Overseas Tariffs and Regulations (OTAR) Section, Export Data Branch, of the Department of Trade.

5. Labelling and language. Regardless of government regulations, the manufacturer requires a label to communicate information to his customers, with a view to facilitating the use of the product, assisting in consumer satisfaction, and encouraging initial and repeat purchases. The label must, therefore, be written in an appropriate local language throughout, except where some national image is particularly important, e.g. in French perfumes.

Occasionally, to reduce costs, a company will use multilingual labels covering several countries. This may be acceptable if a multinational image is likely to make a favourable impression on the customer, but in other instances it may be desirable to incur additional labelling costs to ensure an entirely national image.

SERVICING

6. International importance of servicing. For those goods that require service facilities, servicing is of especial importance internationally; customers tend to give preference to national products if they have the least reason to fear inadequate after-sales service from a remote and foreign company. Some clear international servicing policy is essential.

7. Servicing policy objective. The objective of a servicing policy is to ensure customer satisfaction and goodwill, and hence repeat purchases, at the lowest practicable cost to the manufacturer or seller.

The achievement of that simple objective on an international scale, however, can involve heavy investment in servicing facilities, personnel and training. It presents a major organisational problem.

8. Organising servicing facilities. That organisational problem can be tackled in two principal ways.

(*a*) *Distributors.* Ideally, a company would appoint a reliable distributor with an organised servicing network compatible with the product. In practice, such distributors are rare and involvement by the manufacturer in the distributor's service functions is often essential.

Such involvement may require the training of distributor personnel at the company headquarters, the establishment of travelling teams of trainers, or the secondment of company maintenance staff to the distributor.

(*b*) *Direct servicing.* Direct servicing is normal in the case of major items of capital equipment, when it is economic to fly out maintenance staff from company headquarters. It may occasionally be an option worthy of consideration in the case of other products: preventive maintenance staff may be based abroad where sales are concentrated in one geographical area.

9. Servicing and the product. For some countries where technical skills and maintenance standards are low, servicing requirements may entail product modification, the aim being to produce a simpler or sturdier design (*see* IV, **7**). This is particularly appropriate to agricultural products in relatively isolated areas in developing countries.

> EXAMPLE: The local African government had been buying from . . . an American firm hand-operated dusters for use in distributing pesticides in the cotton fields. The dusters were loaned to individual negro farmers. The duster supplied by the corporation was a finely-machined device requiring regular oiling and good care, but the fact that this duster turned more easily than any other duster on the market was relatively unimportant to the native farmers. Furthermore, the requirement for careful oiling and care simply meant that in a relatively short

time the machines froze up and broke. The result? The local government went back to an older-type French duster which was heavy, turned with difficulty, and gave a poorer distribution of dust, but which lasted longer in that it required less care and lubrication.

TRADE MARKS

10. Definitions. A trade mark is "a brand or part of a brand that is given legal protection because it is capable of exclusive appropriation".

A brand is "a name, term, sign, symbol or design, or combination of them, which is intended to identify the goods or services of one seller or group of sellers and to differentiate them from competitors".

11. Importance of trade marks. A trade mark identifies the origin of the product. It is the customer's assurance of quality, and it enables the manufacturer to promote his product without unduly benefiting his competitors. Its protection (by registration) is often vital, perhaps even to the survival of the company.

12. Trade mark protection. Protection of a successful and well-known brand name is rarely easy. It is particularly difficult internationally, partly because of trade mark registration difficulties (**13, 14**), and partly because brand imitation (**15**) and brand piracy (**16**) are rife in certain countries.

Protection is available to the international company at two levels, national and international.

13. National trade mark protection. Most countries offer a system of trade mark registration and protection for foreign, as well as national, suppliers. The international marketer, however, will need to differentiate between two basic systems:

(*a*) in many countries, registration alone is required—"priority in registration" ensures protection;

(*b*) in the U.K. and some other countries, trade mark protection also requires "priority in use"—registration alone is insufficient and some sales must have been made within the country.

14. International trade mark protection. The Arrangement of Madrid is an agreement covering the international registration of trade marks. A trade mark registered in one member country in the name of a locally domiciled establishment is forwarded to a central bureau for subsequent registration in all other member states, provided it is qualified for registration under the national registration rules of those countries.

Unfortunately, only a very limited number of countries subscribe to the Madrid Convention.

15. Trade mark imitation. Trade mark imitation aims to take advantage of the promotional expenditure and reputation of a major supplier by the production of similar products under the same or very similar brand names, with similar packaging and labelling.

EXAMPLE: Johnnie Walker Red Label is the world's largest-selling Scotch whisky. In recent years the proprietors of the brand have had to bring proceedings to prevent the use of the name and its famous striding-figure device in relation to products as diverse as cigarettes (in the U.S.A.), blue jeans (in Colombia) and sewing thread (in India). For whisky itself, imitation of the packaging and labelling styles, for both Johnnie Walker and other brands, is more usual and the brand owners must be constantly on the alert, ready to take legal action.

16. Trade mark piracy. Trade mark piracy is the registration of brand names with the aim of selling them back to the companies that have originated them if and when such firms wish to enter the market. The firm must either pay the price asked, attempt to register and establish another brand at some expense, or abandon the idea of market entry.

EXAMPLE: Two leading French chemical companies, Péchiney and Ugine Kuhlmann, merged and filed an application for registration of the trade mark "PUK", only to find that "PUK" had been registered, immediately after the merger, by a third party not in any way involved in the actual use of such a brand. Péchiney Ugine Kuhlmann were forced to resort to litigation in order to establish their right to use the brand.

17. Trade mark policy. Under these circumstances the international marketer must adopt a clear policy on trade mark protection. At first sight, it might seem desirable to register the brand in all countries. In practice, some compromise will have to be reached, simply because registration is expensive in terms of initial fees, the renewal fees demanded in some countries, the legal fees involved in registration, and the cost of establishing use, i.e. of achieving limited sales.

Registration is, of course, essential in those countries where the company is operating, or considering operating in the near future. For other countries the following factors should be considered:

(*a*) present and likely future market potential;
(*b*) ease and *total* cost of registration;
(*c*) the expense and inconvenience of selecting a new brand name if that should eventually prove necessary;
(*d*) the importance of the brand name in terms of product sales—often the brand is vital, but in other cases, as with many industrial goods, it is of marginal value;
(*e*) the importance of establishing one standard international brand name.

18. The international brand name. For products bought by travellers, such as films, the establishment of a world brand name is critical. In many other cases, sentiment apart, there is often no real need to insist on use of the same brand in all countries unless it offers significant promotional economies of scale. Such economies might arise, for instance, from:

(*a*) standardisation of advertising campaigns over several countries (*see* XV, **4**);
(*b*) the use of international media (*see* XV, **12**);
(*c*) the opportunities offered by media spillover (*see* XV, **12**).

PROGRESS TEST 5

1. What is meant by (*a*) the "protectional aspect" and (*b*) the "promotional aspect" of packaging? **(2, 3)**
2. Why is servicing of special importance in international marketing? **(6)**
3. How might servicing be organised on an international basis? **(8)**
4. What special problems are faced by the international marketer with regard to trademark protection? **(12)**
5. What factors would you consider in deciding whether or not to register your brand name in a particular country? **(17)**
6. Under what circumstances is it desirable to use the same brand name for a given product in all markets of the world? **(18)**

CHAPTER VI

International Distribution Decisions I: Alternative Channels

INTRODUCTION

1. Definition. Some manufacturers sell and deliver their products direct to the user, e.g. many industrial goods manufacturers. Many companies, however, sell through middlemen, who perform a variety of functions connected with the marketing of the product (*see* 2). Such companies seek to link together the set of marketing intermediaries most appropriate to their profit and other objectives. Such a set of marketing intermediaries is known as the *marketing channel* or the *channel of distribution*. The most obvious example of such a channel is the producer–wholesaler–retailer distribution system adopted for many consumer goods.

2. Functions of middlemen. The functions of middlemen include some or all of the following:

(*a*) the assembly of products from many different producers into an assortment of interest to buyers;
(*b*) breaking bulk to meet the scale of need of the customer;
(*c*) adapting goods to market requirements;
(*d*) physical distribution (transport and storage);
(*e*) price setting;
(*f*) sales promotion and advertising;
(*g*) seeking out buyers and selling to them;
(*h*) extending credit to buyers.

All these are essential functions that must be undertaken by the manufacturer or by middlemen. The manufacturer will decide whether he can himself perform some or all of these functions most efficiently or whether it is desirable to hand the responsibility over to middlemen.

3. Importance of channel decisions. In any country, channel decisions are among the most important policy decisions facing management, for four main reasons.

(a) The channels selected will fundamentally affect almost every other marketing decision, e.g. prices must reflect the mark-up allowed to an intermediary, the size of the sales force must depend on whether sales are made direct to retailers or only to wholesalers.

(b) The channel decision involves the company in long-term commitments to other independent organisations, and these commitments are often extremely difficult to change.

(c) Although these independent organisations work with the producer to their mutual advantage, there is an inherent conflict of interest between them, in that the producer wishes the middleman to sell at the lowest possible margin, thus maximising sales and the producer's profit, while the middleman wishes to sell at the price which will maximise his own profit.

(d) The producer using middlemen necessarily loses a significant degree of control over his own market.

4. Channel design and management. Even in domestic marketing, therefore, a manufacturer must pay special attention both to the initial strategic decision as to *design of channel* and to subsequent *channel management*, i.e. the selection of individual intermediaries, their motivation, control, evaluation, etc. The fundamental aim of channel management is to supply the product to the end customer at the right time and in the manner most profitable to the manufacturer.

5. Channel design and management and the international marketer. Compared with domestic (one-country) marketing, the task of channel design and management internationally is one of infinitely greater complexity. The international marketer must take into account:

(a) channels between nations (market-entry channels);
(b) channels within nations (foreign-market channels).

CHANNELS BETWEEN NATIONS

6. Definition. Channels between nations include:

(a) indirect export, i.e. sales to intermediaries within the U.K. who in turn re-sell to a customer abroad;

(b) direct export, i.e. sales to a customer abroad, who may be the end user of the goods or an intermediary, the latter being perhaps the exporter's own local office;

(c) manufacture abroad, on either a joint-venture or an independent basis.

The principal alternatives open to the international marketer under each of the above headings are shown, with references to the chapters in which they are further discussed, in Fig. 5 (direct and indirect export) and Fig. 6 (manufacture abroad).

7. Selection criteria for channels between nations. Selection of the appropriate market-entry channel will depend in every case on company objectives, company size and product range. There are, however, more general criteria, largely independent of the company or its products, which should be borne in mind.

(a) *Channel availability.* Different markets require different approaches. Licensing, for example, may not be possible because no suitably qualified licensees can be found; in some small markets the only agent of value may already represent the competition.

(b) *Sales volume.* Sales volume depends not merely on market potential, but also on the channel selected.

(c) *Operating costs.* Sales volume figures are not in themselves particularly meaningful; they must be related to the costs involved in achieving that volume. Both the initial and the recurring costs of entry should be considered.

(d) *Investment required.* Investment requirements are clearly highest in wholly-owned overseas production operations, but capital may also be required, for instance, to finance local stocks or extend credit to local distributors.

(e) *Personnel.* The alternative channels described vary greatly in terms of the requirement for skilled managerial and other personnel. Lack of suitably qualified staff may prove a bar to the adoption of certain of the market-entry methods outlined, e.g. own production plant.

(f) *Risk.* The degree of risk is not only a function of the market but also of the company's method of involvement in that market.

(g) *Control.* The degree of control a company can exercise over its distribution channels will usually have a significant bearing on its success. Control will vary widely according to the channel selected, e.g. in the case of sales to export merchants the company will have no control whatsoever, while it is possible to exercise firm control through an overseas marketing or manufacturing subsidiary.

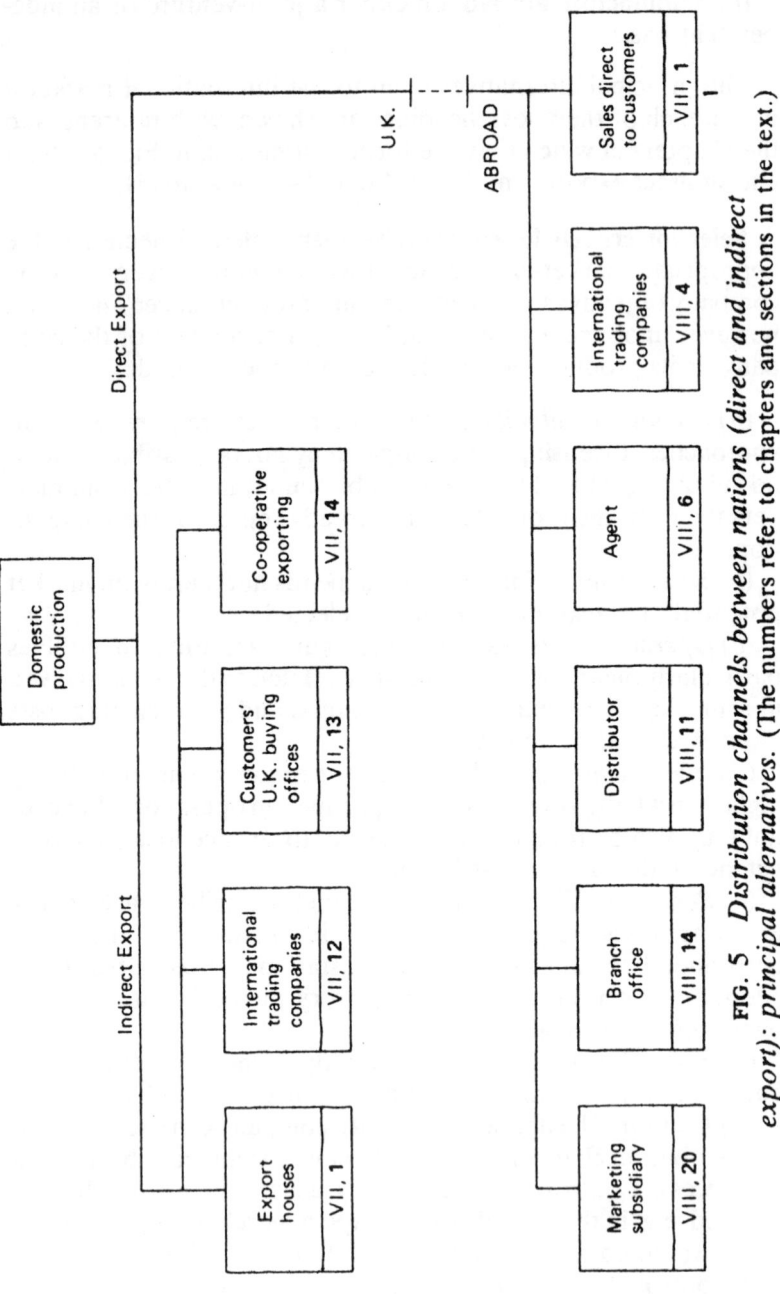

FIG. 5 *Distribution channels between nations (direct and indirect export): principal alternatives.* (The numbers refer to chapters and sections in the text.)

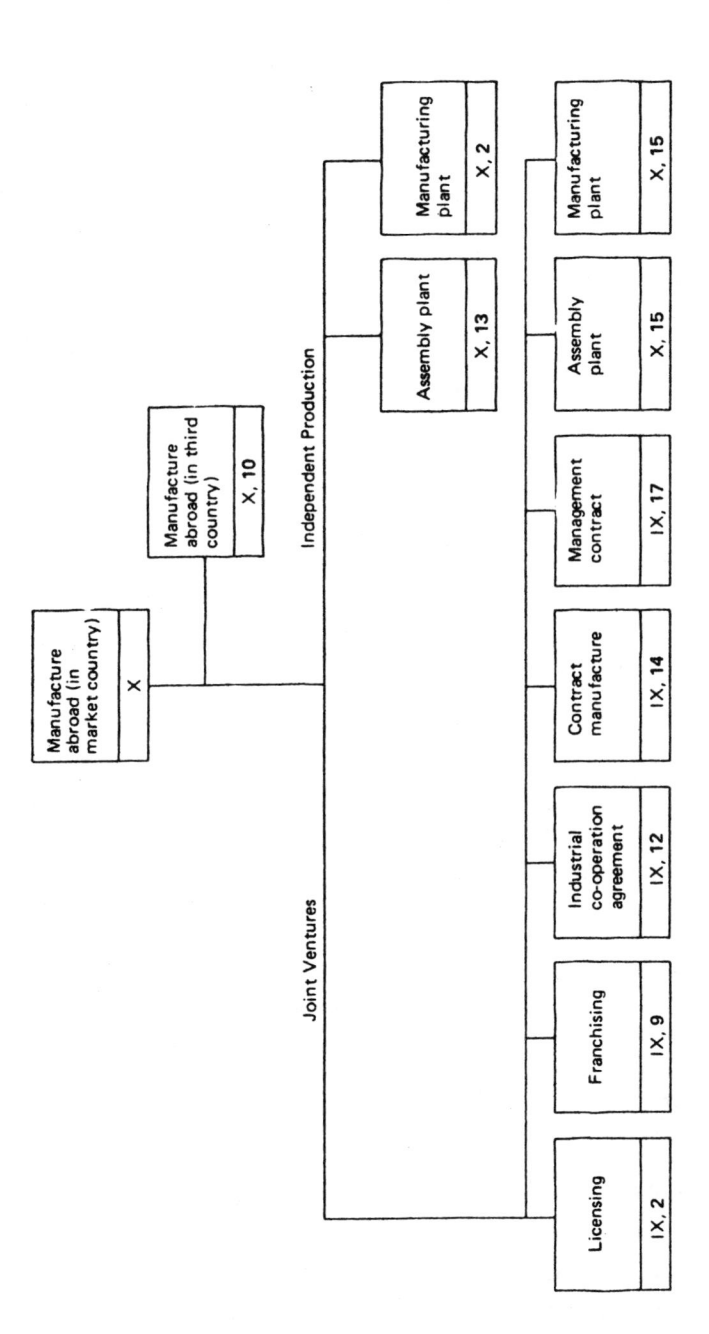

FIG. 6 *Distribution channels between nations (manufacture abroad): principal alternative channels.* (The numbers refer to chapters and sections in the text.)

(*h*) *Flexibility*. A channel which is optimal at the time of market entry may cease to be so as market conditions change, or as sales develop. A company should, therefore, retain flexibility, the ability to change its degree of involvement to meet new conditions. Such flexibility is not easy to achieve under any circumstances (even agencies require a degree of commitment on the part of the principal), but a greater degree of flexibility is likely to be retained if it is planned for in advance.

All the above criteria should be considered, in relation to *all* practicable alternative channels, whenever entry into a new market or a change of established channels is contemplated.

The most appropriate channel will vary from one market to the next, and the correct choice of channel is often far from obvious. A company may quite validly operate simultaneously through several different channels, having licensees in one market, a manufacturing subsidiary in another, agents in a third market, and so on.

CHANNELS WITHIN NATIONS

8. The whole-channel concept. Many manufacturers, especially manufacturers of industrial goods, need consider only the problem of distribution channels *between* nations, as their products are sold direct to the end user (often another company or a government organisation).

Other manufacturers, however, face the additional problem of distribution *within* the foreign market, through local wholesale–retail or other channels. In such cases the task of the international marketer is not complete when the goods arrive (or are manufactured) in the overseas market. *The international marketer should concern himself with the entire channel of distribution, from producer to the final buyer, i.e. industrial end user or consumer, even if it is not always possible for him to exercise a direct influence on the actions and policies of all intermediaries.* This, the *whole-channel concept*, is fundamental to good marketing. It implies, *for each market*, involvement in channel design and channel management (*see* **4**).

9. The whole-channel concept and the exporter. The overseas manufacturing subsidiary, often heavily dependent on the market in which it is located, will usually be closely concerned in channel design and management.

VI. INTERNATIONAL DISTRIBUTION DECISIONS I

The exporter, however, frequently trading with a large number of markets, is all too often content to sell to a foreign importer, ignoring the subsequent distribution channels that link the importer with the final purchaser. In any market of importance, such an approach will usually prove less than optimal in profit terms; a channel is only as effective as its weakest member, and sales may be blocked at any point within the channel. *The whole-channel concept is just as relevant to the exporter as to the overseas manufacturing subsidiary.*

EXAMPLE: Letraset (Canada) and Letraset (U.S.A.) *see* XXVII.

Channels within nations (design and management) are considered in detail in XI.

PROGRESS TEST 6

1. What is a marketing channel? **(1)**
2. Why are channel decisions so important? **(3)**
3. Why are channel decisions especially important, and especially difficult, in international marketing? **(5)**
4. What are the major factors to be considered when making decisions on channels between nations? **(7)**
5. What is meant by the "whole-channel concept"? **(8)**
6. What is the significance of the whole-channel concept to the *exporter*? **(9)**

CHAPTER VII
International Distribution Decisions II: Indirect Export

EXPORT HOUSES

1. Definition. The Directory of British Export Houses defines an export house as "any company or firm, not being a manufacturer, whose main activity is the handling or financing of British export trade and/or international trade not connected with the U.K.". There are from 700 to 800 export houses in the U.K., and between them they handle perhaps 20 per cent of Britain's export trade.

The operations of these export houses are difficult to define in view of the flexibility which is their most marked characteristic. However, from a distribution-channel viewpoint, and ignoring those houses specialising mainly in finance, it is possible to distinguish three major categories:

(*a*) export merchants, who act as principals in the export transaction, buying and selling on their own account;

(*b*) confirming houses and buying/indent houses, who represent the buyer abroad;

(*c*) manufacturers' export agents and specialist export managers, who represent the U.K. manufacturer.

The characteristics of these different types of export house are compared in Table V. They are explained in greater detail below, though it should be realised that many export houses manage to combine several of the functions discussed.

2. Export merchants. In essence, export merchants are domestic wholesalers operating in foreign markets through their own salesmen, agents, stockists and, very often, local branch offices. Their remuneration derives from the difference between the buying price and the selling price. They tend to specialise in certain territories, and sometimes in certain classes of goods.

3. Advantages of trading through merchants. The advantages to a manufacturer of using the services of merchants are:

Table V. Comparison of typical characteristics of U.K. export houses

Category of export house	Representation arrangement	Seeks	Accepts financing and credit risk (short-term)	Shipping, insurance and documentation	Remuneration	Manufacturer's degree of control over market	Handles competing lines	Continuing relationship
Export merchant	Acts as principal	Customers abroad and suppliers in U.K.	Yes	Undertaken	Difference between purchase and resale prices	Nil	Yes	No
Confirming house	Confirms, as principal, order placed by foreign buyer	Suppliers in U.K.	Yes	Undertaken	Commission from foreign buyer	Nil	Yes	No
Buying/indent house	Acts on behalf of foreign buyer, either buying with wide discretion on orders received or placing indents on suppliers specified by buyer	Suppliers in U.K.	Yes if required	Undertaken	Commission from foreign buyer	Nil	Yes	No
Manufacturers' export agent	Represents U.K. manufacturers	Customers abroad	Not usually	Not normally undertaken	Commission from U.K. manufacturer	Fair	No	Yes
Specialist export manager	Represents U.K. manufacturers	Customers abroad	Sometimes	Undertaken	Commission from U.K. manufacturer plus retainer	Good	No	Yes

(a) the manufacturer takes immediate advantage of the merchants' knowledge of foreign markets and their established contacts within those markets, this being particularly important in the case of the more difficult export markets, such as Japan;

(b) he is relieved entirely of the need to finance the export transaction and of the credit risk;

(c) he is, usually, similarly relieved of the mechanics of exporting, i.e. documentation, shipping, insurance, etc.;

(d) he is able to export without any investment of money or of executive time, as there is no overhead load;

(e) many merchants have developed expertise in specialist fields, such as barter trading (see XIII, 14), where, for many companies, their services are essential;

(f) in certain circumstances, merchants carry greater weight in selling than individual manufacturers, e.g. with the Comecon countries (see XXIV, 8), where merchants who import from those countries, as well as export to them, are often more acceptable.

Many of the above advantages are clearly of particular value to the small exporter. It would be a mistake to assume, however, that export merchants have little to offer to the larger company. Such larger exporters may well find it more profitable to concentrate on direct sales in markets of major importance, dealing through merchants in the less important markets, in the more difficult markets (for example, Comecon and Japan), and on those occasions when specialist expertise, e.g. barter dealing, is required.

4. Disadvantages of trading through merchants. There are, of course, certain disadvantages in trading through export merchants:

(a) most serious, the manufacturer has little or no control over his market, and his product may be dropped at any time if a more profitable line appears;

(b) the manufacturer is not building up goodwill in the market as a basis for expansion, i.e. goodwill from the product accrues to the export merchant;

(c) the export merchant needs volume to survive and he may take on so many lines that the product of an individual manufacturer receives little attention;

(d) similarly, the merchant must secure an early return and therefore merchants are not a suitable channel where a long-term

VII. INTERNATIONAL DISTRIBUTION DECISIONS II   57

investment of time or money is essential for maximum exploitation of the market;

(e) if sales in a market expand very significantly, the manufacturer will often find it more profitable to deal direct.

5. Confirming houses. The confirming house confirms *as a principal* an order which a foreign buyer has placed with a U.K. manufacturer who is unwilling to extend credit overseas. It finances the transaction, accepting the short-term credit risk, and receives a commission in return from the buyer.

As far as the U.K. exporter is concerned, trading through a confirming house is little different from trading with a merchant—the advantages and disadvantages are much the same.

6. The buying/indent house. The buying/indent house acts on behalf of the overseas buyer, either buying with wide discretion against orders received, or placing indents on manufacturers specified by the buyer. It may act as a principal in the same manner as a confirming house. For the exporter the advantages and disadvantages are again much the same as for a merchant house.

7. Manufacturers' export agent. The manufacturers' export agent sells abroad on behalf of U.K. manufacturers, either in its own name or, more usually, in the name of the manufacturer. It will usually cover a particular sector of industry, representing to that sector a number of U.K. manufacturers whose products are complementary to one another.

Remuneration takes the form of a commission from the U.K. manufacturers.

8. Trading through a manufacturers' export agent. The advantages and disadvantages of trading through a manufacturers' export agent are similar to those of trading through an export merchant, except that:

(a) export finance, the credit risk, shipping, insurance, and export documentation are usually the concern of the manufacturer;

(b) the manufacturer, since the sale is usually in his name, retains much greater control over his market.

9. The specialist export manager. The specialist export manager, or combination export manager as he is known in the U.S.A., offers a complete export management service, becoming in effect the export department of the manufacturer, acting in the manufacturer's name and normally using the manufacturer's letterhead. He will normally undertake finance and documentation, and will sometimes accept the credit risk.

Remuneration is usually by way of a commission on sales, though in addition a small annual retainer is required.

10. Advantages of the specialist export manager. The specialist export manager offers all the advantages of the export merchant. In addition, the manufacturer:

(a) immediately gains his own export department, at negligible overhead cost;

(b) secures the maximum possible degree of control over his market, short of establishing his own export organisation;

(c) is building up goodwill in the market under his own name;

(d) may expect, as a rule, a continuing and long-term relationship.

11. Disadvantages of the specialist export manager. On the other hand:

(a) the specialist export manager is subject to the same pressures as any other export house, and he must drop or ignore products that do not offer a reasonably prompt return;

(b) as sales develop, the manufacturer may well wish to change to direct export, but he will not have built up the necessary in-house experience and capability;

(c) the specialist export manager will normally expect a world-wide brief—naturally so, if the exporter is not developing his own export department—yet he is unlikely to be able to offer world-wide coverage.

The latter point is perhaps the key issue in the selection of a specialist export manager. The exporter must ensure that his target markets coincide with those in which the specialist export manager has genuine contacts and experience.

12. International trading companies. The international trading companies are highly diversified and large-scale manufacturers and merchants, often operating at both the wholesale and retail levels of distribution. They are of particular importance in South-East Asia and in the former African colonial territories. For a British exporter, dealing with the U.K. trading companies is broadly the equivalent of dealing with a U.K. merchant house, although the size and market coverage of many such companies makes them also attractive as potential distributors. In some countries trading companies alone can provide adequate coverage, market access and political acceptability, though a growing nationalism means that in the long term their influence is likely to decline.

EXAMPLE: U.A.C. International, with headquarters in London, is one of the largest trading organisations in Africa. It consists of some 300 separate (and often competing) enterprises operating in almost all the tropical African states. It was formally established in 1929, as a result of a merger of several British companies, but its origins can be traced back to the first British explorers in the West African coast. Its manufacturing interests (often joint ventures) include timber products, cement, aluminium products, metal furniture, food processing, brewing, vehicle assembly, toiletries, pharmaceuticals and packaging. Its wholesaling interests and distributorships include motor vehicles, agricultural machinery, refrigeration equipment, radio and television, building materials, office equipment, hospital equipment, earth-moving machinery, fork-lift trucks and industrial engines. It also runs its own ocean-going shipping fleet, and operates a chain of department stores. Operations in francophone Africa are controlled from its largely autonomous Paris office.

U.K. BUYING OFFICES

13. Department stores. Many of the major department stores in industrialised countries maintain buying offices in the U.K.; others appoint U.K. export houses as their buying agents.

EXAMPLES: All ten of Japan's leading department stores have buying offices or representatives in London.

Two of the four leading West German department store groups, Karstadt A.G. and Hertie G.m.b.H., maintain their own buying offices in London. These two groups between them control over 250 department or chain stores, which account for between six and seven per cent of the *total* retail turnover in West Germany.

Buyers from many department stores, whether or not they have a London office, make regular visits to the U.K. Notice of many of these visits is given through the Export Intelligence Service or is published in appropriate trade journals.

CO-OPERATIVE EXPORT MARKETING

14. Complementary marketing. Complementary export marketing (often termed "piggy-back exporting") occurs when one manufacturer, the "carrier", uses his established overseas distribution facilities to market the goods of another manufacturer, the "rider", alongside his own.

Two alternative arrangements are possible:

(*a*) the carrier sells the rider's products on a commission basis, effectively acting as his agent;

(*b*) the carrier buys the products outright and re-sells at the best price he can obtain, thus acting as a merchant.

15. Advantages for the rider. It is important, if any such arrangements are entered into, that *both* parties should derive some significant advantage. The advantage to the rider is clear: complementary exporting provides him with a simple and low-risk method of beginning export operations—particularly important for a small company lacking the resources to engage in direct export.

16. Advantages for the carrier. The arrangement should result in increased profit for the carrier. Such profit is most likely to accrue if the rider's products:

(*a*) broaden an otherwise over-limited product range, offering economies of scale in distribution, compensation for seasonal down-turns in the basic product line, or generating distributor enthusiasm; or

(*b*) are related to the carrier's product lines in such a way that they assist in their sale.

> EXAMPLE: The Singer Sewing Machine Co. piggy-backs products closely allied to its own, e.g. fabrics, patterns, thread and other sewing accessories.

17. Export consortia. Continuing piggy-back arrangements are obviously subject to strain. Although reportedly successful in the U.S.A., where the Department of Commerce makes active efforts to introduce prospective piggy-back partners, such arrangements in the U.K. have had results little better than mixed. In recent

VII. INTERNATIONAL DISTRIBUTION DECISIONS II

years the more opportunistic and short-term alternative, the export consortium or the package deal, seems to have proved more successful.

EXAMPLE: Herbert Morris, the Loughborough based crane manufacturer, has just pulled off a $25m. deal with a Korean Shipbuilding and Engineering Corporation which has taken it into a new field of export activity—helping to sell other companies' products. Herbert Morris's cranes and lifting equipment will account for only $10m. worth of the order. The rest will be supplied by firms like G.E.C. Switchgear, Weir Pumps, Atlas Copco, Hugh Smith presses, and B.I.C.C.

"We'd been wanting to get into the package business for some time because it is a very good way of selling the hardware. Most developing countries want someone to come along and build complete plants for them rather than having to order individual bits of equipment."

Export consortia are particularly suited to the construction industry and to those countries, e.g. the OPEC countries of the Middle East, where rapid industrialisation is the aim.

PROGRESS TEST 7

1. What is an export house? What major categories of export house can you define? **(1)**

2. What are the advantages and disadvantages of trading through export merchants? **(3, 4)**

3. Under what circumstances might you envisage the appointment of an export house as a "specialist export manager"? **(10, 11)**

4. What are the characteristics of a typical international trading company? **(12)**

5. What is meant by "piggy-back exporting"? Under what circumstances might you expect such an arrangement to prove successful? **(14–16)**

6. Can you suggest reasons why the export consortium is proving popular? **(17)**

CHAPTER VIII

International Distribution Decisions III: Direct Export

SALES DIRECT TO CUSTOMER

1. Possibilities for direct sales. In many instances sales may, of course, be made direct to customers abroad without the assistance of any kind of agent or intermediary. This applies, for instance, in the case of:

(*a*) many types of industrial goods;
(*b*) goods sold to national government, local authorities, and other official or quasi-governmental organisations;
(*c*) consumer goods sold:
   (*i*) by direct mail to the final consumer;
   (*ii*) to retail stores, especially the major department store groups;
   (*iii*) to mail order houses.

2. Retail stores. Reference has already been made to the London buying offices of the major international retail store groups (*see* VII, 13). Naturally, much greater success is likely if *all* store groups are approached. These may include department stores, variety stores, supermarkets and hypermarkets, and protective groupings of independent retailers (voluntary buying organisations). Again, it is often possible to cover a large number of stores with a very limited number of contacts (*see* Table VI).

3. Mail order houses. Mail order houses, similarly, may be regarded as important outlets worth a direct approach, though abroad, as in the U.K., they tend to be demanding customers: delivery must be strictly guaranteed, and prices must remain unchanged for the period of validity of the catalogue (which could lead to difficulties at a time of varying exchange rates). The larger mail order houses often insist that offers should be sent to them on an exclusive basis and should not be offered to competitors, which limits the value of this channel in any one country.

Table VI. Some central purchasing agencies or groups covering department and variety stores in France

Group or purchasing agency	No. of stores covered (1975)
Prisunic	426
Monoprix	270
Nouvelles Galéries	199
Groupement d'Achats des Grands Magasins Indépendants	140
Au Printemps	95
Parunis	90
Manufrance	83
Paris France	60
Uniprix	34

INTERNATIONAL TRADING COMPANIES ABROAD

4. France. A number of major international trading companies, the counterparts of the U.K. trading companies already mentioned (*see* VII, **12**), are French, with headquarters in Paris. They are of special importance to any exporter wishing to trade with the former French colonies.

EXAMPLE: The Compagnie Française de l'Afrique Occidentale (C.F.A.O.) is concerned with capital goods, consumer goods and services. It is involved in manufacturing, usually through joint ventures, in which it normally takes a minority interest, and wholesaling and retailing through supermarket chains and smaller retail stores. Many of its product lines are of non-French origin.

5. Trading companies in other countries. Other international trading companies are to be found in West Germany, Switzerland, the Netherlands and Denmark.

EXAMPLE: The East Asiatic Company, of Copenhagen, was founded in 1897, with shipping and trading in raw materials as the main activities. Over the years the emphasis has shifted from raw materials to more specialised products, with the emphasis on technical know-how, and to participation in the actual production stage. Initially, the company engaged in trade primarily between Europe and Asia, but its interests now cover also Africa, North America, South America and Australia. The company's world-wide network includes 68 branch offices and 185 companies in which E.A.C. has a controlling interest. These enterprises are located in 51 countries and employ around 40,000 people. Their interests include shipping, industrial and agricultural activities, including timber, oil mills, soap, pharmaceuticals, milk and food processing, and international trading.

East Asiatic, however, is an exception. Few trading companies can match the size, and importance to the U.K. exporter, of the British and French (and Japanese) giants.

For a description of the Japanese trading companies, *see* XXI, 7.

AGENCIES

6. Definition. Agency may be defined as the legal relationship that exists when one person or company (the agent) is employed by another person or company (the principal) to bring that principal into a contractual relationship with third parties. Thus a sales agent is employed to bring about a sales contract between his principal and a third party, the customer.

Strictly speaking, the legal title to goods never passes to the agent; it passes, as a result of the agent's efforts, directly from principal to customer, the agent receiving a commission by way of remuneration. In marketing practice, however, the expression is loosely used to include distributors (*see* **11**).

7. Types of agent. Agents may be classified in many different ways. Some of the types of agent more important in international marketing are described below.

(*a*) *Commission agent.* The commission agent fits most nearly the definition given above. He sells with the aid of, for example, catalogues or samples, and does not hold stocks of the product, merely passing orders on to his principal, who in turn delivers the goods direct to the customer. Such an agency, of course, is particularly appropriate to industrial goods.

(*b*) *Stocking agent.* This agent stocks the product, providing storage and handling facilities, but does not take title to the goods. He will usually receive a commission on sales plus a fixed sum to cover storage and handling.

(*c*) *Agency with spares and servicing facilities.* Similarly, an agency may carry stocks of spare parts and provide servicing and repair facilities, for which he charges the customer, often at a scale of charges agreed with the principal.

(*d*) *Del credere agent.* This is not so much a type of agent as a contractual arrangement that could apply to any agency agreement. In selling through an agent, the principal may find that he has large numbers of customers on his books with whose credit rating he is entirely unfamiliar. The del credere agent accepts the credit risk, agreeing to pay the principal in the event of default by the customer.

Agencies vary greatly in size. They may be individuals, partnerships, or small companies specialising in representation, or they may be large-scale merchant or trading houses or major manufacturers wishing to exploit an established distribution organisation.

8. The appointment of agents: advantages. Agents are heavily relied on in the export trade, since at first sight, as a method of market entry, they offer significant advantages.

(*a*) The exporter obtains the services of (usually) an experienced local national, fully conversant with local business practices, and perhaps also with the exporter's industry.

(*b*) The agent's existing product lines and contracts facilitate the introduction of the exporter's product.

(*c*) The exporter gains market experience and is able to test potential.

(*d*) The investment cost (to the exporter) is nil or negligible.

(*e*) Results in terms of sales can often be immediate.

9. The appointment of agents: disadvantages. It is to be feared that these very obvious advantages have tempted far too many U.K. companies into the over-hasty appointment of an agent (for one example, see the Letraset case study, XXVII). The disadvantages of agencies are often, it seems, unjustifiably overlooked.

(*a*) Any lack of commitment of time or money on the part of the exporter is likely to result in a similar lack of commitment on the part of the agent.

(*b*) The agent, in any case, must offer a number of lines—he cannot give his full attention to the exporter's product.

(*c*) Few agents can afford to take a long-term view—if sales are not readily forthcoming, even the most conscientious agent is likely to leave the product in the range, but make no active efforts to promote it.

(d) If the market proves to have real potential, the agent may not have the resources to exploit it fully.

(e) As with any other intermediary, as sales develop agency commission costs are likely to become disproportionately high in relation to alternatives such as a branch office.

10. The appointment of agents: the correct approach. Clearly no hard and fast rules can be laid down as to when an agency is or is not the appropriate channel. All that can be said is that:

(a) an agency is only one channel, though an important one, among the various channel alternatives considered in VI;

(b) the agency alternative should be compared with these alternative channels in the light of the criteria set out in VI, 7;

(c) the appointment of an agent, if decided upon, requires the most careful planning, selection, motivation and supervision (*see* XVIII).

DISTRIBUTORS AND STOCKISTS

11. Distributors. Distributors have been defined as customers who have been granted exclusive or preferential rights to purchase and re-sell a specific range of products or services in specified geographical areas or markets.

Essentially, therefore, a distributor is a wholesaler, whose remuneration arises from the difference between the purchase price and the re-sale price (and not from any commission granted by the suppliers), and whose functions may include any or all of the 'middlemen functions described in VI, **2**. He differs from a normal wholesaler by virtue of the "exclusive or preferential rights" granted to him, but nevertheless his contractual relationship with the supplier is one of principal and principal, and *not* one of agent and principal.

12. Stockists. Stockists are distributors who receive a special price, discount, purchase terms or credit terms in return for undertaking to hold specified minimum levels of stock of a specified range of products.

13. The appointment of distributors and stockists. Although the relationship between supplier and distributor is one between principals, the granting of exclusivity or preferential terms usually implies the formal appointment of a distributor and the preparation of a distributorship agreement.

Further, most distributors will expect advice and assistance from their suppliers in the marketing of their products, and it will be in the interest of the supplier to provide such assistance.

In these respects, therefore, the appointment of a distributor offers much the same advantages and disadvantages as that of an agent (*see* **8, 9**) and requires similarly careful selection (*see* **10**) and subsequent motivation and channel management (*see* XI).

BRANCH OFFICES

14. Functions. A branch office abroad is simply an extension of the company into another country. There is no clear international definition of what constitutes a branch, and branch functions may vary significantly. In a distribution channel context, however, their responsibilities may include marketing and selling, physical distribution (transport and storage), servicing, repairs and the provision of spare parts. Manufacture is not a usual function of a branch.

15. Establishment of a branch. Not all countries allow branch-office operations; many merely permit branch offices by implication, i.e. they do not actually prohibit their establishment. Where branches are specifically permitted, the rules for their establishment vary, but they usually call for:

(*a*) registration of the name of the owning company, usually by submission to the appropriate registration authority of a certified copy (and sometimes an official translation) of the company's memorandum, articles of association and certificate of incorporation;

(*b*) a statement of the proposed activities of the branch;

(*c*) a declaration to the local tax authorities of the existence of the branch.

16. Legal considerations. A branch office of a U.K. company will usually be subject to the U.K. law as regards its management and operation; it will normally, however, be subject to the laws of the host country for other purposes, including exchange control, employment regulations, and the law of contract.

Before establishing a branch abroad, therefore, a U.K. company should check the legal position on at least the following points:

(a) regulations concerning the number of local staff that the branch *must* employ (many countries lay down a minimum number);

(b) the difficulty and expense of dismissal of such staff;

(c) staff social security and pension entitlements;

(d) mandatory trade union membership;

(e) the capacity and authority necessarily delegated to local staff and their power to bind the owning company;

(f) the general implications of local contract law, where it applies.

17. Taxation considerations. Establishment of a branch normally exposes the owning company to taxation in the country in which the branch is situated. Assessments to local tax may be considerably in excess of the benefit the owning company considers it has derived from the branch. Enquiries as to methods of tax assessment should be made before the branch is established.

18. Advantages of a branch office. A branch is usually established in lieu of a local distributor, often when sales through the distributor have reached a point at which a branch office becomes economic. In these circumstances:

(a) the sales cost per unit should in the future be less than the distributor's margin;

(b) sales may be expected to increase, since sales effort can be concentrated solely on the company's products, rather than dispersed over the wider product range necessarily carried by the distributor;

(c) the company has much greater control over the whole marketing effort, in that it no longer needs to secure the co-operation of an independent organisation;

(d) market information is likely to improve in both quantity and quality;

(e) often the standard of servicing will improve (servicing is an area where distributors tend to be less than satisfactory).

19. Disadvantages of a branch office. The branch office will, however, involve an initial capital investment, and a continuing overhead cost unrelated to the level of sales.

MARKETING SUBSIDIARY ABROAD

20. Functions. A marketing subsidiary abroad performs much the

VIII. INTERNATIONAL DISTRIBUTION DECISIONS III

same functions (*see* 14) and offers much the same advantages (*see* 18) and disadvantages (*see* 19) as a branch office. The difference is simply that the subsidiary is incorporated as a local company. As such, it has a local identity which:

(*a*) may assist in sales, especially to government and official bodies;

(*b*) isolates the parent company for legal or tax purposes (except for remission of profits).

For foreign *manufacturing* subsidiaries *see* X.

PROGRESS TEST 8

1. Under what circumstances might it be possible to make sales direct to customers abroad, without the assistance of agents or intermediaries? **(1)**

2. What is the essential difference between an agent and a distributor? **(6)**

3. What types of *true* agent do you know of? **(7)**

4. What advantages and disadvantages does the appointment of an agent offer? **(8, 9)**

5. What is a distributor, and how does he differ from a wholesaler? **(11)**

6. What are the usual functions of a branch office abroad? **(14)**

7. What advantages does a branch office offer as compared with a distributor? **(18)**

8. What advantages does a marketing subsidiary company abroad offer as compared with a branch office? **(20)**

CHAPTER IX

International Distribution Decisions IV
Joint Ventures

1. Introduction. This chapter considers joint ventures entered into with a partner abroad:

(*a*) licensing;
(*b*) franchising;
(*c*) industrial co-operation agreements;
(*d*) contract manufacture; and
(*e*) management contracts.

Assembly and manufacturing operations may, of course, be undertaken as joint ventures. These are discussed, however, in X.

LICENSING

2. Definition. The term "licensing" covers a wide range of agreements relating to the sale or leasing of industrial or commercial expertise (*see* **3**) by one party to another in return for valuable consideration (*see* **4**).

3. Saleable expertise. The industrial or commercial expertise which is the subject of the licence may include:

(*a*) a patent covering a product or process;
(*b*) manufacturing know-how not the subject of a patent;
(*c*) technical advice and assistance, including, occasionally, the supply of components, materials or plant essential to the manufacturing process;
(*d*) marketing advice and assistance;
(*e*) the use of a trade mark or trade name.

4. Payment for a licence. The valuable consideration (*see* **2**) may take the form of:

(*a*) an initial payment, payable as soon as the licence agreement is signed and often paid to cover the initial transfer of machinery, components, or designs, but sometimes simply for know-how;

(*b*) an annual minimum payment;

(*c*) an annual percentage fee, which may be based on sales or profits;

(*d*) cross-licensing, i.e. a mutual exchange of knowledge and/or patents;

(*e*) any combination of the above.

5. Advantages of licensing. The advantages to the licensor of entering into a licensing agreement are summarised below.

(*a*) *Market access.* Licensing permits entry into markets that are otherwise closed on account of:

(*i*) high rates of duty;

(*ii*) import quotas or prohibitions;

(*iii*) excessive freight charges, on bulky or heavy products; or

(*iv*) simply entrenched competition.

(*b*) *Capital investment.* Licensing requires little capital investment and should provide a higher rate of return on capital employed.

(*c*) *Risk.* Similarly, the penalties of failure are low.

(*d*) *Nationalisation.* The licensor is not exposed to the danger of nationalisation or expropriation of assets.

(*e*) *New products.* Because of the limited capital requirements, new products can be rapidly exploited, on a world-wide basis, before competition develops.

(*f*) *Marketing organisation.* The licensor can take immediate advantage of the licensee's local marketing and distribution organisation and of his existing customer contacts. Local manufacture may also be an advantage in securing government contracts, especially defence contracts.

6. Disadvantages of licensing. The disadvantages of licensing, again from the licensor's viewpoint, are set out below.

(*a*) *Competition from the licensee.* When the licensing agreement finally expires, the licensor may find he has established a competitor in his own former licensee.

(*b*) *Market exploitation.* The licensee, even if he reaches an agreed minimum turnover, may not fully exploit the market, leaving it open to the entry of competitors. The licensor inevitably loses control of the marketing operation.

(*c*) *Revenue.* Licence fees are normally a small percentage, e.g.

between 2 and 7 per cent, of turnover, and will often compare unfavourably with what might be obtained from a company's own manufacturing operation.

(*d*) *Product quality.* Quality control of the product is difficult—and the product will often be sold under the licensor's brand name.

(*e*) *Government.* Governments often impose conditions on remittances of royalties or on component supply.

(*f*) *Disagreements with licensee.* Arguments will arise, however carefully the licensing agreement (*see* 7) is drafted. A disaffected licensee can be a serious problem.

7. Licensing agreement. A licensing agreement is simply a statement, in legally enforceable form, of the details of a commercial contract. It is properly the subject of detailed negotiation and hard bargaining between the parties, and there can be no such thing as a standard form of contract. A check list is given below, however, of the major points that should be considered in drafting a licensing agreement. It is emphasised, however, that this list is necessarily over-simplified and that in all cases competent legal advice should be sought.

(*a*) *Parties to the contract.*

(*i*) Identification of licensor and licensee.

(*ii*) Extension of licence to licensee's subsidiaries/affiliates, if desired.

(*iii*) Reversion of licence in event of take-over of licensee, bankruptcy, etc.

(*iv*) Licensee's right to assign benefits.

(*b*) *Subject of the contract.*

(*i*) Definition of the expertise (see **3**).

(*ii*) Licensee's acknowledgment of validity of all patents and trade marks.

(*iii*) Licensor's right, if any, to subsequent technical developments originating with the licensee, and vice versa.

(*iv*) Capital investment required of licensor, if any.

(*c*) *Territory.*

(*i*) Definition of area for manufacturing rights and sales rights, including exports.

(*ii*) Degree of exclusivity for licensee.

(*iii*) If exclusive, licensee's obligation to meet full market demand, and licensor's rights if licensee fails in this obligation.

(d) *Financial.*
  (i) Licensee's royalty payments or cross-licensing obligations (*see* 4), including level of minimum royalty.
  (ii) Currency of payment, exchange rate, action in event of devaluation.
  (iii) Basis of royalty calculation and dates of payment.
  (iv) Liability for payment of local taxes on royalty payments, e.g. withholding tax.
  (v) Action in event of government prohibition on remittances or other payment difficulties.
  (vi) Possible right of licensor to take a share in the licensee's equity and at what valuation.
  (vii) Licensor's right to audit relevant records.
(e) *Performance of contract.*
  (i) Quality standards required of licensee.
  (ii) Licensor's right to check standards.
  (iii) Extent of technical assistance from licensor.
  (iv) Training by licensor of licensee's staff, secondment by licensor of technical staff, and provision for their expense.
  (v) Licensee's undertaking of confidentiality.
  (vi) Licensee's undertaking not to sell competing products.
  (vii) Licensee's obligation to protect patent in event of infringement by third parties.
  (viii) Conditions as to licensee's use of trademarks, and their protection in case of infringement.
  (ix) Conditions of sale of any components, materials, plant, etc., to be supplied by licensor.
(f) *Legal.*
  (i) The national law applying to the contract.
  (ii) Place of jurisdiction.
  (iii) Stipulation that disputes shall be referred to arbitration.
  (iv) Situation if performance of the contract prevented by events outside the control of the parties (*force majeure*).
  (v) Duration of the contract, provision for its termination in certain eventualities, and its renewal.
  (vi) Responsibility for official registration of the agreement and for any necessary government approvals that may be required.
  (vii) Provision that contract comes into effect only when such government approvals have been secured.

8. Managing licensing operations. For a licensor, the management of licensing operations is just as important as the management of a sales force or of overseas agencies, if profits are to be achieved and pitfalls avoided. Some guidelines for licensing management are given below.

(*a*) *Selection of licensee.* Selection of the licensee is critical; it is just as important as selection of salesmen and agencies, yet far more difficult. Companies should seek out and compare possible alternative licensees; they should not simply respond to an initiative from a foreign manufacturer.

(*b*) *Agreement.* The licensing agreement must be carefully drafted to protect the interests of *both* parties. All points listed in **7** are important, but in addition the licensor should satisfy himself at first hand not only of the technical competence of the licensee but also that he has genuine marketing coverage over the *whole* of the area allotted to him.

(*c*) *Control.* The licensor should endeavour, whenever possible, to maintain some degree of control throughout the duration of the agreement. He may, for instance, retain the right to supply certain ingredients or key components rather than giving a licence for a complete package; alternatively he may allow in the agreement for the acquiring of a sufficiently large equity interest to convert the operation into a joint venture, thus also avoiding the possibility of establishing a competitor at the expiry of the agreement.

(*d*) *Motivation.* The most effective way of encouraging a continuing interest on the part of the licensee is to ensure that he always has something to gain from it. Ideally the licensor should maintain a flow of technical improvements and marketing innovation. At the least he should provide regular assistance with both production and marketing problems, preferably in excess of the letter of the agreement.

FRANCHISING

9. Definition. Franchising is a form of licensing by which:

(*a*) the franchiser provides a standard package of components or ingredients together with management and marketing services or advice;

(*b*) the franchisee provides capital, market knowledge and personal involvement.

Franchising is particularly suitable for products which are not patentable.

> EXAMPLE: Pepsi-Cola relies heavily on franchising. Their franchise holders own the bottling plants, employ local staff, and control their own advertising and sales promotion budgets. Pepsi-Cola International sells its concentrate to the bottlers and provides promotional support and general advice on management of the operation.

10. Advantages of franchising. The advantages of franchising are broadly similar to those of a licensing operation (*see* **5**), except that franchising, with its greater degree of control resulting from the supply of ingredients or components, offers the possibility of revenue from a product that is not patentable.

11. Disadvantages of franchising. Again, these are similar to those of licensing, except that franchising often tends to be a smaller operation. Many more franchisees are required, as a rule, and the search for competent franchisees can be expensive and time-consuming.

INDUSTRIAL CO-OPERATION AGREEMENTS

12. Definition. Industrial co-operation agreements (I.C.A.s) are long-term specialisation agreements entered into by manufacturers with the aim of improving their operating efficiency. Their essential characteristic is that they entail a degree of co-ordination and interdependence in the manufacturing programmes of the partners.

An I.C.A. may involve the interchange between manufacturers of raw materials or components required in the manufacture of a finished product.

> EXAMPLE: Ikarus (Hungary) and Saurer (Austria) co-produce a bus, Ikarus providing the engine and superstructure and Saurer the chassis.

An alternative form of co-operation involves the exchange of finished products. *Each* partner agrees to manufacture only some of the products it needs to supply its home market, but to supply a sufficient quantity of those same products to supply its partner's market as well.

> EXAMPLE: Slovnaft (Czechoslovakia) and Österreichische

Stickstoffwerke (Austria) have an arrangement where each partner specialises in the production of only part of a specified range of chemical products.

13. Advantages of I.C.A.s. The advantages of I.C.A.s, for both partners, will be clear:

(*a*) lower unit production costs resulting from longer production runs;

(*b*) the availability of established marketing and servicing networks.

In addition, when the agreement is between the East and West, as in the examples above, the interdependence of the partners generates bilateral flows of complementary goods which to a large extent eliminate the currency problems so often associated with East–West trade.

CONTRACT MANUFACTURE

14. Definition. International contract manufacture involves merely a formal long-term contract, between parties in two different countries, for the manufacture or assembly of a product. The company placing the contract retains full control over distribution and marketing.

Contract manufacture is thus a half-way house between mere licensing and direct investment in manufacturing facilities.

15. Advantages of contract manufacture. Advantages of contract manufacture, to the company placing the contract, include:

(*a*) limited local investment, with no risk of nationalisation or expropriation;

(*b*) retention of market control;

(*c*) avoidance of currency risks;

(*d*) a locally-made image, which may assist in sales, especially to government or official bodies;

(*e*) possible cost advantages, if local costs are lower;

(*f*) entry into markets otherwise protected by tariffs or other barriers.

Contract manufacture is perhaps most likely to be of interest where a product has no patent protection, and where the market is too small to justify investment in manufacturing facilities.

16. Disadvantages of contract manufacture. On the other hand:

(*a*) contract manufacture is only possible when a satisfactory and reliable manufacturer can be found—not always an easy task;

(*b*) often extensive technical training will have to be given to the local manufacturer's staff;

(*c*) as a result, at the end of the contract, the sub-contractor could become a formidable competitor;

(*d*) control over manufacturing quality is difficult to achieve, despite the ultimate sanction of refusal to accept sub-standard goods.

MANAGEMENT CONTRACT

17. Definition. A management contract is an agreement by which one company, the management company, manages some or all of the operations of another company in return for management fees and, sometimes, a share of the profits.

> EXAMPLE: Hilton Hotels have management contracts with hotels abroad, earning fees for consulting and management services with little or no equity participation.

18. Advantages of the management contract. The management contract:

(*a*) permits low-risk market entry, with no capital investment, and no expropriation risk;

(*b*) capitalises on management skills;

(*c*) provides a guaranteed minimum income and a quick return.

19. Disadvantages of the management contract. On the other hand:

(*a*) the local investor may seek to interfere with the way *his* investment is being managed;

(*b*) training and initial staffing requirements can be a serious drain on the other activities of the managing company—skilled personnel are always a scarce resource.

PROGRESS TEST 9

1. What are the attractions, and what are the dangers of licensing as a method of entry into a foreign market? **(5, 6)**

2. What is a licensing agreement, and what are the more important clauses that it should normally include? **(7)**

3. What is a franchise agreement? **(9)**

4. What is meant by "industrial co-operation agreement"? Why is it of particular importance internationally, especially in relation to the Eastern bloc countries? **(12, 13)**

5. When is contract manufacture feasible, and when is it desirable? **(15, 16)**

6. What is an international management contract and what advantages does it offer to the *managing* company? **(17, 18)**

CHAPTER X

International Distribution Decisions V: Manufacture Abroad

1. Introduction. Manufacturing abroad involves a tangible investment in production plant in a country other than that in which the investing company is established. Such an investment may be merely an extension of existing manufacturing facilities, or it may involve the initial establishment or acquisition of assembly or manufacturing facilities with the aim of gaining entry into, or retaining existing sales in, a market. This chapter considers manufacture abroad from the point of view of market entry, or retention, only.

2. Policy decisions. A company contemplating manufacturing abroad faces a number of policy decisions:

(*a*) whether to manufacture abroad at all (the initial investment decision);

(*b*) if so, in which country to locate the plant;

(*c*) whether to establish a full manufacturing operation or merely an assembly plant;

(*d*) whether to establish an independent operation or seek a joint venture with a local partner;

(*e*) whether to establish a new plant or acquire an existing company.

These decisions clearly have far-reaching implications in terms of company strategy, marketing and financial policy. In this chapter they can be discussed only briefly, with the emphasis, of course, on marketing. For simplicity, each of the decisions is considered separately in turn, though in practice, of course, they are interdependent.

THE INITIAL INVESTMENT DECISION

3. The investment-decision process. In considering a possible investment a company will normally calculate its anticipated rate of return. It will:

(*a*) estimate the current and future market potential;

(*b*) estimate the share of the market it is likely to achieve, and, consequently, company sales;

(*c*) estimate production costs, both present and future;

(*d*) relate sales to costs to provide an anticipated profit (rate of return) on the investment.

There is clearly scope for error in these estimates in any market—an investment decision is among the most difficult faced by management. An international investment decision, however, involves a yet greater degree of uncertainty and risk. Not only are errors in the initial estimates perhaps more likely, given a relative unfamiliarity with the marketing environment, but also political and exchange risks, e.g. nationalisation, devaluation, etc., must be taken into account. The degree of risk will, of course, vary between one country and another. The risk may, in certain circumstances, be insurable with the E.C.G.D.

4. Rate of return. Before making any investment decision, whether at home or abroad, a company will satisfy itself that its anticipated rate of return is at least equal to:

(*a*) its normal target rate of return;

(*b*) the return it might expect from any alternative investment under consideration.

For an investment abroad the company should adopt one additional criterion: that the rate of return should be high enough to compensate for the additional uncertainty and risk. The risk premium, of course, will again vary from country to country.

5. Investment strategy. Investment decisions will usually result from a rational search for additional profit opportunities. International investment, however, may sometimes be a defensive measure, resulting, for instance, from a desire to retain an established export market which the company is in danger of losing, perhaps as a result of a change in currency values. In these circumstances, the company is tempted to depart from its investment strategy and make an isolated and urgent decision, without fully considering alternative investment possibilities.

It is important, however, that the company should still apply the same objective criteria as for any other international investment, including the required rate of return (*see* **4**). The present or future loss of profit resulting from the loss of the export market is simply one factor, even if an important one, to take into account.

6. Factors influencing the investment decision. A full discussion of all the factors to be considered in arriving at a decision to invest abroad is beyond the scope of this book. Below are listed the more important items that typically require consideration, other than market potential (it is assumed that research has already selected the appropriate markets).

(*a*) *Political.*
   (*i*) Political stability or uncertainty.
   (*ii*) Attitude of host government to private enterprise, and, in particular, to foreign private investment.
   (*iii*) Special inducement for foreign investors, such as tax holidays, grants, loans at favourable rates, tariff protection for newly-established industries.
   (*iv*) Membership of a free-trade area, or trade agreements with other countries that might offer export opportunities.

(*b*) *Legal.*
   (*i*) Legal discrimination against foreign companies or their expatriate employees.
   (*ii*) Percentage of company that may be foreign-owned.
   (*iii*) Patent protection laws and ease of enforcement.
   (*iv*) Trade mark protection.
   (*v*) Price control legislation.
   (*vi*) Restrictive trade practice legislation.

(*c*) *Costs.*
   (*i*) Cost increases resulting from smaller scale of production, product modification to meet market needs, etc.
   (*ii*) Wage costs, related to productivity.
   (*iii*) Additional labour costs, e.g. company share of social security payments.
   (*iv*) Availability and costs of local raw materials and components.
   (*v*) Availability and cost of transport services.
   (*vi*) Freight, packing and insurance savings, if product previously exported to the country.

(*d*) *Taxation.*
   (*i*) Existence of a double-taxation agreement between host country and parent-company country.
   (*ii*) Withholding tax payable on remittances to parent company.

(*iii*) Level of company taxation.
(*iv*) Method of calculation of depreciation allowances, stock valuation, etc.
(*e*) *Exchange Control.*
(*i*) Restrictions on remittances to parent company, e.g. maximum percentage of foreign capital invested.
(*ii*) Restrictions on repatriation of capital.
(*iii*) Convertibility of local currency.
(*f*) *Finance.*
(*i*) Local sources of capital, and interest rates payable.
(*ii*) Practicability of supplying capital from the U.K. (*see* 7).
(*iii*) External sources of capital (*see* 7).
(*iv*) Local accounting requirements and conventions.
(*v*) Rate of inflation.
(*g*) *Personnel.*
(*i*) Availability of labour, e.g. skilled, unskilled, clerical.
(*ii*) Availability of local managerial talent.
(*iii*) Percentage of employees that must be local nationals.
(*iv*) Availability of work permits for expatriates.
(*v*) Living conditions for expatriates, e.g. housing, education, medical, etc.
(*vi*) Labour laws and regulations, especially regarding appointment and dismissal of staff.
(*vii*) Industrial relations, trade unions, worker participation in management.
(*viii*) Existence of compulsory profit-sharing schemes for employees.

7. Insurance of overseas investment. International marketers should be aware that it is possible to insure overseas investment with the Export Credits Guarantee Department against expropriation, war damage and restriction of remittances of profits. The E.C.G.D. scheme covers virtually all countries, though it is intended primarily for developing nations.

The investment must be *new*, and the investor must apply for cover *before* becoming irrevocably committed to invest. Injection of new capital into an existing enterprise is regarded as new investment. In certain circumstances, reinvestment of retained earnings, or the purchase of a foreign interest in an existing enterprise, may also be regarded as new investment.

E.C.G.D.'s commitment is normally for a maximum of fifteen years and for 90 per cent of any loss from the insured causes. An

X. INTERNATIONAL DISTRIBUTION DECISIONS V

overall maximum insured amount will be determined at the outset, within which the investor proposes a *current* insured amount at the beginning of each twelve months of the insurance contract. E.C.G.D. may restrict or refuse cover at its discretion, especially where the risks appear exceptional.

8. Financing investment abroad (grants and loans). Many governments are anxious to encourage foreign investment in manufacturing plant, especially in designated development areas. A variety of grants, loans, and other incentives is available to the Investor.

> EXAMPLE: DATAR, the French national government agency for regional planning and development, offers French or foreign firms investing in new plant in certain designated development areas cash grants of between 12 per cent and 25 per cent of the total value of the investment. Extension of existing facilities in those same areas attracts grants of between 12 per cent and 20 per cent. Subsidies are also payable for the cost of staff training (50 per cent) and instructor training (100 per cent). Other incentives available through DATAR include tax reductions and tax exemptions, and a proportion of personnel relocation costs. Local government bodies and other authorities offer additional assistance, including the sale of prepared industrial sites at less than cost, and standard factory buildings.

LOCATION OF INVESTMENT

9. The location decision. The investing company must decide:

(*a*) in which country to invest;
(*b*) exactly where in that country its plant should be located.

The second decision is outside the scope of this book and is not considered further. It will also be realised that the decision as to the country of investment is closely linked with the initial decision to invest at all. The factors listed in **6**, therefore, are again relevant.

An investing company, however, should consider two additional location possibilities: third-country manufacture and free-trade areas.

10. Third-country manufacture. The obvious site for a production plant would seem to be within one of the markets it supplies.

Sometimes, however, it will pay to site the plant in a third country which enjoys free access to the markets served but offers additional advantages, e.g. lower tax rates, lower wage rates, inducements for foreign investors.

> EXAMPLE: A rum manufacturer set up a distillery in Puerto Rico in order to serve the United States market. Puerto Rico is a commonwealth of the U.S.A., with free access to the U.S. market as a whole. It offers significant inducements to investors, and a supply of not over-expensive labour, skilled in this trade. The raw material for rum, sugar cane, is grown locally. To supply the U.K. market, a distillery was established in the Bahamas, where a particular advantage was the right to supply the U.K. and other E.E.C. countries up to a permitted quota. As the quota was inadequate to supply the whole of the company's requirements within the E.E.C., supplies for France were drawn from a distillery on the island of Martinique, which is legally part of metropolitan France and has, therefore, unrestricted access to the French market. It was decided to supply the Australian market from an existing distillery in Brazil, largely because of the highly attractive export incentives paid by the Brazilian Government.

11. Free-trade areas. A free trade area is an enclosed zone, under customs supervision, in or near a port of entry, into which foreign goods not otherwise prohibited may be imported without payment of duty. A free port is a port designated as a free-trade area.

Free-trade areas are usually operated by government or local governments. The government's aim is to increase business activity within its borders, i.e. activity that would normally be discouraged by high import duties. With this aim in mind, most free-trade areas permit processing, assembly, sorting and repacking. In some countries, a company can arrange for a part of its own plant to be declared a free-trade area.

> EXAMPLE: There are several free trade areas located throughout the U.S.A. These areas, known as Free Trade Zones, are situated in New York City, New Orleans, San Francisco, Seattle, Toledo, Kansas City (Missouri), Kansas City (Kansas), McAllen, San José (California), Little Rock, Sault Ste. Marie, Omaha, Dorchester County, Chicago, Orange County, Pittston, Port Everglades, and Shenandoah. Goods imported into these zones may be stored, sold in wholesale quantities,

exhibited, broken up, replaced, assembled, mixed with foreign or domestic merchandise or otherwise manipulated or manufactured. Goods are not subject to the payment of duty until withdrawn from the foreign trade zones.

12. Advantages of free-trade areas. Free-trade areas offer the following advantages:

(*a*) lower freight costs, because:
  (*i*) it becomes economic to ship in bulk, since duty is not paid until the goods are imported into the country from the area;
  (*ii*) it is possible to ship components and assemble in the area;
(*b*) reduction in stock costs, again because duty payments are delayed;
(*c*) complete avoidance of duty on:
  (*i*) components or ingredients imported into the area and subsequently re-exported in finished products;
  (*ii*) items damaged in transit and rejected;
(*d*) improved security resulting from the customs supervision.

ASSEMBLY OPERATIONS

13. Advantages of assembly operations. An assembly operation is a half-way house between exporting and a complete manufacturing operation abroad. It offers many advantages:

(*a*) lower freight costs;
(*b*) lower import duties (lower in any case if duty is charged *ad valorem*, but sometimes the *rate* of duty is lower as well);
(*c*) easier modification of the product to suit local market requirements;
(*d*) possible cost advantages, e.g. from lower wage rates for the assembly operation, or from local purchase of cheaper components;
(*e*) creation of a national image, which may help in marketing;
(*f*) initial experience of the market, which will be of value if a full manufacturing operation is to be established.

14. Disadvantages of assembly operations. Apart from the fact that some capital investment is required, a disadvantage of an assembly operation is that the host country may eventually apply pressure to bring about extension into full manufacture.

JOINT VENTURES

15. Definition. An international joint venture involves some degree of association with an organisation in another country. Licensing and contract manufacture (*see* IX, 2 and 14), for instance, are two examples of joint ventures.

In the context of assembly or manufacture, however, an international joint venture is an operation in which:

(*a*) two or more companies, in different countries, join forces, not merely for manufacturing purposes but also (usually) for marketing, financial and management advantages; and

(*b*) in which all participants have both a share in the equity and a voice in management.

The proportion of shares held by each of the participants may vary widely, but, for the purposes of the present discussion, the essential feature of a joint venture is that no one participant holds a sufficient shareholding to exercise effective managerial control. (If this latter case does arise, the venture takes on many of the characteristics of an independent operation for the dominant partner, and becomes largely an investment in shares, though an important one, for other partners.)

16. Circumstances favouring joint ventures. Joint ventures are usually contemplated as an alternative to a wholly-owned manufacturing operation abroad. In such a case a joint venture will often be preferred when:

(*a*) 100 per cent foreign equity ownership is not permitted by local laws, as in Nigeria;

(*b*) local government attitudes towards foreign investment are such that an independent operation, though legally possible, is not an attractive alternative;

(*c*) it is important to acquire quickly local marketing expertise or an established distribution network;

(*d*) there is inadequate capital to exploit fully all markets offering potential;

(*e*) managerial and other personnel resources are limited (this is particularly relevant in the case of the smaller company);

(*f*) political and other uncertainties, e.g. fear of expropriation, call for some limitation of investment risks;

(*g*) a manufacturing company wishes to safeguard its sources of supply of raw materials, e.g. a steel works may enter into a foreign venture for the exploitation of iron ore deposits.

17. Conflict of interest. In *any* joint venture there is an inherent conflict of interest; each partner will inevitably wonder whether his reward is proportionate to the share of the profits his efforts have earned.

Disagreements are yet more likely to arise, however, in the case of an *international* joint venture, simply as a result of:

(*a*) national differences in culture, business practices and management styles;

(*b*) inadequate communications, arising from both distance and language problems.

18. Minimising conflict. It is therefore essential to minimise the possibility of conflict by:

(*a*) undertaking the most careful and detailed evaluation of joint-venture partners;

(*b*) negotiating a joint-venture agreement of benefit to *both* sides;

(*c*) covering in that agreement all eventualities that might reasonably be expected to give rise to differences of opinion, e.g.:

(*i*) dividend policy, i.e. amount to be distributed to the partners, and amount to be retained in the business for further investment;

(*ii*) basis of transfer prices for components supplied to the venture by any of the partners;

(*iii*) export sales by the joint venture to countries in which either of the partners is operating, or to which they are exporting;

(*d*) arranging in advance some mechanism by which any unforeseen disagreements can be resolved, e.g. arbitration.

19. Achieving control. Companies are often unwilling, as a matter of policy, to accept a minority (or 50/50) interest in any venture, being unwilling to lose control. It is possible however, to arrange to retain effective control over at least the key decisions, even with a minority shareholding. Subject to local regulations, a U.K. partner may, for example:

(*a*) arrange a management contract;

(*b*) retain ownership of key patents and trademarks;

(*c*) retain the right to appoint the directors, or the key managers;

(*d*) arrange for the issue of voting and non-voting shares, retaining a majority of voting shares;

(*e*) encourage equity participation by banks or insurance companies that have no interest in management;
(*f*) spread the majority shareholding over a multitude of small investors.

ACQUISITION OF A COMPANY ABROAD

20. Definition. Acquisition of a company abroad involves the purchase of all or a majority of the shares of that company; otherwise the operation becomes at most a joint venture (*see* **15**).

Often, of course, the acquisition question will simply not arise, since:

(*a*) local government regulations and attitudes may make acquisition by a foreign company difficult, if not impossible;
(*b*) there may be, in the relevant country, no suitable candidate for acquisition;
(*c*) the suitable companies may not be interested in a take-over and a direct appeal to shareholders may be impracticable.

21. Advantages of acquisition. In comparison with an independent operation, acquisition offers three immensely important advantages:

(*a*) market entry, and revenue earning, are immediate;
(*b*) the purchase price includes not merely the production facilities but an established marketing and distribution organisation, market knowledge and contacts, and trained and experienced local staff;
(*c*) the cash requirement for the purchase may be minimal, e.g. it may be possible to issue shares in payment.

22. Disadvantages of acquisition. Two principal disadvantages must be considered:

(*a*) the grants of capital, low-interest loans, tax holidays, tariff protection for infant industries, etc., so often offered to foreign investors in new plant will not normally be available in the case of an acquisition;
(*b*) integrating *any* newly-acquired company is a difficult, expensive and time-consuming task that is not invariably successful, and it is a yet more difficult task in the case of a foreign company.

X. INTERNATIONAL DISTRIBUTION DECISIONS V
PROGRESS TEST 10

1. What are the major policy considerations that management will need to take into account in arriving at a decision to manufacture overseas? **(2)**

2. What factors would you take into account in selecting a particular country for the establishment of a manufacturing operation? **(6)**

3. How might a company finance a manufacturing investment in a foreign country? **(7, 8)**

4. What is a free-trade area, and what advantages might it offer to a multinational company? **(11, 12)**

5. Assembly operations are a half-way house between exporting and manufacture abroad. What advantages do they offer in comparison with each of these alternatives? **(13)**

6. Under what circumstances might a company decide on a joint-venture manufacturing operation with a foreign partner? **(16)**

7. In any joint venture, but especially an international joint venture, conflict is likely to arise. How can such conflict be minimised? **(18)**

8. How might a company with a minority interest in a joint venture still retain effective control over the operation? **(19)**

9. Why might a company prefer the acquisition route to obtaining wholly-owned manufacturing facilities overseas? **(21)**

CHAPTER XI

International Distribution Decisions VI: Foreign-Market Channel Design and Management

CHANNEL DESIGN

1. Foreign-market channel structures. For the reasons mentioned in VI, 3, channel decisions in any market are among the most important facing management. For any given product, several alternative channels may be practicable and it is often difficult to make the right choice between them.

The task facing the international marketer is infinitely more complex, simply because distribution systems vary so significantly between nations. Within each nation distribution systems have evolved over many years and they inevitably reflect not merely differences in economic development but social and cultural diversity. Figure 7 shows typical wholesale–retail distribution patterns for four different countries by way of example. Even with these necessarily generalised analyses of the distribution systems, fundamental differences become obvious.

Under these circumstances, every product and every country presents the international marketer with a unique problem to which no general solution can be propounded. Unless, therefore, he is already well acquainted with the market, the international marketer will need to undertake careful research into the established distribution systems relevant to his product. Only on the basis of reliable information can he hope to design the most effective marketing channel.

Such research is likely to cover the market characteristics discussed below.

2. Examination of market characteristics. Channel design will involve consideration of such factors as:

(*a*) customer characteristics, e.g. number, geographical location, purchasing pattern, purchasing preferences;

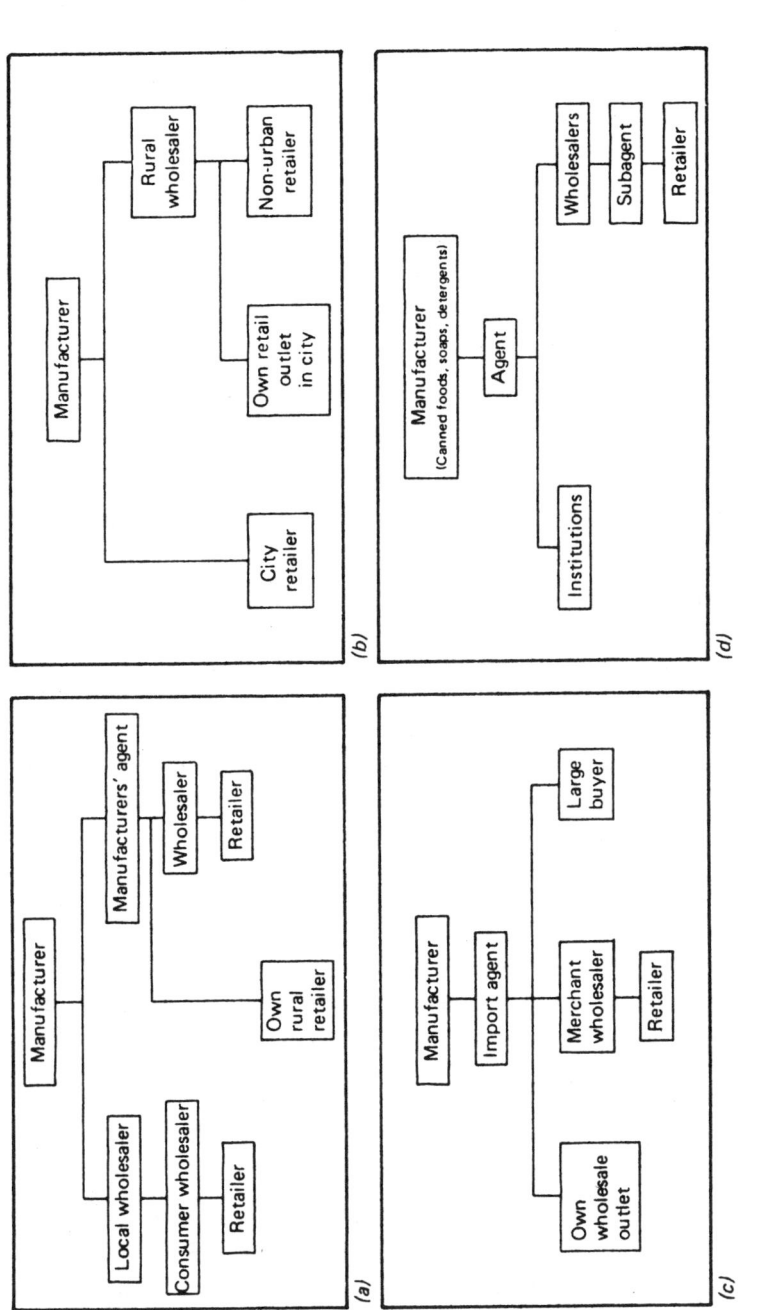

FIG. 7 Typical wholesale-retail distribution patterns (a) India. (b) Turkey. (c) Venezuela. (d) Egypt.

(b) product characteristics, e.g. bulk, weight, perishability, unit value, servicing requirements;

(c) existing intermediaries and their activities, e.g. physical distribution, storage, advertising, selling, customer credit;

(d) competitor characteristics, e.g. need to avoid, or to take advantage of, competitors' channels, degree of exclusivity offered to competitors;

(e) legal restrictions imposed by certain governments, e.g. Norway lays down specific licensing requirements for middlemen; in Italy, municipalities have some discretion over the product lines that may be handled;

(f) company characteristics, e.g. size, financial resources, product mix, previous channel experience, and overall marketing strategy.

3. Consideration of alternative channels. It is at this stage that the international marketer will encounter some of the special problems of foreign-market distribution. Often the channels adopted elsewhere will simply not exist. In other cases the obvious channel will not be available: the number of middlemen available in many developing markets is small, and these may already have been attracted on an exclusive basis to competitors; or associations of middlemen may have joined in an agreement to restrict distribution to a limited number of suppliers (usually domestic).

Under these circumstances, a foreign company has a number of alternatives:

(a) to take over local distributors;

(b) to "buy distribution" by offering extra-high margins or other financial inducements;

(c) to build up its own parallel outlets from scratch;

(d) to develop a completely different type of channel from scratch, e.g. door-to-door selling of soap, for instance, is economically possible in some developing countries;

(e) to use its ingenuity in developing original methods of distribution, or transferring such methods from other countries.

> EXAMPLE: Tupperware Home Products Inc. sold in the U.S.A. through its "party-plan", i.e. housewives organised parties in their own homes, at which the products were on display, and received commission on sales. This system was transferred unchanged to Japan where, despite all the social, cultural and economic differences, it was highly successful.

It should be borne in mind, however, that building up new channels is one of the most difficult tasks in international business.

4. Evaluation of alternative channels. The final choice between the various alternative channels, existing or new, will depend on the balance between anticipated distribution costs on the one hand, and, on the other, control, coverage and continuity (which in turn will affect likely sales volume).

(*a*) *Cost.* Two kinds of channel cost may again be distinguished:
   (*i*) the capital or investment cost of building or developing the channel; and
   (*ii*) the continuing cost of maintaining it, e.g. the cost of the company's own salesmen, or the commission, mark-ups, etc., taken by intermediaries.

(*b*) *Coverage.*
   (*i*) Market coverage may be on an *intensive* basis, with the product available in as many outlets as economically possible. Intensive coverage is not easy to develop in many markets and the international marketer will often have to be satisfied with intensive coverage of urban areas only.
   (*ii*) Alternatively, it may be on a *selective* basis, with a limited number of outlets committed to the product, often with an exclusivity agreement.
   (*iii*) A further consideration is coverage of *all* product lines: middlemen may take on the lucrative parts of a line but reject or ignore others. Occasionally, separate channels of distribution must be developed in foreign markets for products which would in other markets be regarded as a homogeneous line.

(*c*) *Control.* Channel control is a critical question: it is, after all, the main reason why the international marketer involves himself in the difficult area of foreign-market distribution. A manufacturer enjoying intensive coverage can achieve control, just as in his domestic market, by heavy advertising to the ultimate consumer, i.e. the "pull" strategy, by which customer demand, generated by advertising, draws the products through the distribution chain. This policy is, however, expensive and open only to the larger companies.

Manufacturers without the resources necessary for such an approach should still, however, seek the maximum degree of control. Usually coverage will have to be selective, and a degree of exclusivity offered. In return, the manufacturer should expect to exercise a degree of influence over the middleman's market coverage, prices, services, etc. Not all levels of distribution, of course, can be controlled to the same degree and by the same methods, but quotas, reports and personal visits by company staff can all assist.

(*d*) *Continuity.* Channels of distribution pose problems of continuity which should be considered at the evaluation stage. Many distributors in developing countries are small organisations—retirement of one or two partners can mean closure of the business. In many countries, too, distributors dependent on imports have learnt that political changes, exchange control or exchange-rate variations can radically affect their competitive position. They may tend, therefore, to be less than loyal to their principals.

CHANNEL MANAGEMENT

5. Selection of individual channel members. Selection of middlemen is particularly difficult in foreign markets. Many distributors, for instance, will suffer from low sales volume or under-financing; not all will prove reliable. Often the ideal will have to be rejected in favour of the expedient, especially in developing countries.

6. Motivation. Once the channel has been established, a motivational programme must be instituted to maintain a high level of middleman interest in the manufacturer's products. The manufacturer faces much the same problems of motivation as in his domestic market and any motivational programme assumes as a pre-requisite that the middleman is achieving an adequate volume at an adequate margin. Additional motivational factors often of particular importance in many foreign markets, however, are:

(*a*) training of dealer staff;
(*b*) credit terms;
(*c*) local advertising support;
(*d*) company communications, e.g. letters, newsletters, promotional conferences (often at company headquarters), publicity in company media, personal visits by company staff.

7. Control. The control designed into the system must be firmly exercised as a matter of conscious policy, not merely to exclusive dealers but as far down the channel as possible. Direct influence will not always be feasible, but the indirect approach can often be successful.

EXAMPLE: A spirits manufacturer introduced his product into West Germany. Initially the product was regarded as a luxury item and distributor margins were necessarily high. As sales developed the manufacturer persuaded his main agents to reduce their prices. The large retail groups and grocery chains responded by reducing their own prices accordingly, but most smaller retailers maintained their original prices and margins. Retail margins soon became a bar to further market penetration. The manufacturer offered special discounts to the retail groups and grocery chains, provided most of the discount was used to advertise the price reductions. The smaller retailers were forced to quote lower prices in order to compete. Sales (and profits for the manufacturer) showed a marked increase.

8. Performance evaluation. As with any managed and controlled distribution channel, the performance of channel members should be regularly evaluated, preferably, in the case of exclusive dealerships, against standards agreed in writing. Where these standards are not met the causes should be investigated.

9. Separation. Occasionally, it will be necessary to dispense with the services of a dealer/distributor whose performance is not up to the required standard. Where some form of agreement has been entered into between the distributor and the manufacturer this is, in some countries, by no means an easy matter.

(*a*) In many countries the business community is very small, and mishandling of the separation arrangements can provoke hostility in the trade.

(*b*) In other countries, the law recognises that middlemen invest time and effort in developing the manufacturer's business and heavy compensation may be payable.

10. Channel obsolescence. In any country, there should be a constant watch for channel obsolescence, which will usually occur when a competitor steals a march by opening up entirely new channels. This is perhaps more difficult in foreign markets, but it is just as important.

11. New channels. Similarly, the manufacturer should himself actively seek possible additional or alternative channels as market conditions change. This is particularly important in the smaller developing countries.

PROGRESS TEST 11

1. Why do distribution channels vary so markedly between one country and another? **(1)**

2. What market information would you require to assist you in designing a channel of distribution for your products in a foreign country? **(2)**

3. What factors would you take into account in evaluating the various alternative channels open to you in a foreign country? **(4)**

4. What methods of middlemen motivation are of particular relevance in markets abroad? **(6)**

5. Why is it especially difficult abroad to terminate distribution agreements? **(9)**

CHAPTER XII

International Pricing Decisions I: Pricing Strategies

1. Introduction. The alternative pricing strategies discussed in most marketing text-books are, of course, relevant to both domestic and international markets. They are briefly reviewed in this chapter, with special emphasis on their international application.

2. Pricing orientation. Three different approaches are usually distinguished in relation to pricing policy: competitor orientation, cost orientation, and demand orientation.

(*a*) *Competitor-oriented pricing.* The extreme example of competitor-oriented pricing is found in the commodity markets, e.g. wheat, tea, coffee, etc., where world market prices are known and prevail. These prices are established through the collective interaction of a large number of buyers and sellers. For any one individual producer to quote above the prevailing price would merely invite a catastrophic fall in orders; to quote below it would mean a pointless reduction in profit.

In commodity marketing and similar situations, the company really has no pricing decision to take, except to concentrate on cost reduction. The strategies discussed below are not open to it.

(*b*) *Cost-oriented pricing.* The cost-oriented company will quote as its price its total unit cost plus a percentage of profit, demand considerations having little influence on the final price. The approach is not unusual for those industrial goods where differentiation between products, in terms of value to the customer, is often difficult.

Some of the pricing strategies discussed below (*see* **4–8**), however, are open to the cost-oriented producer.

(*c*) *Demand-oriented pricing.* Demand-oriented pricing requires an assessment of the intensity of demand: high prices are charged when and where demand is buoyant, and low prices are charged when and where demand is weak, even if unit costs are the same in both cases. Price-setting is flexible, several alternative strategies, including those discussed below (*see* **4–8**), are open to the company, and pricing becomes an effective weapon in the marketer's armoury. Demand-oriented prices are usual in the case of branded consumer goods and are a practical possibility with many industrial goods.

3. The long-run pricing objective. The long-run objective of commercial organisations may be taken to be profit maximisation, subject to ethical or legal constraints which are often merely implicit, e.g. the company will not enter into price-fixing agreements with competitors where such agreements are forbidden by law.

In pursuing the objective of profit maximisation, however, a company may adopt several different short-run strategies, including a market penetration strategy, a market-skimming strategy, early cash recovery, and a strategy aimed at ensuring a satisfactory rate of return on investment. The international marketer is faced with an additional dimension: standardisation or differentiation of prices between countries.

4. Market penetration. A market-penetration strategy implies the establishment of a relatively low price, with the aims of stimulating market growth, capturing a high market share, and discouraging competition. Essential pre-conditions for such a strategy are a price-sensitive market and significant manufacturing economies of scale.

Some degree of courage is also required: by definition, results in terms of profits are not quickly achieved. The export marketer, in particular, will think carefully before adopting a market-penetration strategy; he may find the market lost to him, e.g. by significant variations in exchange rates, or by import restrictions, before he has achieved a satisfactory profit position.

5. Market-skimming. The aim of market-skimming is initially to obtain a premium price from buyers to whom the product has a high present value; prices are subsequently reduced to attract the more price-conscious market segments. Books, for instance, are usually produced first in a limited hard-cover edition; the cheap paper-back edition follows later, in the light of demand indications.

A market-skimming strategy is particularly relevant to the international marketer who has selected a policy of undifferentiated marketing rather than concentration (*see* **II, 6**). With limited commitment, and possibly only through limited distribution channels, he can try his hand profitably in several markets.

EXAMPLE: A U.K. manufacturer of men's suits decided he was unable to compete on a price basis in export markets. A fundamental problem of high production costs was exacerbated by fashion differences which implied, at least initially, uneconomic short-run production. He therefore promoted a range of standard U.K.-style suits as the "British Look" at a premium price in the U.S.A., restricting sales efforts to the better department stores. Results were sufficiently encouraging to justify the extension of this strategy to selected European markets.

6. Early cash recovery. A cash-recovery strategy aims at rapid cash generation. The company may simply be short of funds, or it may regard its future in the market as too uncertain to justify patient market cultivation. The international marketer who rejects a market-penetration strategy for fear of import restrictions, for instance, may incline to a policy of early cash recovery.

7. Satisfactory rate of return. The aim of this strategy is to achieve a satisfactory rate of return but no more: a level of profit that may be considered normal for a given amount of investment and a given level of risk. It is often the strategy (at least implicit) of the cost-oriented industrial-goods company.

At first sight this strategy may seem to be at variance with the long-term objective of profit maximisation, but in the domestic market this is not necessarily so; manufacturing costs of all companies in the domestic industry are likely to be broadly similar, so the approach makes for market stabilisation and avoidance of damaging price wars.

This advantage will often not apply internationally, however, since manufacturing costs can vary significantly between one country and another. It might be thought, therefore, that exporters would avoid a policy of satisfactory rate of return and the resultant near-standardisation of price quotations. Nevertheless, many companies remain content to quote prices in export markets which provide a uniform rate of return on a given product. Some will even quote the same ex-works price for both domestic and export markets, as the Betro report disclosed:

EXAMPLE: The prices at which products will sell in the export markets are determined as a rule in Britain and prices are often the same for all markets. This practice tends to deprive companies of flexibility that could help in maximising profits and also in meeting competition.

8. Differential pricing opportunities. Many companies, particularly in the consumer-goods field, establish a different price in each significant market segment, charging what the market will bear. This, the strategy of the demand-oriented company, is the nearest possible approach to the simultaneous achievement of both short-run and long-run profit maximisation. It is only possible, however, when:

(a) the market is clearly segmentable;
(b) the segments show differing elasticities of demand;
(c) there is effective separation between market segments, i.e. the lower-priced segments cannot re-sell the product to the higher-priced segments.

These requirements are clearly much easier to meet in international, as opposed to domestic, marketing; the international marketer has a real opportunity to maximise profits by taking advantage of varying price levels in different countries. Such variations in price are by no means uncommon, and may be very significant.

9. Difficulties of differential pricing. Effective separation of markets is becoming increasingly difficult, however, for a number of reasons:

(a) regional economic groupings result in increasing pressure towards price uniformity;
(b) competition is becoming increasingly international;
(c) international communications are improving, e.g. distributors tend to meet frequently, often at supplier-organised meetings, and prices are inevitably compared;
(d) governments exert an influence towards price uniformity, partly by their own purchasing practices, e.g. many make it a condition of purchasing contracts that the prices are at least as favourable as those quoted to anyone else, and partly by legislation designed to promote free competition, e.g. Articles 85 and 86 of the Treaty of Rome (*see* XIV, **5**).

Thus a differential pricing system is by no means easy to operate. Nevertheless, there are still many opportunities open to the profit-oriented international marketer, and it may be doubted whether all of them are seized.

PROGRESS TEST 12

1. What is meant by "competitor-oriented" pricing, "cost-oriented" pricing and "demand-oriented" pricing?'**(2)**
2. What is a market-penetration strategy, and how far might an exporter adopt such a strategy? **(4)**
3. When might an exporter adopt a market-skimming strategy? **(5)**
4. What consideration might deter an exporter from adopting a "satisfactory rate of return" pricing policy? **(7)**
5. It is easier to adopt a differential pricing policy in international, as opposed to domestic, marketing. Why? **(8)**
6. Separation of markets for differential pricing purposes is becoming increasingly difficult, even in the international field. Why? **(9)**

CHAPTER XIII

International Pricing Decisions II: Export Pricing

THE EXPORT QUOTATION

1. Build-up of the export price. Whatever the pricing strategy adopted, every price must be set with cost considerations in mind. The true cost of the goods in the market place is, at the least, a yardstick against which pricing decisions can be made on an informed basis.

In some companies the export price is based on the domestic price, plus appropriate additions for freight, duty, channel mark-ups, etc. The domestic price, however, will usually include cost elements inapplicable to export sales, e.g. the cost of the home sales force, advertising and publicity in the home market, domestic transport fleet, warehousing and storage charges, cost of financing stocks, etc.

Conversely, exports attract additional costs not incurred in the home market. Some of these costs, e.g. freight, duty, etc., will be immediately obvious; others are not so obvious and may be overlooked.

2. Profitability of export sales. The level of profitability of export sales has implications not merely for short-term profit, but for pricing policy and overall marketing policy. It is vital that it should be correctly calculated. It may be the case that an export price *lower* than the home market price is nevertheless *more* profitable.

> **EXAMPLE:** An important element in this context (of export profitability) is the way prices (for the home and export markets) are determined and the way overheads are allocated as between home and export sales. We noted earlier that many companies would reject an order from abroad if it were, say, 5 per cent or 10 per cent lower than that ruling in the home market. Yet the company might have to devote vastly more time and effort to the sale of the same product in the home market. Many elements of cost—if rationally appor-

tioned—would present an entirely different picture of the relative profitability of operations in the home and export markets. In fact, on statistical grounds alone, a solid logical case could be made out for the proposition that, where a company exports only a small proportion (say, 10 per cent or 20 per cent) of its output at the same price as in the home market, exports *subsidise* the home market sales.

Below is given a check list that will help to avoid the more serious errors and omissions in calculating the profitability of exports.

(*a*) *Ex-works price.*
  (*i*) Direct cost of manufacture, including the cost of any special modifications required by the market.
  (*ii*) Appropriate allocation of company overheads, *excluding any overhead expenditure of relevance solely to domestic sales or to sales in other export markets.*
  (*iii*) Allocation of part of total export overheads, e.g. part cost of export department.
  (*iv*) Allocation of overheads specific to the market, e.g. local advertising costs.
  (*v*) Allocation of an appropriate proportion of the company's total research and development expenditure.
  (*vi*) Relevant agency commission(s).
  (*vii*) Appropriate profit margin.
  (*viii*) Special export packing costs.
(*b*) *F.o.b. price.*
  (*i*) Transport and insurance to docks/airport.
  (*ii*) Handling and other f.o.b. charges.
(*c*) *C.i.f. price.*
  (*i*) Transport to country of destination.
  (*ii*) Insurance in transit.
(*d*) *Local market price.*
  (*i*) Landing charges.
  (*ii*) Import duty.
  (*iii*) Internal transportation, storage and handling charges, unless covered in channel mark-ups.
  (*iv*) Main distributor mark-up.
  (*v*) Wholesale mark-up.
  (*vi*) Retail mark-up.
  (*vii*) Local turnover and/or other taxes.
(*e*) *Additional costs.* These costs will often be included in the

export overheads, but may on occasions be significant enough to warrant separate treatment.

(*i*) Increased financing costs resulting from the delays in transit and payment inseparable from even the normal export transaction; delays in payment which are almost inevitable in some countries, especially in the case of government contracts; necessary assistance to under-financed distributors.

(*ii*) Insurance of credit risks, political risks, etc., with E.C.G.D. (Export Credits Guarantee Department).

(*iii*) Forward exchange cover.

(*iv*) Import certificates, consular invoice fees, etc., which, though usually trivial, can occasionally reach such levels that they become *de facto* an import tax.

(*v*) Additional expenses resulting from the inevitably small-scale operations in some export markets, such as the minimum handling and storage charges for small shipments, the extra cost of a small-scale service and repairs organisation, and replacement of parts under guarantee, perhaps by air.

3. Quotation in the exporter's currency. Perhaps the first instinct of any exporter is to quote export prices in his own currency. This offers two principal advantages:

(*a*) it is administratively simple;
(*b*) the risk of variation in the exchange rate is borne by the foreign customer.

4. Quotation in a foreign currency. An exporter may also quote prices in a foreign currency, normally one of the major international currencies (it makes no sense to accept payment in currencies that are not freely convertible or are rapidly depreciating).

By quoting in a foreign currency the exporter automatically accepts the exchange risk, which he will usually cover in the forward exchange market (the major international currencies can now be bought and sold forward for several years ahead). There is, of course, no obligation on the exporter to cover the transaction forward; significant, even dramatic, profits can be made by an exporter who bears the exchange risk himself. Equally, of course, dramatic losses can be incurred, and few exporters are equipped to be currency speculators.

The forward exchange contract does not in itself, however, offer complete protection against the exchange risk. The contract matures on a fixed date, normally the date on which payment is

XIII. INTERNATIONAL PRICING DECISIONS II

due to be received from the foreign customer. In the event of delay in payment (or of non-payment) the exchange risk subsequent to the date payment is due is borne by the exporter. For exporters insuring credit risks with E.C.G.D., however, this is an insurable risk.

5. Advantages of quoting in a foreign currency. Quoting in a foreign currency on the basis outlined above (*see* **4**) offers significant advantages to the exporter.

(*a*) Forward exchange cover does not mean that an exporter loses all the potential exchange profit: if sterling is at a discount on the forward exchange market, he can sell his anticipated foreign currency receipts at a premium, thus securing a greater sterling return.

(*b*) The exporter may take this additional return in the form of extra profit, or, knowing that he will eventually receive a higher sterling sum, he may reduce his price at the quotation stage, i.e. *foreign currency invoicing can help the exporter to secure the contract in the first place.*

(*c*) Foreign currency invoicing can sometimes provide access to finance abroad at rates of interest significantly lower than those obtaining at home.

(*d*) To the importer, a quotation in his own currency is administratively more attractive, though not all customers will react favourably to a change to invoicing in their own currencies, especially if, at a time of a decline in the value of the exporter's currency, they have become accustomed to an exchange profit.

MARGINAL-COST PRICING

6. Relevance of marginal-cost pricing to exports. Manufacturing costs may be divided into two categories, which can be defined, though with admitted over-simplification, as follows:

(*a*) *fixed costs*, i.e. those costs, such as factory rental, which, at least in the short or medium term, remain unchanged regardless of the level of output;

(*b*) *variable costs*, i.e. those costs, such as raw material purchases, which vary directly according to the level of output.

Once the company has reached an output which gives sufficient revenue to cover *all* the fixed costs, *plus* all the variable costs incurred in achieving that output, it is said to have reached break-even point.

At break-even, total revenue is equal to total cost. Above break-even, since *fixed* costs have already been fully covered, *any* price which is above the *variable* cost per unit will give a profit.

In its established markets, however, the company will continue to sell at the price already fixed. It may wish to offer a price reduction to gain extra sales, but any price reduction would merely depress the general level of prices to all customers, thus increasing the volume of output required to reach break-even. If, however, the company can find an isolated market or market segment in which, without jeopardising price levels in its established market, it can quote prices based on marginal cost, i.e. below the established market level but still above the variable cost per unit, the additional sales to these isolated segments will increase the *total* profit of the company, though *percentage* profit per unit would clearly be reduced.

It is difficult to find an isolated market segment within any one country. In the export field, however, communications difficulties, import restrictions, tariffs, etc. tend to divide one country from another, so that marginal-price selling has become common practice. The typical situation is that a manufacturer maintains high prices in his domestic market, sheltering behind high tariff barriers, and from time to time sells any surplus capacity abroad at marginal prices.

7. When to quote marginal prices. The profit-conscious export marketer will realise that marginal-cost pricing is worthwhile only when:

(*a*) all decisions on marginal business are taken against an agreed profit plan, to ensure that it does not form too high a proportion of total business;

(*b*) it is unlikely that there will be speedy intervention by the government of the importing country, such as the imposition of dumping duties (*see* **8**);

(*c*) there is no more profitable use of resources, such as an alternative market which might offer a higher price level, or an alternative and more profitable product that could be manufactured on the same plant (the true cost of marginal pricing is the opportunity of more profitable business that is foregone);

(*d*) as already explained, the markets are clearly segmentable, so that price levels in the principal market(s) are not depressed. In this context not only the domestic but all major export markets, not protected by tariffs, should be considered.

EXAMPLE: A U.K. manufacturer of razor blades enjoyed a lucrative trade in the U.S.A. He also seized an opportunity of sales in bulk to Eastern Europe at marginal prices. These Eastern European blades subsequently appeared in U.S. retail outlets at prices significantly below the established market level.

It should be noted that all the above conditions must be met simultaneously before a decision is made to seek marginal business. Most companies would probably add one further condition: that it should be short-term business, aimed at remedying, for example, a purely seasonal fall-off in orders or temporary overcapacity after the construction of new plant.

8. Dumping. The beneficiary of goods exported at marginal prices is, of course, the importing country, which is able to buy on highly favourable terms. Where the importing country has a competing industry, however, the government may try to protect that industry from low-price and, arguably, unfair competition by the imposition of a dumping duty.

One rather loose definition of dumping is the export of goods at prices below their full cost of production, i.e. at marginal prices. From a legal viewpoint, however, such a definition is less than adequate: it is difficult to ascertain a foreign company's costs and the reasonableness or otherwise of its allocation of such overheads as marketing expenditure. Article VI of the General Agreement on Tariffs and Trade (G.A.T.T.), which is incorporated in the anti-dumping legislation of most of the major free-market industrialised nations, therefore concentrates first on the concept of "normal value":

... a product is to be considered as being introduced into the commerce of an importing country at less than its normal value, if the price of the product exported from one country to another is less than the comparable price, in the ordinary course of trade, for the like product when destined for consumption in the exporting country; or, in the absence of such domestic price, is less than either: the highest comparable price for the like product for export to any third country in the ordinary course of trade; or, the cost of production of the product in the country of origin plus a reasonable addition for selling cost and profit.

The investigative procedures needed to establish dumping are lengthy and involved, and the exporter must be allowed to present his side of the case. As a result, anti-dumping legislation poses less of a threat to the exporter than might have been feared, at least for the occasional or short-term dumper.

The G.A.T.T. rules, however, do permit the imposition, in certain circumstances, of provisional duties. The U.K., for instance, is prepared to impose provisional duties, especially in the case of seasonal products or where irreversible damage to the domestic industry may occur before the necessary investigations have been completed.

The exporter, therefore, needs to be increasingly aware of the constraints imposed on his pricing policy by anti-dumping legislation.

DEVALUATION

9. Devaluation and the exporter. When a country changes the value of its currency by devaluation (or revaluation), a company exporting to that country will suddenly find that its competitive position has been radically altered. With the recent trend towards floating exchange rates currency movements are less sudden, but the performance of the pound sterling in 1976 showed that even a floating currency can decline in value with disconcerting speed. The exporter must be alert to take the maximum possible advantage of any change in currency values.

10. Alternative courses of action. The alternative courses of action open to a U.K. exporter in the event of a sterling devaluation are, in respect of any given market:

(a) to leave his sterling price unchanged, thus reducing the price to the foreign buyer;

(b) to maintain unchanged the price in foreign currency, increasing the sterling price accordingly;

(c) to set an intermediate price somewhere between these two extremes.

11. Maintaining the sterling price. This course requires no positive action by the U.K. exporter, but it can only be sustained in the short term, since cost increases resulting from devaluation, e.g. increases in prices of imported raw materials and pressure for cost-of-living wage increases, are likely to force price increases within months. In fact this first alternative makes sense only if:

(*a*) price elasticity of demand in the market is such that the increase in sales at the new (reduced) price will be of sufficient magnitude to increase total profits even after the inevitable cost increases have been incurred;

(*b*) there is available capacity, e.g. plant, labour, finance, etc., to support such an increase in production.

12. Maintaining the price in foreign currency. This course results in an immediate increase in profit and automatically more than covers the cost increases which can be expected to result eventually from the devaluation. Unfortunately, however, it will often be impracticable, since:

(*a*) distributors, and possibly customers, will be expecting some price reduction as a result of the devaluation, and some goodwill, and orders, may be lost unless at least a gesture is made;

(*b*) other U.K. competitors may reduce their prices in the market, with a resulting loss of business for those U.K. companies that maintain their prices;

(*c*) local competitors and exporters in third countries, anticipating U.K. companies' price reductions, may reduce their own prices, even though this is at some sacrifice of profit.

13. Setting an intermediate price. The most appropriate course of action, therefore, will usually lie somewhere between the two extremes. Ideally, the exporter will:

(*a*) estimate the cost increases which will eventually result from the devaluation, consider the timing of such increases, and prepare cost estimates accordingly;

(*b*) compare the new estimated costs with the elasticity of demand in the market, and establish the price which maximises profit contribution, considering also the possible effect of increased advertising on the demand curve;

(*c*) take into account the actions or likely actions of competitors, and adjust his price accordingly.

In practice, each of these three requirements presents too many imponderables for the ideal ever to be achievable. Quantitative techniques in marketing, however, can be of assistance, and the exporter's task is to arrive somewhere near the ideal in those markets of real significance.

BARTER TRADING

14. Barter. Strictly speaking, barter is the direct exchange of goods for goods, the economic system of the primitive economies. Occasionally, such direct exchanges still occur.

> EXAMPLE: Pakistan recently sent cotton to Bangladesh and received jute in return. No hard currency was exchanged and no credit was extended. The two countries are still not friendly, so the trust that is normally present in international trade made a routine sale impossible. The negotiators agreed on the quantity to be traded and agreed that the transactions would occur simultaneously.

15. Compensation trading. Direct exchange on so crude a basis, however, presents too many complications in terms of the simultaneous physical transfer of merchandise between the parties. In the modern form of barter trading an exporter agrees to accept payment or part-payment in goods from the buyer's country, in lieu of cash; but the deal is organised as two separate cash transactions, entered into simultaneously. Modern barter arrangements are variously described as "compensation trading", "contra-trading", or "reciprocal trading".

> EXAMPLE: Cadbury-Schweppes uses its international group purchasing resources as a means of entering the Eastern European markets in a big way. Its Swedish subsidiary manufactures tomato paste and Schweppes in Britain accepts deliveries of Bulgarian tomatoes as part of a deal to sell its beverages into Bulgaria.

16. Special forms of barter trading. The simple forms of barter trading instanced above (*see* **14, 15**) are rarely possible. Several variations on the basic barter-trading theme have therefore developed in modern commerce, in order to meet special trading conditions or seize particular opportunities. Three such variations are described below:

(*a*) *buy-back contracts;*
(*b*) *clearing arrangements;*
(*c*) *switch dealing.*

The student is warned, however, that in this area there is no general consistency of nomenclature: most of the terms pertaining

XIII. INTERNATIONAL PRICING DECISIONS II

to barter trading are used loosely or in some cases interchangeably.

17. Buy-back contracts. In the buy-back contract a supplier of plant, usually a complete factory, agrees to accept part-payment in the form of finished goods from that factory.

EXAMPLES: General Motors is selling paint and know-how to Poland to manufacture light vans and is becoming the distributor in the West of the Polish vehicles.

Wilkinson Sword has provided the U.S.S.R. with a razor blade factory and has agreed in return to buy blades from the factory.

18. Clearing arrangements. Clearing arrangements are agreements between two governments to exchange products not easily sold on the open market. Such agreements define the goods to be exchanged, their respective values and the settlement date. At the expiry of the contract any deficit on either side is cancelled either by the payment of a previously agreed financial penalty or by the acceptance of unwanted goods.

EXAMPLE: East Germany and a West African country agree that they will exchange machine tools for cocoa. The Germans ship machine tools whose open market value is 20,000 English pounds and agree to take cocoa beans in return. The beans will be shipped regularly during the year. The total value of the beans will come to 20,000 pounds by settlement day a year later.

19. Switch deals. Few companies find themselves in a position to buy their raw materials from a country interested both in barter and in the purchase of their finished products; perhaps fewer still are in the business of supplying complete plant. For most companies barter trading involves the disposal of the barter goods to a third party, usually a party in a different country. The larger company may employ its own specialist executives to find a buyer for such goods, but most companies will find it safer and more convenient to arrange in advance for a merchant house specialising in barter trading to take the goods off their hands at a discount. The merchant then finds a buyer for the goods at a reduced price, taking advantage, of course, of part of the discount.

EXAMPLE: Greece has accumulated the equivalent of $1 million of credit in Rumania through its sales of cotton and fresh oranges, but has agreed to take Rumanian goods—which it does not want—as payment. It asks a bank in Vienna to act as its switcher. The bank offers the equivalent of $700,000 in hard currency for the overvalued Rumanian credit position. The Greeks accept the offer and purchase aircraft parts from Boeing in Seattle, something they wanted all along. The switcher finds a customer in Africa who is willing to accept the Rumanian canned goods if the price is right. If the switcher has done his job properly the prices will be acceptable to the Africans, and everyone else will benefit too.

20. Advantages of barter to the bartering nation. Barter is becoming increasingly popular in the international field, usually with Eastern European countries and the smaller developing nations. It enables these countries:

(*a*) to import goods without using up scarce foreign exchange;

(*b*) to take advantage of the exporting company's contacts with the marketing system of the industrialised western countries;

(*c*) through that system to dispose of goods they are themselves unable to sell for cash.

Recently certain OPEC (Organisation of Petroleum Exporting Countries) countries have engaged in barter trading, apparently with the aim of reducing the time taken up by the normal buying and selling processes—a particularly important consideration in times of high inflation and fluctuating exchange rates—though it has also been suggested that the barter arrangements served to circumvent the OPEC price agreements.

> EXAMPLE: Some of the Organisation of Petroleum Exporting Countries (OPEC) recently were accused of bartering away oil at less than the fixed price by accepting overpriced goods in return. Petroleum exporting countries have been swapping oil for goods and services since before OPEC was established. But in recent years such arrangements attracted attention because they may suggest a crack in the OPEC wall.

21. Advantages of barter to the exporter. Few companies, of course, like to exchange their products for goods offered by the buyer; they prefer hard cash. Nevertheless, barter deals can offer significant advantages:

(*a*) barter can provide access to some markets that would otherwise be out of reach;

(b) those markets, particularly in Eastern Europe, are often of significant size and the typical barter contract is much larger than might be expected in the normal course of trade;

(c) in the case of the buy-back contract, lower wage rates in the manufacturing country may provide the plant supplier with what amounts to additional low-cost manufacturing capacity.

22. Precautions for the exporter engaging in barter. Clearly, a company engaging in barter faces rather more pitfalls than are usual even in the international field. The prudent company will:

(a) be certain, first of all, that a barter deal is essential if the export is to take place;

(b) endeavour to obtain at least part-payment in cash, keeping the barter element to the minimum possible;

(c) ensure *in advance* that it can dispose of the barter goods, either direct or through a specialist merchant house;

(d) allow in the export contract price for the cost of arranging the barter deal, taking into account the world market price of the goods received in exchange and any possible discount allowed to a specialist merchant house;

(e) if a U.K. company, and if the barter goods are to be imported into the U.K. and not shipped direct to a third country, ensure that the goods are not subject to U.K. import restrictions;

(f) again if a U.K. company, contact E.C.G.D. at an early stage to check whether the export sale is insurable (E.C.G.D. insist that the export sale, and the buyer's obligation to pay the U.K. exporter in cash, are kept completely separate from the import transaction).

PROGRESS TEST 13

1. What costs over and above the ex-works price might it be necessary to allow for in establishing the true delivered price of goods in an overseas market? (2)

2. What are the advantages to an exporter of quoting prices in a foreign currency? (5)

3. Under what circumstances might it be worthwhile for an exporter to quote marginal-cost prices? (7)

4. What alternative courses of action are open to a U.K. exporter when the pound sterling is devalued? **(10)**

5. What is meant by "compensation trading"? **(15)**

6. What is a buy-back contract and how does it operate? **(17)**

CHAPTER XIV

International Pricing Decisions III: Foreign-Market Pricing Decisions

1. Introduction. This chapter discusses foreign-market pricing decisions, i.e. those pricing decisions that relate to products that are both produced and marketed in the same country, but with some centralised guidance or direction from outside that country, e.g. as is the case with multinational companies.

GOVERNMENT INFLUENCES ON PRICING

2. Governmental influences on pricing and the international marketer. The exporter and, to a much greater extent, the multinational company, face a bewildering maze of legislation imposed by government. Pricing decisions cannot safely be made in ignorance of such legislation.

3. Price control.

(*a*) *Control of price increases.* Some years ago continuing price control was associated largely with countries facing constant and serious inflation. In other countries, price control was limited to temporary "freezes". With the spread of inflation, however, price control is now encountered with increasing frequency and permanency.

(*b*) *Other price controls.* Government have also intervened:

(*i*) to set minimum prices, e.g. California's Unfair Practices Act;

(*ii*) to set price ceilings, usually on staple food products;

(*iii*) to lay down specified mark-ups in the distribution channel, e.g. as in Norway;

(*iv*) to control manufacturer's profit margins, e.g. as in Ghana.

4. Restrictive trade practices and monopolies. Restrictive trade practices may be broadly defined as all agreements or concerted practices tending to prevent, restrict or distort competition. They include:

(*a*) horizontal price fixing, i.e. price agreements between competitors;
(*b*) allocation of markets between competitors;
(*c*) discriminatory pricing or terms of sale;
(*d*) refusals to supply, boycotts.

Monopolies are usually taken to mean not merely a monopoly in the literal sense but mere market dominance, or mergers and acquisitions that might lead to market dominance.

5. Government attitudes to restrictive trade practices and monopolies. The views of governments vary according to the national attitudes to free competition and the economic state of the nation. Most governments, however, have introduced some form of legislation against both restrictive trade practices and monopolies. Two areas of particular interest to the international marketer, the U.S.A. and the European Community, are discussed below by way of example.

(*a*) *U.S.A.* In brief, any restrictive trade practice is illegal; penalties for contravention are heavy, both for the company and for responsible corporate officials. Landmarks in legislation are:

(*i*) *Sherman Antitrust Act 1890:* prohibited "monopolies or attempts to monopolise" and "contracts, combinations or conspiracies in restraint of trade";

(*ii*) *Federal Trade Commission Act 1914:* established a Commission to investigate unfair methods of competition and issue "cease and desist" orders;

(*iii*) *Clayton Act 1914:* prohibited certain restrictive practices such as price discrimination, exclusive dealing and tying arrangements, inter-corporate stockholdings, etc., where the effect was substantially to lessen competition;

(*iv*) *Robinson Patman Act 1936:* strengthened the Clayton Act, and defined price discrimination as unlawful except in certain instances—the Federal Trade Commission was given the right to establish limits on quantity discounts and other allowances;

(*v*) *Antimerger Act 1950:* broadened the power of the Clayton Act to prevent mergers where these might have a substantially adverse effect on competition.

These laws apply only within the U.S.A. The Webb–Pomerene Act of 1918 specifically permits, between U.S. companies competing in foreign markets, all forms of co-operation, including price-fixing and allocation of export business.

(*b*) *European Community.* The international marketer should be aware of the Community's rules of competition set out in Articles 85 and 86 of the Treaty of Rome.

(*i*) Article 85 prohibits all agreements or concerted practices likely to affect trade between member states which have as their object the prevention, restriction or distortion of competition (again, trade outside the Community is ignored, as is trade within one member state). Price-fixing, market sharing, restriction of production or technical development, and discriminatory terms of supply are specifically mentioned. Article 85 is particularly wide in its terms, but a general exemption is allowed to agreements/ practices which improve production or distribution or promote technical or economic progress. The Commission of the Community may in other cases grant exemption from Article 85.

(*ii*) Article 86 prohibits any improper advantage being taken of a dominant position within the Community in so far as it affects trade between member states. "Improper advantage" includes *inter alia* the direct or indirect imposition of any inequitable purchase or selling prices or the application to parties to transactions of unequal terms in respect of equivalent supplies.

INTERNATIONAL TRANSFER PRICING

6. Definition of transfer pricing. When a company decentralises, organising itself into separate profit centres, it will usually find it necessary to transfer components or finished products between units. To enable the profit performance of each unit to be evaluated, a price must be established for each inter-unit transaction. This price is known as the transfer price.

7. Fixing the transfer price. Transfer prices may be established on a number of bases, such as cost, cost plus a standard margin, or arm's length transfer, i.e. the same price as would be quoted to an independent customer. Central corporate management will usually establish the basis of the transfer price, with the aim of ensuring both a realistic assessment of the contribution of any one unit and the maximisation of the profit of the enterprise as a whole (narrow unit interests may not coincide with this latter aim). Even within a single country, transfer pricing can give rise to problems in terms of accounting systems, inter-unit co-operation, and motivation of executives. When products are transferred across national frontiers, however, entirely new considerations arise, both financial and strategic, which can have a major impact on total corporate profit.

8. Financial aspects of international transfer pricing. The transfer price between nations can be manipulated to minimise tax or import-duty liability, or (in effect) to transfer funds. For example:

(*a*) products may be transferred into high-duty countries at an artificially low transfer price, so that, assuming duty is charged *ad valorem*, the duty paid will be low;

(*b*) products may be transferred into high-tax countries at high transfer prices, so that profits in the high-tax country are virtually eliminated and, in effect, transferred to low-tax countries;

(*c*) products may be transferred at high prices into a country from which dividend repatriation is restricted or subject to government taxes—in effect, invisible income replaces a formal dividend;

(*d*) similarly, it is possible to avoid an accumulation of funds in a country with high inflation rates, or where an early devaluation is thought to be a probability, or where expropriation is feared.

9. Strategic aspects of international transfer pricing. International transfer pricing can also be used as a weapon in the overall marketing strategy: profits can be concentrated, by vertically integrated corporations, at the stage of production where there is least competition. Competitors operating at other stages of production can thus be discouraged by the relatively low profits to be earned.

> EXAMPLE: The integrated oil companies keep the prices of crude oil, and, hence, profits of crude production, at high levels. There are many reasons for high crude oil transfer prices, not the least of which is pressure from the governments of crude oil producing countries, and the desire by the companies to take maximum advantage of oil depletion allowances. Another reason for keeping transfer prices and market prices of crude oil at relatively high levels, however, is to discourage entry into refining and distribution by firms without captive sources of crude oil. Since entry into refining and distribution is easier than entry into crude production, the transfer-pricing strategy pursued by integrated producers helps to reduce competition all along the line.

10. Governmental attitudes to transfer pricing. The manipulation of international transfer prices clearly offers the prospect of very significant financial gain. Such manipulations, however, whether practised for financial reasons or for reasons of marketing strategy, have attracted the attention of governments. For instance:

(*a*) the government of the *exporting* country has an interest in seeing that the transfer price is not artificially low, and it will endeavour to ensure that appropriate profits are made, and taxes paid, within its jurisdiction;

(*b*) in the *importing* country, the tax authorities are usually on the look-out for unreasonably high transfer prices which will reduce local profits, and consequently, liability to income tax; while the customs authorities will, in contrast, be watching for low transfer prices designed to minimise duty liability.

11. Company attitudes to international transfer pricing. It will now be clear that the financial and strategic aims of international transfer pricing will usually be irreconcilable with the initial aim of good corporate management.

In these circumstances, international companies adopt varying attitudes towards transfer pricing. Some regard it solely as a means of encouraging and measuring corporate efficiency; others emphasise the opportunities for financial gain or market manipulation.

Either way, the international marketer must be aware of the alternatives open to him, both in formulating his marketing strategy and in setting his market prices.

PROGRESS TEST 14

1. In what ways do governments attempt to control prices? **(3)**
2. What varying attitudes do governments adopt towards restrictive trade practices? **(5)**
3. What is the effect of Articles 85 and 86 of the Treaty of Rome? **(5)**
4. What is meant by "international transfer pricing"? **(6–8)**
5. In what way might international transfer pricing be used as a weapon in overall marketing strategy? **(9)**

CHAPTER XV

International Communications I: Media Advertising

INTRODUCTION

1. Communications. Communications is a general term covering all methods of influencing a target audience. In a marketing sense it will include advertising (*see* **2**), sales promotion (*see* XVI), public relations (*see* XVI) and personal selling (*see* XVII and XVIII).

2. Advertising. Advertising has been defined as "any paid form of non-personal presentation and promotion of ideas, goods or services by an identified sponsor". Media are the channels used to convey the advertising message to the target audience, e.g. radio, newspapers, posters.

3. International advertising. The principles and concepts of advertising are the same the world over. Internationally, advertising is modelled very much on the U.S. pattern and the American influence is strengthened by the proliferation of branches of U.S. advertising agencies throughout the world. Thus the international marketer requires a good knowledge of basic advertising principles.

Paradoxically, in its application and practice, advertising internationally offers greater problems than almost any other aspect of international marketing, simply as a result of the environmental differences between nations (*see* I, **5**). Differences of particular relevance to advertising are culture, language, government attitudes towards advertising, and the availability or otherwise of certain advertising media.

These environmental differences present special problems for the international marketer, which may be summarised under the following headings:

(*a*) the advertising message;
(*b*) the selection of appropriate media;
(*c*) the selection of advertising agencies.

XV. INTERNATIONAL COMMUNICATIONS I

Despite these differences, significant economies may be achieved by standardisation of international communications, a subject which has already been touched upon in connection with product policy (*see* IV, 4).

It is with the standardisation of international advertising and the special international problems of advertising that this chapter is concerned.

STANDARDISATION

4. Extent of standardisation. Complete standardisation of all aspects of a campaign over several different countries is rarely practicable—language difficulties alone would often make such an approach impossible. Standardisation usually implies a common advertising strategy, a common creative idea and message, and, as far as possible, similar media.

> **EXAMPLE:** Two days of earnest persuasion failed to overcome the European affiliates' reluctance to accept that what had been successful advertising half the world away was an ideal ready-made package for their own market. A similar reception for the Esso "Tiger in your Tank" campaign was a prospect never far from the minds of the planners in New York five years later; they did their homework accordingly. Returning to square one, what, they asked themselves, was the definition of a co-ordinated, multinational advertising programme? They came to the conclusion that it was a programme which expressed, in different countries and different languages, a common creative idea—an idea based on a commonly-established strategy. This did not imply that the advertisements appearing in any one country should be exact reproductions of those running elsewhere, but the programme should be such that the advertiser was satisfied that, in all the different countries concerned, he was directing the same message through the same illustrative material, sound effects, and verbal expression—translated as necessary—in all the markets where his product was available.

5. Advantages of standardisation. Like any other businessman, the advertiser should select that course of action which is most likely to prove profitable in terms of sales achieved in relation to costs incurred.

At first sight it might seem that sales would invariably be maximised by a campaign tailored to the cultural influences and buying motives of each specific market. Often, however, buying motives are identical in all or many markets. In such cases, genuine creativity in advertising—a scarce commodity the world over—may more than compensate for a standardised theme. Thus, by taking international advantage of creativity, wherever it may originate, standardisation may actually improve sales.

> EXAMPLE: The Avis Rent-a-Car Co. used its theme "We try harder" in the U.S.A. and (translated) throughout Europe, with considerable success.

Standardisation will certainly reduce costs, in terms of artwork, copywriting, block production, printing, film production, and creative staff, though only exceptionally will it reduce media costs, since most media operate within national boundaries. Because such costs are usually low in relation to media and product costs, they tend too often to be ignored. Yet savings can often reach highly significant levels.

6. The standardisation decision. There can be no universal solution to the problem of standardisation; each campaign must be separately considered. The following factors should be taken into account:

(*a*) the general similarity or otherwise of the markets to be covered by the campaign, e.g. where cultural differences are limited, and income, education, etc. are similar, buying motives are likely to be the same;

(*b*) the nature of the product, e.g. industrial goods, for instance, are purchased more on objective criteria, and are therefore particularly suitable to a standardised approach, as are "tourist" products such as films and petrol;

(*c*) local advertising agency standards, especially in terms of creativity, the importance of which has already been stressed (*see* **5**), and which in some countries is of a low standard;

(*d*) government and other restrictions, which may prohibit certain copy themes (*see* **8**) or the use of certain media (*see* **14**);

(*e*) the non-availability of media, e.g. television, in certain countries (*see* **14**);

(f) media spillover possibilities (see **12**);
(g) the availability of suitable international media (see

7. The prototype campaign. Where standardised campaigns prove impossible, prototype campaigns may be a useful alternative. Such campaigns are normally prepared by corporate headquarters and are based on common denominators drawn from consumer research in a number of markets regarded as generally representative. The prototypes are then modified by local subsidiaries, licensees or distributors to suit each particular market. In this way:

(a) the subsidiaries, etc. can benefit from the central creative approach;
(b) at least some cost savings can be achieved, even if only in terms of creative staff.

THE ADVERTISING MESSAGE

8. Legal restrictions. As in the U.K., so in most other countries the law restricts the advertiser's freedom, particularly with regard to the advertising message. Regulations vary from country to country and must be checked in every individual case. It is unsafe to assume a general similarity with English law; some of the regulations, even in Europe, would appear surprising to the U.K. marketer.

EXAMPLES: Germany forbids superlatives or comparative claims: "better" and "best" are words to be avoided. In the case of product comparisons, the manufacturer with whose products the advertised products are compared may be able to sue for damages. In France, if an advertiser is unable to substantiate the claims he has made, the courts may order corrective advertising at his expense.

9. Social constraints. Social and other conventions may affect both the advertising message and the way it is expressed.

EXAMPLE: What to British eyes would be a quite normal illustration of men and women dining together may be quite unacceptable in some Middle East countries.

10. Translation of advertising copy. Where there is no advantage in standardisation, the question of translation of the advertising message will not arise, since copy can be prepared in each individual country.

Often, however, ideas will be generated in the U.K. and used in many different countries; this is particularly the case, of course, with exporting companies.

Seemingly straightforward translation offers a number of far from obvious pitfalls which can negate the value of the entire campaign. The apparently correctly translated message may become incomprehensible, or, worse, may make both the advertiser and his product look ridiculous.

> EXAMPLE: Consider this observation of a Danish executive working for a European trading company in Indonesia: "I have read many sales pieces written by Americans that were translated into the local language. Often they miss the point entirely. Sales psychology is different in every country and you can get the feel of it only if you know the language". A countryman of his, based in Thailand, echoed that point. "Check them out", he suggested, "by having a different translator put back into English what you've translated from the English. You'll get the shock of your life. Once, I remember, 'Out of sight, out of mind' had become 'Invisible things are insane' ".

11. Some rules for copy translation. Some rules for translation of copy are given below.

(*a*) Understand that the task of the translator is to translate the thought and ideas, not to provide a literal translation from the English. The latter can only rarely be a success as advertising copy.

> EXAMPLE: Once it had been agreed [by Esso] in Washington that all the European affiliates would adopt the original Tiger artwork, the difficulties of rendering exact translations of the slogan, "Put a Tiger in your Tank" became only too apparent. As research had established, it was the crispness and alliteration of the slogan which had contributed significantly to the campaign's success in the United States. It was essential that, where possible, these qualities should be carried over into the European translations, but not if it meant departing from the basic exhortation to the motorist to put a Tiger in his tank. In Italy, the word "tank" could not be literally translated; and "motor" was chosen as a substitute. . . . Finally, their slogan emerged as

XV. INTERNATIONAL COMMUNICATIONS I

"Metti un tigre nel motore", retaining the alliteration of the original and the same pithy delivery.

(b) Design and write the copy from the outset with possible translation in mind.

(c) Avoid unusual idiomatic expressions or slang.

(d) Select a professional translator whose mother tongue is the language into which the translation is to be made. Ideally, this translator will be living in the country where the advertisement will appear, but this may not always be possible.

(e) Bear in mind that languages common to several countries nevertheless show important national differences, e.g. Spanish in Colombia differs from Spanish in neighbouring Venezuela.

(f) Always have the translation checked by local nationals with experience in the relevant product area; agents and distributors are the obvious choice. Alternatively, have the advertisement translated back into English by a different translator, as suggested in an earlier example.

(g) Arrange for printing either by a U.K. printer specialising in the relevant language or by a printer within the market.

(h) Have the printed proofs re-checked by both the translator and agents/distributors.

(i) Allow adequate time for all the above operations in the campaign plan.

ADVERTISING MEDIA

12. International media. An option open to the international marketer in a position to standardise his appeal is the use of international media, i.e. publications aiming, as a matter of policy, at coverage in several different countries. Such media include:

(a) consumer magazines such as *Reader's Digest* or *Business Week*;

(b) a number of trade and technical magazines;

(c) newspapers in several different countries offering a package deal;

(d) international commercial radio, e.g. Radio Luxembourg, and television, e.g. Télé Monte Carlo, whose transmissions are directed principally to audiences in France.

In addition, the international marketer may be able to take advantage of media spillover, e.g. television programmes in the north of the U.S.A. can also be seen in Canada.

13. National media. Purely national media, however, account for the vast bulk of world advertising. It is not possible here to discuss the diversity of media available.

14. Media selection. The principles of media selection are universal; the desirable media in every country are those that reach the target market most effectively in cost-benefit terms.

The application of those principles, however, will vary from one country to the next. Some of the points the international marketer will need to bear in mind are discussed below.

(a) *Media availability.* Very often what would normally be regarded as the most suitable media are available only on a limited basis or do not exist at all.

> EXAMPLE: Television advertising in France is state controlled and advertising time is strictly limited both in terms of number of minutes of advertising per day and in terms of number of minutes per product per annum.

(b) *Legal restrictions.* Local laws may forbid the advertising of certain products.

> EXAMPLE: France does not permit television advertising of a wide range of goods and services. These include not merely cigarettes, tobacco and certain alcoholic drinks, but also books, records, theatres and cinemas, air travel and personnel recruitment.

(c) *Media information.* There is often a lack of reliable basic information on circulation or audience characteristics, particularly outside the industrialised countries.

(d) *Literacy.* Low levels of literacy may mean that the normally appropriate medium is unsuitable. Radio, for instance, is particularly suitable in developing countries, and may be preferred to press advertising.

(e) *Taxation.* High taxation on certain media result inevitably in distortion of the media plan. Apart from V.A.T., many countries tax advertising, e.g. the U.K., though the tax is now disguised as a levy on the programme companies. Some countries charge a special tax on *imported* advertising material.

(f) *Regionalisation.* Distinct regional characteristics, especially linguistic, may require the use of regional media. Switzerland, with three major languages, is an obvious example.

(g) *Print reproduction.* The appropriate media may be unsatisfactory from the point of view of quality of reproduction. This applies particularly in the case of half-tone illustrations.

ADVERTISING AGENCY SELECTION

15. Options available. The international marketer wishing to advertise abroad will normally have the following principal options open to him:

(*a*) selection of his domestic advertising agency, which will work either directly with the overseas media or through the U.K. representatives of those media;

(*b*) selection of a domestic agency with branch offices, affiliates or association agreements with agencies abroad;

(*c*) selection of foreign agencies in each national market.

16. Selection criteria. Again, there can be no general rule, but in selecting his agency the international marketer should take into account the following criteria.

(*a*) *Extent of market coverage.* Although many of the larger agencies have a remarkably wide international coverage, that coverage may not coincide with all markets of interest to the advertiser.

(*b*) *Quality of service.* The standard of advertising agencies varies from market to market, and even between branches of the same agency. A company with its own advertising department may find a weak local agency acceptable.

(*c*) *Size of appropriation.* A certain minimum appropriation is necessary to interest the major international agencies or to interest any one foreign agency. The small advertiser, e.g. of industrial products, may have to rely on his domestic agency.

(*d*) *Need for international co-ordination.* A company aiming at a standardised international campaign will require good co-ordination and control, which is most likely to be achieved through a single international agency.

(*e*) *Company organisation.* International companies organised on a decentralised basis may prefer to leave agency selection to the local subsidiary. Similarly, in joint-venture arrangements, or co-operative advertising in conjunction with a distributor, local influence would be significant in the final choice.

PROGRESS TEST 15

1. What is meant, in a marketing context, by "communications"? **(1)**

2. What advantages might be expected to accrue to a company that standardises its advertising on a world-wide basis? **(5)**

3. What criteria would you consider before taking a decision to standardise your advertising programme internationally? **(6)**

4. What is meant by "prototype advertising campaign" and under what circumstances might you adopt such an approach internationally? **(7)**

5. What basic rules should be borne in mind when considering translation of advertising copy into a foreign language? **(11)**

6. What are "international media" and under what circumstances might an advertiser consider their use? **(12)**

7. What criteria should the international marketer take into account in selecting an advertising agency abroad that he would not need to consider in a purely domestic context? **(16)**

CHAPTER XVI

International Communications II: Sales Promotion and Public Relations

INTRODUCTION

1. Sales promotion. Sales promotion consists of those marketing activities, other than personal selling, advertising and public relations, that stimulate consumer purchasing and/or dealer effectiveness, such as demonstrations, exhibitions, catalogues, films, trading stamps, premium offers, contests, coupons and free samples.

After a short discussion of international aspects of sales promotion in general, this chapter considers in some detail overseas exhibitions and store promotions, two aspects of promotion of special interest to the international marketer.

2. Public relations. Public relations has been defined as the non-personal stimulation of demand for a product, service, or business unit by placing commercially significant news about it in a published medium or by obtaining favourable presentation of it on radio, television or stage that is not paid for by the sponsor.

In an international context two aspects of public relations are of special importance:

(*a*) placing press releases with overseas media—particularly difficult for the exporter;

(*b*) for the overseas subsidiary of an international company, earning the reputation of being a "good citizen" in the host country.

SALES PROMOTION IN GENERAL

3. Legal restrictions. Legal pitfalls abound for the international marketer employing sales promotion techniques abroad. Each promotion must be checked against local regulations.

>   EXAMPLE: In West Germany, premiums are forbidden if they constitute a real financial incentive to buy. Samples must not be

larger than is absolutely necessary to provide an adequate trial for the product. A promotion should not normally require the purchaser to send in labels or packet tops.

4. Retailer co-operation. Promotions will often require retailer support in terms of processing coupons, handling on-pack gifts, setting up display material, etc. Securing co-operation is often much more difficult abroad, as a result not so much of dealer attitude but of lack of space and handling facilities.

5. Competition. Promotion may occasionally be forced on the international marketer by the actions of competitors. If the competition is offering trading stamps, for instance, he may have little option but to follow suit.

EXHIBITIONS

6. International importance of exhibitions. Exhibitions are, of course, a regular feature of the business scene in the U.K. Internationally, however, they assume much greater significance since:

(*a*) they play a much more important role in business in many other countries;

(*b*) the ever-present problems of time, distance and cost in meeting customers and potential customers are at least partially solved;

(*c*) product demonstrations automatically surmount all communications barriers;

(*d*) in Eastern Europe, trade fairs are one of the few methods by which face-to-face contact with the end-purchaser company is possible. Normally, all contact must be with the state trading organisations.

7. Marketing planning. Occasional participation in trade fairs on an *ad hoc* basis is usually a recipe for failure. Exhibitions must be:

(*a*) an integral part of the overall marketing plan;

(*b*) supported by a planned promotional programme designed to ensure that the maximum possible benefit is derived from participation.

8. Categories of exhibition. The first essential is to plan participation well in advance. A list of all major overseas exhibitions is published two years in advance in the *Trade Promotions Guide*, a quarterly supplement to the Department of Trade's magazine *British Business*.

Essentially the choice will lie between:

(*a*) a general trade fair or a specialised (industry) exhibition;
(*b*) a national or international exhibition;
(*c*) exhibitions open to the trade only and those open to the general public;
(*d*) special-event exhibitions (the majority) and permanent exhibitions, e.g. the British Export Marketing Centre in Tokyo.

It may also be worthwhile to consider the company's own exhibition, perhaps as a mobile exhibition in a train, or as a "spin-off" exhibition, i.e. one held at the same time as, and in the vicinity of, a major exhibition.

9. Selecting an exhibition. Usually, within any one category of exhibition, the intending exhibitor will have a wide choice. Final decision criteria are likely to include:

(*a*) the relationship between the company's target audience and the composition of the exhibition audience in previous years—organisers sometimes provide appropriate research data on attendance;
(*b*) the length of time the exhibition has been established—as a rule new fairs attract only a small attendance;
(*c*) the standing of other exhibitors, in past years, and intending exhibitors;
(*d*) the authority of the exhibition sponsors and their organising competence—efficiency matters;
(*e*) the timing of the exhibition—it may clash with another similar exhibition, but, on the other hand, it may immediately follow, at a reasonably near venue, another relevant exhibition, thus encouraging a "spin-off" attendance.

10. Purpose of exhibiting. At the same time the objectives of exhibiting must be fully and clearly defined. They may include:

(*a*) taking orders on the stand;
(*b*) obtaining inquiries for subsequent follow-up;
(*c*) general market publicity, with a view to securing orders in the longer term;
(*d*) *assistance* in meeting a selection of prospective agents or distributors;

(*e*) *assistance* in the assessment of market potential or of product acceptability.

11. Advance marketing programme. As mentioned (*see* **7**), mere participation in an exhibition is not sufficient. The advance marketing programme should include:

(*a*) target audience identification;
(*b*) direct-mail publicity to that audience;
(*c*) advance press publicity.

12. Advance stand planning. Arrangements for the stand itself should be made well ahead of the exhibition date. They might include:

(*a*) a decision as to which products are to be exhibited;
(*b*) a design brief for the stand designer;
(*c*) a decision as to the exact position of the stand in the exhibition hall;
(*d*) preparation of a shell stand;
(*e*) assurance regarding electrical connections and other services that might be required, such as water or compressed air;
(*f*) a decision as to precisely which staff will attend;
(*g*) hotel reservations for all such staff;
(*h*) booking of interpreters, when necessary;
(*i*) a timetable for the above and for all other preparatory work.

One senior executive, who will attend the exhibition, should be given entire charge of the project.

13. Budget. A careful and comprehensive budget should be prepared. It might cover:

(*a*) design costs;
(*b*) the transport of exhibits and their possible return;
(*c*) stand construction and removal;
(*d*) hire of furniture from local sources;
(*e*) the cost of stand space;
(*f*) stand cleaning expenses;
(*g*) staff travel costs and other expenses;
(*h*) interpreter costs;
(*i*) telephone installation;
(*j*) stand photography, for current publicity and future guidance;

(k) local public relations;
(l) support advertising, including stand leaflets;
(m) customer entertainment expenses;
(n) insurance;
(o) contingency allowance.

14. Stand organisation. A successful stand is a well-organised stand. The senior executive responsible should make arrangements for, and control:

(a) the activities of all staff on duty on the stand, including local interpreters;
(b) security of the stand, its exhibits, and publicity material;
(c) customer hospitality, both on and off the stand;
(d) inquiry forms and visitors books.

15. Evaluation and follow-up. After the exhibition:

(a) results should be compared with the original objectives;
(b) actual costs should be compared with budget;
(c) enquiries should be followed up promptly;
(d) market information obtained should be evaluated;
(e) a decision should be reached as to whether to exhibit at the same exhibition in the following year.

16. Government support for exhibitors. The U.K. Government provides financial support to companies participating in overseas exhibitions, provided such companies are sponsored by an approved trade association or chamber of commerce. Such support includes:

(a) sub-letting of space and shell stand for a nominal participation fee or low rental;
(b) up to 50 per cent of the travel costs outside Western Europe of two representatives of the company, who will man the stand;
(c) up to 50 per cent of the freight cost of returning unsold exhibits after the exhibition (from outside Western Europe).

STORE PROMOTIONS

17. Definition. The term "store promotion" can refer to a variety of promotional activities within retail stores. In the international marketing sense, however, it is used specifically to describe the more elaborate promotions staged in favour of consumer goods from one or more countries.

18. Selection of store. Usually the international marketer will have little choice. Only a limited number of promotions is arranged in any one year. Details can again be found in the *Trade Promotions Guide* (*see* **8**).

19. Value of store promotions. The long-term value of store promotions is difficult to assess and opinions differ on the subject. A few generalisations, however, can be made:

(*a*) as with exhibitions, they should be considered only as part of a long-term marketing plan;

(*b*) the aim should normally be the continuing supply of the products in the future, so evaluation should take place, say, a year afterwards;

(*c*) they are most likely to be successful if the products concerned are already being purchased and sold by the store, and are not simply purchased specially for the event;

(*d*) such continuing sales may require the establishment of the product at other stages of the distribution chain, e.g. for food products, which are not normally purchased direct by department stores.

20. Government support. The U.K. Government assists the *promoting store* by providing an agreed contribution towards promotional expenses. No contributions are made to participating British companies.

PUBLIC RELATIONS

21. Press releases in overseas media. The U.K. company is particularly well situated with regard to obtaining space in overseas media.

(*a*) *Press correspondents.* Some 700 correspondents of overseas newspapers, periodicals, radio and television are based in London. The B.O.T.B. provides a list, which is periodically updated.

(*b*) *Central Office of Information.* The C.O.I. will prepare a professional news release from any newsworthy item submitted to it and will distribute it to media in all relevant countries. The service is entirely free and perhaps too few companies take advantage of it.

EXAMPLE: The C.O.I. now reckons, through British Information Services abroad, to publicise 2,000 new products and processes every year. Last year, 74 out of the 114 new foreign products listed by America's *Journal of Commerce* came from the U.K. Two weeks out of every three, the C.O.I. has at least one spot in the "New Products and Processes" column of the American weekly magazine, *Newsweek*. On television it has five minutes every week in Mexico with a programme called *24 Hours*, which promotes U.K. products; a feature programme, *This Week in Britain*, for Australia and Canada; and a scientifically-based series, *Living Tomorrow*, which has a world-wide distribution. The C.O.I. can prove an admirable dirt-cheap springboard into export markets.

(c) *B.B.C.* The B.B.C. External Services broadcast in English and in 39 other languages. A significant part of their programmes is concerned with developments in British industry, commerce and technical research. New products, export successes and exhibits at trade fairs are of particular interest. Enquiries resulting from the broadcasts are forwarded by the B.B.C. to the company concerned.

22. Public relations for subsidiary companies. The overseas subsidiary, located within its major market as a rule, has fewer problems in organising press releases. Its more usual problem is that of earning and retaining a reputation as a good corporate citizen of the host country. The standards required of a subsidiary company vary from country to country, but as a general rule most subsidiaries would do well to adhere to the guiding principles laid down by the Government of Canada Foreign Investment Review Agency, an abridged version of which is given below:

(*a*) pursue a high degree of autonomy in the exercise of decision-making and risk-taking functions;

(*b*) develop as an integral part of the Canadian operation an autonomous capability for technological innovation, and for production, marketing, purchasing and accounting;

(*c*) retain in Canada a sufficient share of earnings to give strong financial support to the growth and entrepreneurial potential of the Canadian operation, having in mind a fair return to shareholders on capital invested;

(*d*) strive for a full international mandate for innovation and market development, when it will enable the Canadian company to improve its efficiency by specialisation of productive operations;

(e) aggressively pursue and develop market opportunities throughout international markets as well as in Canada;

(f) extend the processing in Canada of natural resource products to the maximum extent feasible on an economic basis;

(g) search out and develop economic sources of supply in Canada for domestically produced goods and for professional and other services;

(h) foster a Canadian outlook within management, as well as enlarged career opportunities within Canada, by promoting Canadians to senior and middle management positions, and by including a majority of Canadians on boards of directors of all Canadian companies;

(i) create a financial structure that provides opportunity for substantial equity participation in the Canadian enterprise by the Canadian public;

(j) pursue a pricing policy designed to assure a fair and reasonable return to the company and to Canada for all goods and services sold abroad, including sales to parent companies and other affiliates;

(k) regularly publish information on the operations and financial position of the firm;

(l) give appropriate support to recognised national objectives and established government programmes, while resisting any direct or indirect pressure from foreign governments or associated companies to act in a contrary manner;

(m) participate in Canadian social and cultural life and support those institutions that are concerned with the intellectual, social, and cultural advancement of the Canadian community.

PROGRESS TEST 16

1. Why should exhibitions be regarded as being of greater importance in international, rather than domestic, marketing? **(6)**

2. What various categories of international exhibition may be distinguished? **(8)**

3. The international marketer is usually faced with a wide choice of exhibitions. On what criteria should he make his choice? **(9)**

4. What factors should be taken into account in planning for an exhibition? **(11–13)**

5. What government support is available for U.K. exhibitors at international fairs? **(16)**
6. What is a store promotion? **(17)**
7. How can the Central Office of Information help the exporter? **(21)**

CHAPTER XVII

International Communications III: International Sales Management

INTRODUCTION

1. Sales management. Sales management includes the recruitment, training, motivation, compensation, organisation, evaluation and control of a sales force, i.e. the personal selling function.

For obvious reasons, personal selling, more than any other marketing activity, is closely linked to national, or even regional, social or cultural characteristics and to language. Most face-to-face selling is organised within national frontiers. In the E.E.C., for instance, despite the progress made towards integration, few sales forces cross political or cultural boundaries; international selling is limited mainly to industrial goods or to quantity sales of consumer goods to wholesalers and major retail groups.

Purely national selling is not further considered.

2. International sales management. The international sales management function may involve:

(*a*) the management of a team of travelling export salesmen based at company headquarters;

(*b*) the management of salesmen based abroad, within their market areas; such salesmen may, of course, be either expatriates or nationals of the market country;

(*c*) ultimate responsibility for the nationally organised and managed sales forces of an overseas subsidiary or branch;

(*d*) responsibility for sales through agents.

The first three subjects are considered in this chapter. Agencies are discussed in XVIII.

THE TRAVELLING SALES FORCE

3. The export salesman. In sales management a prime requisite for success is the selection of the right sales team: a difficult task for any sales manager, but doubly difficult in the export field. An export salesman must possess all the qualities of his domestic counterpart, plus the characteristics discussed below.

(*a*) *Managerial competence.* The export salesman must be able to make prompt decisions, often with limited information and with less consultative support, on risks and opportunities of much greater magnitude than are usual in the home market. Overseas buyers are unlikely to react favourably to a salesman who is constantly referring back to headquarters for instructions.

Furthermore, the export salesman is likely to be responsible for guiding agency operations and for training agency staff.

(*b*) *Research competence.* The export salesman must know where to look for advice and information and how to interpret data obtained. He will have many of the characteristics of the market researcher.

(*c*) *Cultural adaptability.* The ability to adapt to and, better still, identify with cultures very different from his own is essential in an export salesman. Much more is required than mere tolerance or acceptance.

(*d*) *Dependability.* Far more than his domestic counterpart the export salesman will be required to work without supervision; business abroad is often frustrating, and temptations to take time off are greater. The export salesman must be relied upon to persist in his sales task.

(*e*) *Health.* Travel in itself is physically demanding. Extremes of climate, strange foods, indifferent hotels, and customer entertainment all combine to increase the strain on a salesman's constitution.

(*f*) *Linguistic ability.* On the one hand, linguistic skills may be overvalued: competence in appropriate languages, without the qualities discussed above, is not enough. Conversely, some companies even today fail to realise the weakness of a sales approach that relies on a bi-lingual customer.

4. Size of the export sales force. The size of a sales force is a function of:

(*a*) market potential;
(*b*) the extent to which personal selling is the most effective method, in terms of eventual profit, of exploiting that potential;
(*c*) the work load involved, in terms of sales calls and other related activities, in exploiting the potential.

These basic principles hold good whether sales are national or international. It is necessary to mention them in an international context only because so many companies ignore them in relation to their export markets. The Betro report *Concentration on Key Markets* commented on this fact and on the resultant damaging effect on the sales and profits of U.K. exporters.

> EXAMPLE: (1) Even allowing for the use of overseas agents British companies employ a relatively small number of people on the export side of their activities (small in relation to the numbers employed on the selling side for the home market, and small in relation to the number of countries they have to service).
>
> (2) There are many companies where almost the entire export effort revolves around one man (including a number exporting from 50 per cent to 80 per cent of their production). It is his task to keep in touch with all the markets (often over 100), customers and problems overseas; attend to the problems of administration and finance; appoint and supervise agents and so on.

5. Deployment of the export sales force. Sales forces are normally organised into territories, again on the basis of market potential and work load. In exporting, the same principles hold good, except that the sales contribution of the agent must also be taken into account. Assessing the agent's contribution on a realistic basis is not always easy—his efforts are usually spread over a range of products and may, as a result, be sporadic. Nevertheless, such an assessment must be attempted and the sales force must be deployed accordingly. The Betro report also commented on the deployment of U.K. export salesmen.

> EXAMPLE: Yet another reason for the small export sales force is that companies organise their selling operations for exports in an entirely different manner from that in the home market. In the latter they split up the country into small sales territories, effectively manageable by one man. In the export markets, as a rule, they hand over their products to an agent who covers an entire country. Thus one export sales specialist can "look after" ten or more countries. Even allowing for the different situation, this approach would be regarded as monstrously inefficient in the home market.

THE EXPORT SALESMAN ABROAD

6. Expatriate salesmen. In the case of expatriate salesmen the problems of sales management are similar to those of a travelling export sales force. Two additional problems arise:

(*a*) employee conditions of service;
(*b*) the high cost of expatriate staff.

7. Conditions of service. With any sales force, one of the most important problems is the maintenance of morale. This is doubly important when a salesman, or, perhaps more usually, a sales manager, is posted overseas with only limited contact with headquarters. Inadequately thought-out conditions of service are a frequent source of dissatisfaction, and it is important to consider salary, expenses and career development *before* any employee is posted abroad. Below is a check list of the major items to be considered.

(*a*) *Salary and allowances.*

(*i*) How does the proposed salary compare with local cost of living *for expatriates*?

(*ii*) Is a clothing allowance to be paid? For *all* members of the family?

(*iii*) Is a car provided? With driver?

(*iv*) How is the salary, if expressed in sterling, protected against devaluation?

(*v*) Is the salary to be linked to the local cost of living? How often should cost of living adjustments be made?

(*vi*) If there are exchange controls on remittance of capital to the U.K., should part of the salary be paid into a U.K. bank? Or a bank in some other country with a freely convertible currency?

(*b*) *Travel.*

(*i*) Are *all* family passages to be paid? Class?

(*ii*) What quantity or value of household goods may be shipped over at company expense? And who pays duty on these items?

(*iii*) If children attend boarding schools, how many times per annum can they fly out to join their parents at company expense?

(*iv*) Who pays fares home in the event of compassionate leave, e.g. sickness/death of near relative, etc.?

(*v*) For what regular home leaves will travel be paid for by the company?

(*c*) *Local housing.*

(*i*) Does the company provide accommodation? If so, of what standard? Furnished or unfurnished? If furnished, what exactly will be provided?

(*ii*) If accommodation is not provided, what allowance should be made towards its cost? And will hotel expenses be paid to enable an employee to look around for accommodation? If so, for how long?

(*iii*) Who pays for electricity, water, gas, and other utilities? And local property taxes? And maintenance charges?

(*d*) *U.K. housing.*

(*i*) If the expatriate is to sell his U.K. house will the company pay legal fees, estate agent's costs, etc.?

(*ii*) If the house is retained but not let, will the company assist in payment of mortgage interest, rates, insurance, etc.?

(*iii*) If the house is retained but let, will the company contribute to any shortfall between outgoings and rental income?

(*iv*) Does the company pay the cost of any furniture storage?

(*e*) *Education.*

(*i*) Will the company pay for or subsidise local school fees? Or U.K. boarding-school fees?

(*ii*) What exactly may such fees include? (For example, are optional subjects such as music, elocution, etc. allowed?)

(*f*) *Medical.*

(*i*) Who pays for initial inoculations?

(*ii*) Is appropriate medical advice available locally? And hospital accommodation? And who pays?

(*iii*) Will all dental treatment be paid for? Or merely emergency treatment?

(*g*) *Social.*

(*i*) Who pays club entrance fees and annual membership fees?

(*ii*) Is an entertainment allowance desirable?

(*iii*) Will the company pay for language courses for the employee? *And* his wife?

(*h*) *Career prospects.*

(*i*) How long is the employee expected to serve abroad?

(*ii*) Where is he likely to fit in at headquarters after his tour of duty abroad?

Actual salary levels, or the allowance for the local cost of living, must, of course, be established separately for each relevant country. The larger company, regularly sending employees overseas, may find it worthwhile to subscribe to the service of Employment Conditions Abroad Ltd., which monitors economic conditions, salaries and tax structures in some seventy-five countries.

8. Cost of expatriate staff. The advantages of posting a man abroad are perhaps greater than appear on the surface. The

XVII. INTERNATIONAL COMMUNICATIONS III

average export salesman spends, as a rule, a very limited amount of his time actually in the market; he may be out of the U.K. for perhaps six months of the year, but absences much longer than six months would be unusual. The expatriate salesman is based in the market and may be regarded as the equivalent of two travelling salesmen, while he achieves a significant saving in air fares and hotel bills.

The cost of maintaining an expatriate abroad, however, can be surprisingly high, as merely the briefest consideration of 7 will suggest. For the not-too-distant markets the travelling salesman may be the more cost-effective alternative.

EXAMPLE: If, like a good number of United Kingdom concerns, you were thinking of seeking increased export business by basing a senior sales executive for the first time in the Middle East, how much do you think this move would cost? According to Michael Egan of P.A. International Management Consultants the answer to the question is much more than the average employer is likely to expect.

Let's say the company concerned prides itself on good, as distinct from best, employment practice and is to transfer a 35-year-old sales manager earning £9,000 in Birmingham to not-unusually-expensive Tehran, where he will be paid £15,000 tax-free. Let's say also that he is married, with children aged ten and seven, one of whom will be going to boarding school in the U.K.

In these circumstances, P.A. estimates the total cost of the new appointment as follows:

	£
Pre-posting: medical, language training	600
Disturbance: house sale, storage, etc.	1,600
Relocation: transport, insurance, etc.	3,300
Installation: hotels, settling-in, etc.	2,350
Remuneration: pay, tax, pension, etc.	21,650
Accommodation: rent, furnishing, etc.	15,600
Education, including travel expenses	2,950
Leave	2,420
Car purchase and running	3,500
Other costs: Medicare, clubs, U.K. administration	800
Total	£54,770

This calculation, in which costs of car and furniture are spread over two years, takes no account of "on-site" expenses such as office services, travel and entertaining, which altogether could add a further £15,000–£20,000.

9. The national salesman. Partly on the grounds of cost, but perhaps also on the grounds of language and cultural compatibility, exporters are turning increasingly to the local national salesman, already based in the market. Again, a superficial estimate of costs can be deceptive: apart from the higher salary probably needed, the increased cost of supervision of a newly appointed salesman, based a long way from headquarters, can be significant.

Many of the comments made throughout this chapter are relevant to such an appointment (*see* **3–5, 7, 11**).

THE NATIONAL SALES FORCE

10. Organisation. A full sales force abroad will usually be managed through a branch office or subsidiary company. For obvious reasons it will normally consist of local nationals.

11. Recruitment. Simply because personal selling varies so much with the social and business environment, recruitment is best undertaken within the foreign market by local managers. If a sales force is being recruited from scratch, and, therefore, without the benefit of local sales management advice, it will usually prove advisable to rely on local personnel recruitment agencies.

Regional differences within the country should, of course, be taken into account at the recruitment stage, e.g. a French Canadian would be recruited for Quebec.

12. Managing the sales force. No hard-and-fast rules can be laid down; face-to-face selling varies so much not merely between nations and between regions, but also between industries and individual companies. Generally, however, the international sales manager is likely to find that:

(*a*) training, motivation, methods of remuneration, organisation and control of the sales force are best left in the hands of local managers;

(*b*) in all these areas he has a significant role to play as an adviser on sales management techniques and in facilitating the international exchange of experience.

XVII. INTERNATIONAL COMMUNICATIONS III

Chapter XXVI, concerned with a Brazilian sales force, may help to illustrate some of the cultural differences likely to be encountered in other countries.

PROGRESS TEST 17

1. What does *international* sales management involve? **(2)**
2. What qualities must the export salesman possess, over and above those of his domestic counterpart? **(3)**
3. On what bases would you decide on the size of an export sales force? **(4)**
4. What items would you consider in establishing the conditions of service for a sales manager posted, with his family, abroad? **(7)**
5. What contribution might an international sales manager expect to make to the success of the established sales force of a foreign subsidiary? **(12)**

CHAPTER XVIII

International Communications IV: Agency Sales

AGENCY SEARCH

1. Consideration of alternative channels. Before seeking any agent (*see* VIII, **6**) the exporter should have undertaken sufficient research, or have sufficient experience of the market, to be sure that, among all the alternatives open to him, an agent is the channel most appropriate to his profit and other objectives (*see* VIII, **8–10**).

2. Agency profile. The exporter should be clear in his own mind as to exactly what type of agency he is seeking; similarly, he must give as detailed a brief as possible to those organisations who are likely to assist him in his search (*see* **4–9**). Preparation of a formal and detailed profile of the ideal agency is a useful step, even if in practice the ideal is unlikely to be achieved.

Such a profile will vary from one company to the next, but is likely to include, as a minimum:

(*a*) the precise geographical area the agent should *already* cover;

(*b*) the types of customers or distribution channels to which the agent should *already* be selling;

(*c*) the completeness and frequency of the agent's sales coverage;

(*d*) the types of products ideal as complementary lines;

(*e*) requirements in terms of servicing, repair and stockholding facilities.

The first three items are particularly important, and are often the basic reason for selecting an agent rather than recruiting a local salesman, yet intending principals often fail to inquire about the *extent* of sales coverage, let alone its *quality*. If an agent has to introduce himself to a new range of customers, he incurs a significant outlay, while the principal, at best, has an expensive delay before sales result.

3. Principal profile. Any competent agent who is seriously interested will require the fullest possible information on the prospective principal. Such information is best drawn up initially in the form of a profile of the principal. The profile should be a selling document, designed to interest as many prospective agencies as possible. It should cover not merely the usual and obvious subjects, such as product range, factories, number of employees, etc., but, as far as possible:

(*a*) the company's recent performance in the home and other export markets;

(*b*) the special advantages and selling points of the product range offered;

(*c*) the recommended marketing approach;

(*d*) the assistance the company normally provides in the marketing of the products, e.g. co-operative advertising, the provision of sales literature, training of agency's technical and sales staff.

Commission rates payable are often best left for more detailed discussion with agents at the face-to-face negotiation stage.

4. Finding the agency. The more usual sources of information on likely candidates for the agency are:

(*a*) the British Overseas Trade Board;
(*b*) chambers of commerce;
(*c*) banks;
(*d*) trade associations;
(*e*) agents' associations;
(*f*) advertising in appropriate trade magazines.

5. British Overseas Trade Board. The B.O.T.B. arranges for commercial officers overseas to undertake an agency search. The objective is to provide the U.K. exporter or intending exporter with a list of suitable and interested agencies. Status reports, giving information on the business operations and commercial standing of the agencies, and a general assessment of the exporter's prospects in the market, are also prepared.

A small charge is made for each separate enquiry, and this is payable whether or not names of prospective agents can be provided.

6. Chambers of commerce. The functions and importance of chambers of commerce vary significantly according to country, some being very much official bodies with legal standing, others being fairly informal trade bodies. Similarly, the value of the assistance they can give to companies in search of agencies will vary.

Many chambers of commerce, however, will make efforts to provide introductions, or will pass on enquiries to other chambers abroad. The London Chamber of Commerce and Industry offers an "Openings for Trade" service to which members can subscribe for a small additional fee. The service issues a regular publication which includes the names of overseas agencies interested in representing U.K. principals.

Chambers of commerce abroad may also be contacted direct. These include specialist two-country chambers, e.g. the Anglo-Venezuelan Chamber of Commerce in Caracas.

7. Banks. Most of the major banks have an overseas business development service, whose task it is to help customers *or prospective customers* of the bank to enter or to expand in foreign markets. It is not as a rule necessary to have an account at the bank to take advantage of such a service.

Bank information is not limited to financial status reports. Many banks are specially organised to provide introductions between principals and agents.

8. Trade associations. Trade associations can assist in the agency search by contacting their equivalents abroad and by publishing agency opportunities in their newsletters.

The service may cover not only equivalent associations, i.e. those covering the same products, but also associations covering the complementary side of the industry, e.g. an electrical manufacturers' association might contact an association of electrical wholesalers abroad.

9. Agency associations. In many of the major industrialised markets of the world agents have formed themselves into official bodies for the better regulation of their industry. The International Union of Commercial Agents and Brokers (I.U.C.A.B.), based in Amsterdam, covers the industrialised nations of Western Europe and the U.S.A. It has a total membership, direct or through affiliated associations, of some 50,000 agents. One of its most important functions is the introduction of principals to prospective agents.

The appropriate national agency federations can be located

through I.U.C.A.B. These national associations offer lists of their members for sale.

10. Advertising. Appropriate trade and technical magazines can be identified from the international or national press guides used by advertising agencies, e.g. *Tarif Media* in France.

AGENCY SELECTION

11. Market visit. A visit to the market is absolutely essential. A company which lacks either the financial resources or the management time necessary for such a visit should seriously ask itself whether it should be contemplating entering, or remaining in, the market at all. Further, the visit should be made by a senior executive, who will be either immediately or ultimately responsible for the subsequent results from the territory.

12. Selection procedure. Essentially, the selection decision should be based on:

(*a*) the fullest possible discussion with agency executives, salesmen and other relevant staff, e.g. service engineers;

(*b*) whenever possible, discussions with customers and potential customers, i.e. the companies to which the agent will sell your products and to which he is already selling, or should be selling, other lines.

13. Agency selection check list. Some companies have also found it helpful to establish a formal comparison procedure, or check list. Such check lists will vary from company to company, but are likely to include the points listed below.

(*a*) Ownership of agency.
(*b*) Career histories of executives.
(*c*) Other agencies held, and extent of success with those agencies.
(*d*) Geographical area genuinely and regularly covered.
(*e*) Types of outlet covered.
(*f*) Frequency of visits per outlet.
(*g*) Number of salesmen and their length of service.
(*h*) Agency's knowledge of the market.
(*i*) Agency's apparent marketing competence, particularly in relation to how it is intended to market the new product line.
(*j*) If required, serving and spares facilities.

(*k*) If relevant, number and qualifications of service staff.
(*l*) Bank and other trade references.
(*m*) Agency's interest in and enthusiasm for the new product.

THE AGENCY AGREEMENT

14. Nature of the agreement. The agency agreement is a commercial contract and is quite properly the subject of detailed negotiation between the parties. Agreements are likely, therefore, to vary significantly between one company and another, or between markets. Nevertheless, there are a number of common features that should be taken into account in drawing up almost any agency agreement. These features are summarised below.

(*a*) *Parties.* Identification of parties to the agreement and their capacity to contract.

(*b*) *Purpose.* One party appoints the other as agent and the other agrees to act.

(*c*) *Products* (*see* **15**).

(*i*) Definition of products subject to the agreement.

(*ii*) Position regarding other products sold by the principal, now and in the future.

(*d*) *Territory* (*see* **16**). Definition of territory in which agent is entitled to act.

(*e*) *Exclusivity* (*see* **17**).

(*i*) Agent's sole and exclusive right to represent principal.

(*ii*) Extent to which principal may operate in the territory without the agent's assistance.

(*iii*) Agent's right, if any, to commission on orders placed direct with principal.

(*iv*) Prohibition on agent's dealing in competing products.

(*f*) *Duties of principal* (*see* **18**). Sales and marketing assistance, e.g. training of agent's staff, provision of information, etc.

(*g*) *Duties of agent* (*see* **19**).

(*i*) Right, *if any*, to enter into binding agreements on behalf of principal, and, if so, to what extent.

(*ii*) Extent to which agent is bound to comply with principal's instructions on prices and other conditions of sale.

(*iii*) Stipulation of minimum turnover required, if any.

(*h*) *Consignment stocks* (*see* **20**). Provision for sale of, and payment for, such stocks, and their storage, maintenance, and insurance.

(*i*) *Servicing.* Provision of after-sales and spares service by agent, if required, and his remuneration.

(*j*) *Commission* (*see* **21**).

(*i*) Percentage rate of commission.

(*ii*) Variations in rate for different origins of orders, e.g. for orders through a London export house.

(*iii*) Basis of calculation of commission, e.g. f.o.b. price, c.i.f., etc.

(*iv*) Indication of when commission is earned, e.g. on receipt of order, on delivery of goods, on payment by customer, etc.

(*v*) Position in event of subsequent order cancellation, buyer bankruptcy, etc.

(*vi*) Dates for payment of commission by principal, e.g. quarterly.

(*k*) *Duration* (*see* **17**). Date agreement comes into force and *expiry date.*

(*l*) *Termination* (*see* **22**). Provisions for termination before expiry date, e.g. breach of agreement, bankruptcy, etc.

(*m*) *Arbitration.* Provision for arbitration in event of disagreement.

(*n*) *Assignment.* Stipulation that agent cannot assign the benefit of the contract.

(*o*) *Authentic text.* Indication of which text is authentic, if agreement in two languages.

(*p*) Law of agreement (*see* **23**). Indication of the national law that governs the agreement.

The check list given above is necessarily an over-simplification. Many of the points listed require the most careful and detailed consideration; some brief indication of problems that may arise is given below (*see* **15–23**).

Further, the laws of many countries make special provisions for agency contracts, usually with a view to protecting the position of local agents or defining the position of the principal in relation to any possible liability to local taxation. Some reference is made below (*see* **19, 20, 22, 23**), to the more important and more usual of such provisions, but it is emphasised that no international agency contract should be entered into without the benefit of professional legal and fiscal advice. The U.K. exporter can obtain initial information on agency legislation in foreign countries from the B.O.T.B.

15. Products. In many markets, the exporter is unlikely to find one single agent suitable for his entire product range. Two or more agents may need to be appointed if adequate market coverage is to be secured.

There should be no implication whatever in the agreement that new products to be introduced by the principal in the future will automatically be included in the agreement. Such products may bear no relation to existing products in terms of sales outlets or marketing programmes.

16. Territory. The territory should normally relate to the agent's existing sales area, as has already been emphasised (*see* **2**). This area will not necessarily coincide with national boundaries, and may require careful definition in geographical terms.

It may also be desirable to define the territory in terms of sales outlets. For instance, two agents could quite validly be appointed to cover the same products and the same area, one covering retail outlets and the other covering industrial outlets.

17. Exclusivity. It is not normally in the principal's interest to grant exclusivity—he leaves the entire rights to the market in the hands of an independent party who may fail to exploit its potential. On the other hand, no agent can really be expected to invest his time and money in the sale of his principal's product unless he is granted exclusivity for a reasonable period of time. Normally the principal's aim should be to grant exclusivity but to limit the duration of the agreement to the shortest reasonable period.

18. Duties of principal. The agreement should consider in detail all likely future marketing activities and indicate who is expected to foot the bill. Constantly recurring areas of friction include:

   (*a*) servicing and repairs;
   (*b*) guarantee arrangements;
   (*c*) local advertising;
   (*d*) the provision of promotional material;
   (*e*) translation costs;
   (*f*) training of agent's staff; and
   (*g*) stockholding, especially consignment stocks (*see* **20**).

19. Duties of agent. The agency agreement should specifically state whether the agent has any power to enter into binding agreements on behalf of his principal and, if so, to what extent. It should be borne in mind that in some countries if an agent has, and exercises, a general authority to negotiate and conclude contracts on behalf of his principal, that principal becomes liable to tax *in the agent's country*.

A frequent clause in agency agreements is that the agent must maintain the prices and conditions of sale quoted by the principal, but in some countries such a clause is not legally valid.

Another favourite clause stipulates a minimum acceptable turnover from the territory, below which either the agreement is terminated or the agent loses exclusivity. Such clauses often take up much valuable negotiating time and then are finally fixed at so low a level of turnover that they are virtually useless as a form of motivation. A competent principal will offer a better approach to agency motivation (*see* **24–29**).

20. Consignment stocks. Consignment stocks remain the property of the principal but are physically within the agent's territory, under his control, and are sold by him to customers. The possible causes of friction under such an arrangement are legion, and any agreement covering consignment stocks must make the most careful and detailed provision for storage, maintenance, insurance, terms of sale, stock checks, etc.

A further danger is that in some countries the establishment of a consignment stock may render the principal liable to taxation in the country in which the stock is held.

21. Commission rate. These days few sales managers would pay a fixed percentage of turnover to their domestic sales force; most would vary the commission so as to achieve maximum incentive effect. Nevertheless, such a fixed percentage of turnover is still very much the normal and expected form of remuneration for overseas agents.

It is often worthwhile to devise a scheme which acts as a genuine incentive to the agent to direct his selling efforts into the channels desired by the principal, at the same time increasing profits for both parties. For instance, higher percentage rates can be paid on orders from new clients, or for particularly profitable items in the range.

22. Termination. The termination clause is of vital importance. Termination of agency agreements offers special difficulties in many countries and heavy compensation may be payable. *Termination requires the most careful consideration, in the light of local laws, before the contract is even signed.*

23. Law of agreement. The agreement should state which national laws govern the interpretation of the contract. It should be noted that in some countries, *regardless of what is agreed by the parties and stated in the contract*, the law of the agent's country must apply.

AGENCY MOTIVATION

24. The need for motivation. For the principal, the fundamental problem of agency distribution is that of ensuring that his product, among all the different lines the agent handles, receives at least its fair share of attention, and preferably more. The agency agreement is important for the avoidance of disputes that might damage the agent's goodwill, but it is only the starting point, the base from which a positive programme of motivation can be launched.

25. Market visits. The first essential is frequent visits to the territory by the principal. Interest and support simply *must* be demonstrated in this way if success is to be achieved, a point which might seem obvious if it were not for the fact that so many U.K. exporters seem to ignore it.

> EXAMPLE: The relatively few export salesmen are away from their home base for 5 to 7 months of the year. But because they have so many countries to look after, even the best markets are visited once or at most twice a year only—seldom more. The others, once every two or three years—or never.

26. Profit. The fundamental motive of the agent is, of course, profit—profit for his agency and himself. The principal must work closely with the agent and help him to make money.

This is especially important with a newly appointed agency. Many agents tend to be salesmen at heart; in any case, they are, not unnaturally, unwilling to invest time in market enquiries. The principal, with the advantage of the market research that should have been undertaken, may be able to suggest one or two hitherto neglected possibilities and assist in initial sales.

27. Marketing plans. The principal can provide valuable assistance in preparing annual plans covering all aspects of the marketing of the product.

28. Communications. Quite apart from market visits, regular *two-way* communication is essential. The uninformed agent soon becomes uninvolved and uninterested; the uninformed principal directs his attention to other markets where opportunities seem more obvious.

The communications system should cover:

(*a*) formalised and regular reporting of results, not merely by the agent, but by the principal *to* the agent, e.g. of overall company results;

(*b*) essential information, e.g. changes in agency executives, new product developments by the principal;

(*c*) informal personal matters, preferably in an informal manner.

29. Interpretation of agreement. However carefully the agreement is drafted, some difficulties of interpretation, or some unforeseen special circumstances, . will occasionally arise. Whenever possible the agreement should be interpreted in favour of the agent; his goodwill is worth much more than the commission paid in borderline cases.

PROGRESS TEST 18

1. In a search for an agent, it is quite usual to draw up a profile of the ideal agency. What points should such a profile cover? **(2)**

2. What organisations are likely to be of help in the search for agents abroad? **(4)**

3. What points should be included in an agency agreement? **(14)**

4. Why is the question of exclusivity of particular importance in an agency agreement? **(17)**

5. Why is motivation of overseas agents so important and how can it best be achieved? **(24–29)**

CHAPTER XIX

Organising for International Marketing

INTRODUCTION

1. Company organisation. Company organisation includes:

(*a*) the analysis of the work that needs to be accomplished in order to meet company profit and other objectives;

(*b*) the division of that work into manageable tasks;

(*c*) grouping those tasks together on a logical basis and defining the relationships between them;

(*d*) the appointment of staff to control the tasks and ensure that the work is carried out as planned.

The aim of any organisation structure is to achieve maximum operating efficiency and, hence, maximum profit.

2. Principles of organisation structure. Over the years a number of guiding principles of organisation have been developed.

(*a*) There should be a clear line of authority from top to bottom of the organisation, i.e. the "chain of command" principle.

(*b*) Everyone in the organisation should know to whom he reports, and who reports to him, while no-one should report to more than one superior, i.e. the "unity of command" principle.

(*c*) Managers responsible for results should be given the authority necessary to achieve them.

(*d*) Conversely, those managers are then fully responsible for the acts of their subordinates.

(*e*) Authority should be delegated as far down the line as is possible.

(*f*) The number of different levels of authority should be kept as low as possible.

(*g*) There is a limit to the number of subordinates who can be controlled by one executive, i.e. the "span of control" principle.

(*h*) The organisation should be flexible, so as to enable it to adjust to a changing environment.

XIX. ORGANISING FOR INTERNATIONAL MARKETING

These principles must be regarded as guidelines rather than rigid rules. This is a point that is particularly important to bear in mind in a marketing context, where the organisation should be adjusted to the needs of the market(s) the company intends to serve.

3. Marketing organisation structures. A company's marketing activities will usually be organised on the basis of:

(*a*) marketing functions;
(*b*) geographical regions;
(*c*) product groups.

Each of these alternative approaches is illustrated in simplified form in Fig. 8. In practice, in a company of any significant size, the organisation structure will usually combine two or more of the basic alternatives.

4. International marketing organisation. The same basic organisational principles apply also in an international context, but in addition the organisation structure will vary according to the company's degree of involvement in international operations. It is possible to distinguish, in international marketing, three principal stages as regards organisation structure:

(*a*) the export department;
(*b*) the international division; and
(*c*) the multinational organisation.

It is these three organisational stages that are considered in this chapter, against a background of the general principles of marketing organisation illustrated in Fig. 8.

THE EXPORT DEPARTMENT

5. The occasional exporter. Many companies begin their international marketing activities by responding to one or two initial orders received from abroad, with little or no marketing effort. At this stage, the order will be processed by the existing (home) sales administration.

6. The exporting company. If international sales increase, the company, recognising the special nature of exporting, will usually organise a small export department consisting of an export sales manager and the necessary administrative assistance, perhaps a

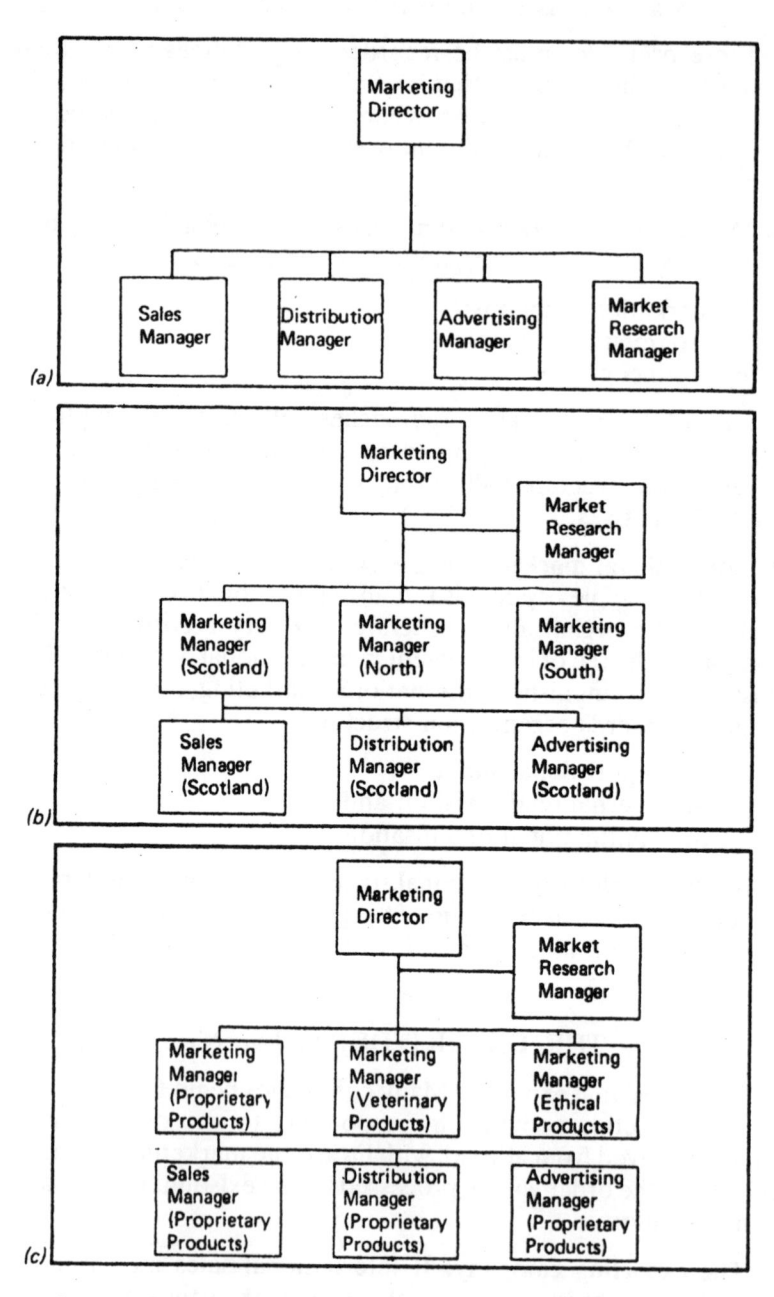

FIG. 8 *Marketing organisation structures: simplified illustrations of the three principal alternatives*

XIX. ORGANISING FOR INTERNATIONAL MARKETING

secretary and a sales clerk. The danger at this point is that, as sales continue to expand, the company may fail to realise the need for corresponding changes in the organisation of the department: the export manager is allowed to struggle unaided with an ever-increasing volume of business (*see* XVII, **4**). Just as the field sales organisation should develop with increasing business, so must the export department develop back at headquarters. What might be a typical export department for a company with a significant export turnover is illustrated in Fig. 9. Such a department has its own functional specialists, for export market intelligence, publicity, etc., and can seek export business more independently and more aggressively than it could if it depended on the part-time services of a home marketing staff that is, perhaps, already over-extended. The example given is, of course, only one of many possible alternatives, but, *however the export department is organised, it must be a marketing, not merely a sales, organisation.*

7. Licensing operations. In Fig. 9 the export manager is shown as not being responsible for licensing operations. Licensing agreements go beyond marketing, involving manufacturing at least to the extent of quality control and probably well beyond that. When a company becomes seriously involved in licensing, a separate manager for licensing should probably be appointed.

THE INTERNATIONAL DIVISION

8. Need for an international division. When a company moves beyond exports into manufacturing abroad, on either an indepen-

---

FIG. 8.
(*a*) *Functional organisation.* Activities are organised by function (sales, advertising, etc.). All geographical areas and products are covered by each function. The approach offers good co-ordination and co-operation between managers, but its value declines as the company expands geographically or extends its product range. (*b*) *Regional organisation.* Activities are organised by geographical region, each region covering all functions, including marketing. The approach is appropriate where significant differences exist between regions. (*c*) *Product organisation.* Activities are organised by product group, each product group controlling all functions, including marketing. The approach is appropriate where the products are quite separate, requiring entirely separate marketing programmes, or where product groups coincide with customer groupings or distinct marketing channels.

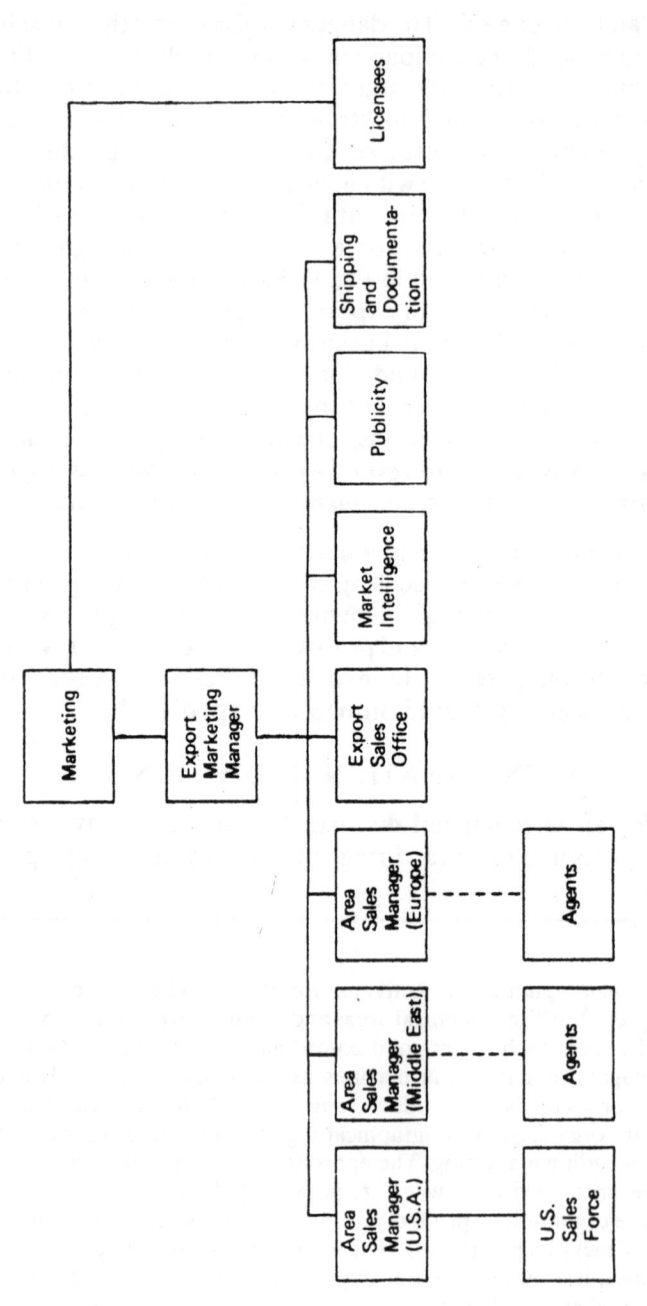

FIG. 9 *An exporting company: development of the export function as export sales increase*

XIX. ORGANISING FOR INTERNATIONAL MARKETING

dent or joint-venture basis, an export department no longer serves its purpose, and an international division should probably take its place. Essentially, the aim of establishing such a division will be to minimise the problems arising from:

(*a*) the great distances separating the various units within the organisation;
(*b*) the diversity of operating conditions and personnel.

9. Organisation of an international division. The international division may be organised in a variety of ways. Usually, however, it will have a central headquarters staff consisting of functional specialists in marketing, manufacturing, finance, personnel, etc. This staff will plan for, and provide services to, the various operating units located around the world.

Decentralisation may be organised on any of the three bases discussed in Fig. 8, i.e. function, region or product. Regional organisations are by far the most common, however, while a functionally-organised division is perhaps most appropriate as a first development from an export-department organisation. Regional and functional divisional organisations are illustrated, with explanatory comment, in Fig. 10. The examples shown are again highly simplified; in practice, of course, it is again possible to combine two or more of the basic organisational principles.

10. Limitations of the international division. The major disadvantage of the international-division approach is that higher management may regard the international division merely as one among many, on a par with the various domestic divisions. Ignorant of world market opportunities, they may fail to give the international division the management attention and the resources it merits. The largest international companies tend to think of organising along multinational lines (*see* I, 9).

Mere size, however, is not in itself a limitation on the international division structure. Whilst the international division is a particularly suitable organisational approach for companies involving themselves for the first time in international manufacturing operations, it is also relied upon by some of the world's largest corporations.

MULTINATIONAL ORGANISATION

11. The nature of multinational organisation structure. In a multinational company, corporate management and staff are *fully*

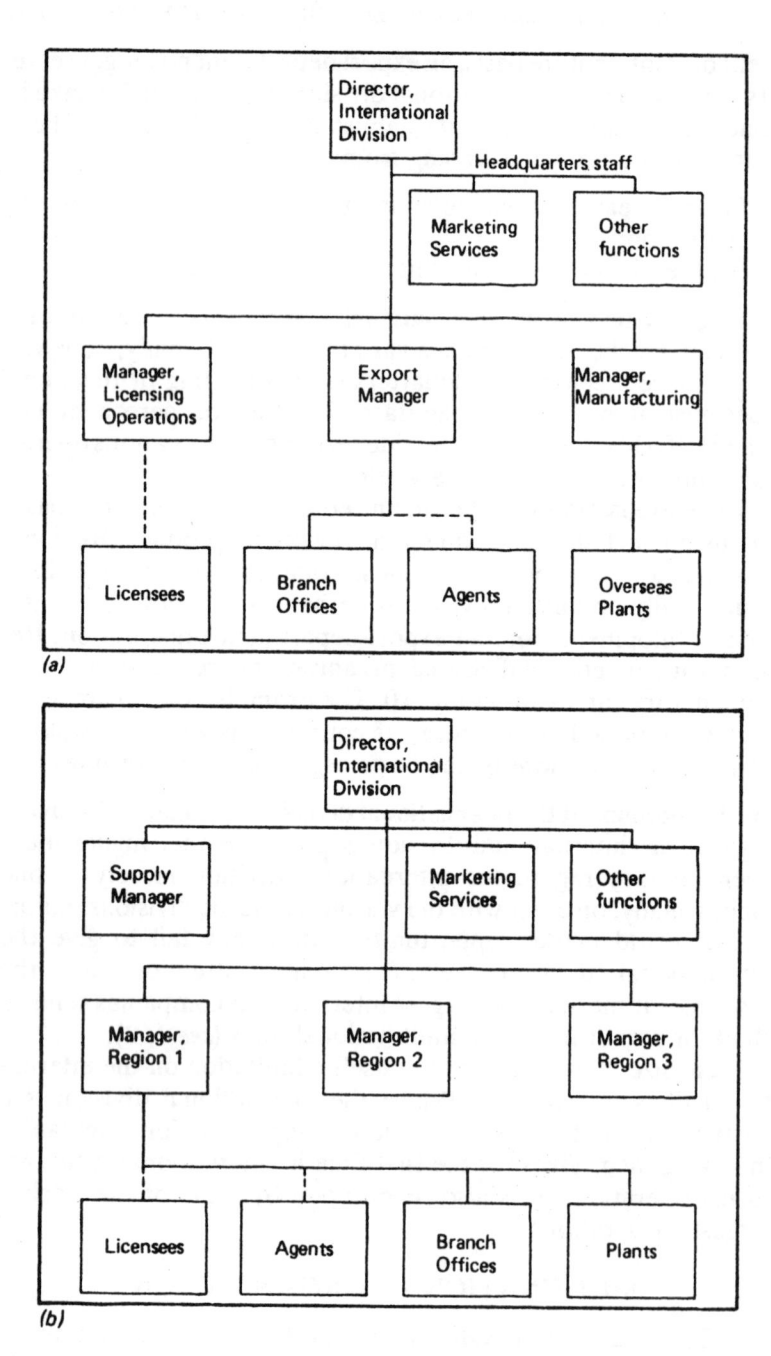

FIG. 10 *The international division: simplified illustrations of functional and regional organisation structures*

XIX. ORGANISING FOR INTERNATIONAL MARKETING 163

involved in the world-wide planning of manufacturing facilities, marketing policies and financial flows. All the operating units around the world report directly to the chief executive of the group, not to an international division.

Multinational organisation structure is a major management subject which is still developing as the multinational companies seek improved organisational approaches. Here it can only be touched upon, with the emphasis largely on the marketing function.

12. The aim of the multinational organisation structure. The basic aim of the organisation structure of a multinational company is to capitalise on the advantages of internationalism while at the same time minimising its inherent disadvantages. More specifically, the objectives are:

(*a*) to maximise the operating performance of the individual units by making available the resources of company headquarters in terms of management expertise, technical know-how, financial assets, market intelligence, etc.;

(*b*) to minimise the problems that arise from distance between operating units and from diversity of operating conditions and personnel, e.g. the exercise of too much or too little initiative, or actions taken with inadequate knowledge of the local market;

FIG. 10

(*a*) *Functional organisation.* For supervisory purposes, foreign units are grouped by the nature of their activities. Executives can develop their skills in exporting, licensing, etc. The approach is usually best adopted where the operations in any one country are all of one type; problems are likely to arise if a company has a plant in a country and also exports to that country. It is for this reason that the functionally organised division is most suitable as a first step from exporting. As international operations grow, problems of co-ordination arise. (*b*) *Regional organisation.* The regional managers are the key executives at headquarters: they have full and sole responsibility for all activities in their area. Marketing and other functional executives support the regional operations with information, analysis and advice, applying the know-how of the parent for the benefit of the foreign units. The supply manager is responsible for the deliveries from home plants to foreign units. Unlike the functional organisation, the international division organised on regional lines is capable of indefinite expansion.

(c) to co-ordinate the activities of individual companies where these are interdependent.

13. Interdependence of individual companies. Interdependence of companies is most obvious, perhaps, in the case of manufacturing operations; for instance, one plant may supply components to another. It is important to consider also the extent of *marketing* interdependence.

(a) Marketing activities may be competitive, now or in the future. The organisational implications should be considered in advance, and not when both companies find themselves in competition in the same export market.

(b) Marketing activities may be complementary, e.g. when:

(i) common marketing channels can be utilised for different products from different manufacturing units;

(ii) standardisation of advertising and promotion may be possible (*see* XV, **4**).

14. Centralisation. For an organisation structure to achieve its objectives (*see* **12**) some degree of centralisation is clearly essential. At the very least central management must retain control over what are regarded as the three key areas of:

(a) basic policy decisions, e.g. changes in marketing policy, such as product elimination or introduction, or expansion of manufacturing facilities;

(b) major capital expenditure;

(c) appointment of key executives.

Usually this limited degree of centralisation will be quite inadequate to capitalise on the advantages of internationalism. On the other hand, centralisation of decision-making offers serious drawbacks (*see* **15**). In fact, the problem of centralisation versus decentralisation is fundamental to any consideration of a multinational organisation structure.

15. Disadvantages of centralisation. The principal disadvantages of centralisation of decision-making may be summed up under two headings: motivation and communication.

(a) *Motivation.* Centralisation of the important decisions is likely to have an adverse effect on the motivation of senior managers in the individual operating units. Most managers are motivated by the need to achieve results in profit terms, and they

XIX. ORGANISING FOR INTERNATIONAL MARKETING

expect to be judged on those results. When the decisions most vitally affecting profits are taken out of their hands, they not unnaturally tend to lose interest.

(*b*) *Communications.* Centralisation requires international communication, which in turn leads to expense (though not usually significant), possible misunderstandings, and certain delays. Delay, of course, is particularly important in a marketing context: opportunities may be missed that could have been seized by a decentralised or independent organisation.

16. The usual approaches to multinational organisation. Most multinationals adopt one or more of the three basic approaches to decentralisation already mentioned: the functional, regional or product approach.

(*a*) *Functional organisation.* The functional organisation is more likely to be favoured when:

(*i*) the company offers a limited or homogeneous product line, with few modifications required for international markets;

(*ii*) variations between countries are not significant in marketing terms.

These conditions are rarely met in the case of multinational companies and the functional organisation is uncommon.

(*b*) *Regional organisation.* The regional organisation is more likely to be favoured when:

(*i*) the company is exploiting regional market groupings, such as the European Community;

(*ii*) the market countries are grouped in close proximity, but at some distance from headquarters;

(*iii*) the product line is limited or homogeneous, as above.

(*c*) *Product organisation.* It will now be evident that the product organisation is most likely to be favoured when the company offers several quite unrelated products, or when modification of products to meet various national requirements is of fundamental importance.

The very real danger of a product organisation is that international market opportunities are likely to be missed, especially if the domestic market has been historically important and the product division staff lack international marketing experience and expertise.

(*d*) *Combined structures.* Any organisation structure, of course, must allow for functional, regional and product inputs, and reliance on only one of the above organisational approaches would, in a multinational context, be highly improbable. The organisation structures of most multinational companies are likely to show either:

(*i*) initial reliance on product decentralisation, with subsequent regional groupings; or

(*ii*) initial reliance on regional decentralisation, with subsequent product groupings;

with, in all cases, a functional input from corporate headquarters staff. The principle of product decentralisation followed by regional groupings is illustrated in Fig. 11.

17. Recent alternative approaches to multinational organisation. All the above approaches provide for the co-ordination of activities in only one dimension: for instance, a regional organisation permits co-ordination of all activities within a region. Interdependence, however, may not be confined within one region; in marketing, in particular, a decision taken within a region may have world-wide implications for the company as a whole. The traditional organisation structure is not adequate to cope with multidimensional interdependence. For this reason some multinational companies have been searching for structures that permit simultaneous co-ordination in terms of product, area and function, while still achieving the benefits of decentralisation. The alternative approaches that have been propounded all involve the overseas executive in reporting not merely to his regional superior but also to a functional superior at headquarters. The headquarters staff cease to play a merely supportive role and exercise executive authority.

This type of organisation, the matrix organisation, would seem at first sight to violate the "unity of command" principle (*see* **2**). In practice, the most careful and detailed job descriptions need to be prepared, indicating, for a number of possible eventualities, who initiates a possible course of action, who must be consulted, and who decides. No organisation chart can hope to show the complexity of the relationships involved. The matrix organisation is in any case suitable only for organisations already confident in their ability to handle sophisticated inter-company communications problems.

PROGRESS TEST 19

1. What is meant by "company organisation"? **(1)**

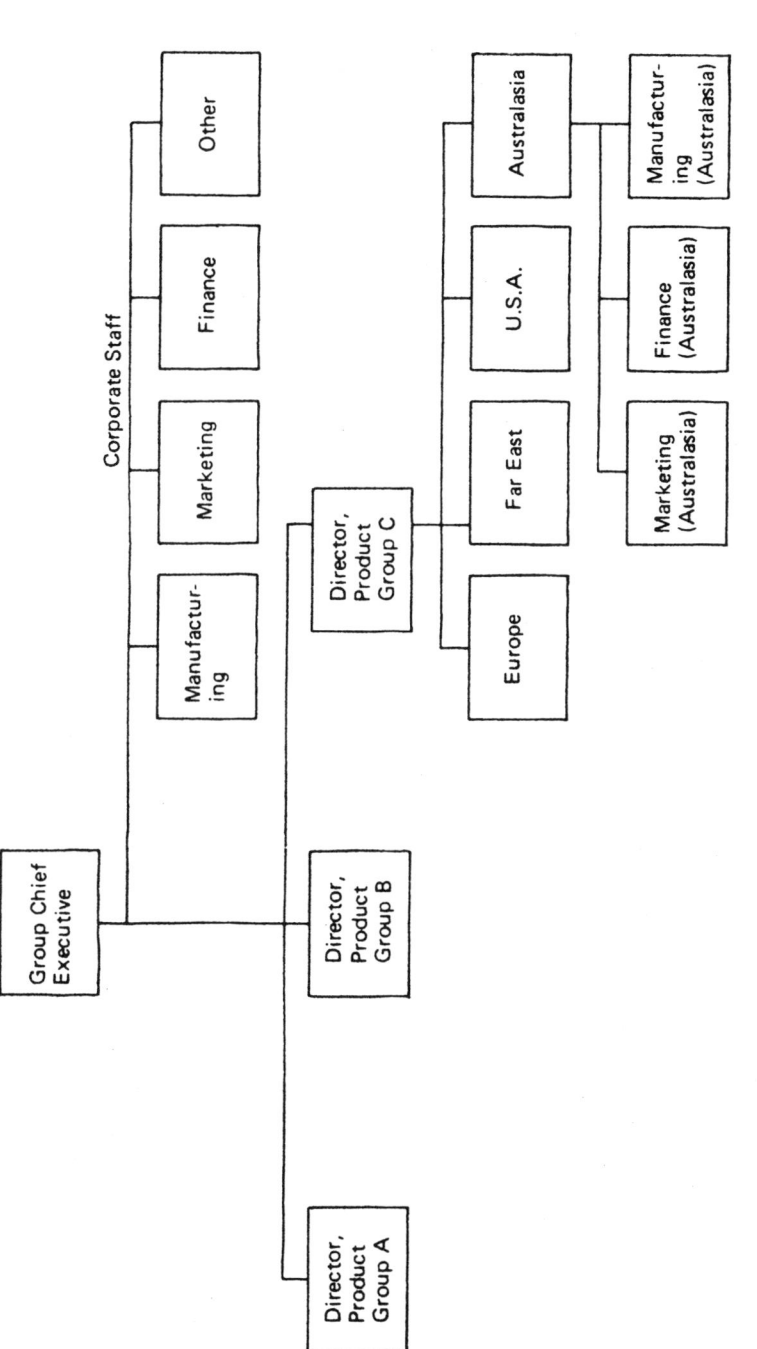

FIG. 11 *Multinational company organisation (simplified): product basis, with subsequent regional and functional decentralisation.*

2. On what three principal bases may a company's marketing activities be organised? **(3)**

3. How might a company's export department be organised? **(6)**

4. What are the limitations of an international divisional organisation structure? **(10)**

5. What is the principal distinction between an international divisional organisation structure and a multinational organisation? **(11)**

6. In a multinational organisation, what are the major disadvantages of centralised control? **(15)**

7. What is meant by a matrix organisation, and what problems might you foresee in its adoption by a multinational company? **(17)**

PART TWO

MARKETING IN SELECTED COUNTRIES

The principles of international marketing as set out in Part One are of world-wide application. From a marketing viewpoint, however, every country has its own special national characteristics, deriving usually from a political philosophy, varying distribution systems, or legal restrictions (often designed, especially in developing countries, to protect a country's economic independence or the interests of its nationals). Part Two examines these special characteristics in relation to a limited number of countries.

Each of these countries offers real profit opportunities to the international marketer, both now and in the foreseeable future: this has been the first criterion for their selection. Thereafter, however, the aim has been to illustrate the divergences between countries and to indicate how such divergences might affect marketing decision-making.

It is emphasised that no attempt has been made—or could be made, in a few short chapters—to provide a complete treatise on marketing in any of the countries selected. The intention has been more to highlight features of special interest in each country.

In some instances, it has been thought best to quote specific figures, e.g. percentage rates of duty. It should be noted, however, that such figures can be changed at short notice.

CHAPTER XX

Marketing in Brazil

1. Introduction. Brazil is the largest country in Latin America, about the size of the whole of Europe excluding Russia. The population is around 123 million, of which about half is under the age of eighteen.

After the remarkable growth of industry in recent years Brazil must be numbered among the industrialised nations, though the

2. Inflation. Like so many South American nations, Brazil has for many years suffered from an extremely high level of inflation, which has reached an annual rate of over 100 per cent on occasion.

However, Brazil is the country that has learned to live with inflation. Its system of monetary correction encourages investment despite inflation, while the crawling peg system, i.e. frequent small devaluations at irregular intervals, keeps Brazilian exports competitive.

3. Regional nature of the country. Inevitably in a country of this size, there are marked differences between one region and another. Economic activity and growth are heavily concentrated in the states of Rio de Janeiro, São Paulo and Minas Gerais; the north-east has been referred to, in contrast, as the "underdeveloped country within a country", while the centre-west and northern regions, vast as they are, account for only 10 per cent of the total population.

4. Import regulations.

(*a*) *Import certificates.* Imports are subject to the issue of an import certificate by the Bank of Brazil. Since the oil-price crisis, import certificates for virtually all consumer goods have been unobtainable.

(*b*) *Import duties.* In any case, import duties have for years been prohibitively high for consumer goods, sometimes in excess of 200 per cent on the c.i.f. value.

For machinery and equipment, import duties are lower, usually between 15 per cent and 55 per cent, and may be nil.

It is possible to obtain duty reductions on goods for which there is no "national similar". Before the oil-price crisis, such reductions were automatically granted but they are now limited to imports for approved projects.

(*c*) *Other taxes.* Several other taxes are levied on imported goods. Those of real significance are sales taxes, levied also on locally produced goods, but, since they are levied on the duty-paid value, they still represent a further discrimination against imported goods.

XX. MARKETING IN BRAZIL 171

(*d*) *Free zones.* A free-trade zone is established at the river port of Manaus.

5. Government purchasing. Brazilian Government departments, official bodies and nationalised industries may not purchase foreign goods at all, if "national similars" are available. Even when such similars are not available, imports are subject to strict controls.

6. Agents. Inflation and import restrictions have taken an increasing toll of commission agents, many of whom have gone out of business. It is therefore increasingly difficult to find a good agent.

Few agents can hope to cover the whole country, but concentration on Rio de Janeiro, São Paulo and Minas Gerais is clearly an acceptable approach for many U.K. companies.

Brazilian law protects the agent from unilateral termination of his contract by a foreign principal without just cause. Compensation for such termination may amount to 6 per cent of total sales effected during the life of the contract.

Brazil is one of the countries in which an agency agreement granting to the agent a general authority to conclude contracts may render the exporter liable to local income tax on the grounds that he has a "presence" in the country (*see* XVIII, **19**). The tax payable in such cases is 20 per cent of the total price of the products. It is normally desirable to state formally in the agreement that the agent has no power to bind the principal in sales contracts.

7. Licensing. Licensing agreements with foreign companies must be registered with the Brazilian Central Bank and with the National Institute for Industrial Property (INPI), the equivalent of the U.K. Patent Office. These bodies assess the value of the technology and set a limit on the percentage rate of remittance, each contract being separately considered. The assessment procedure is often slow, and the remittances are often limited to a short period, generally no more than five years, i.e. considerably less than the life of a patent. Permitted royalties range from 1 per cent to a maximum of 5 per cent of sales. The remittance of royalties to the U.K. is in any case subject to a Brazilian withholding tax.

Brazilian law lays down in some detail the terms of a licensing agreement, some of which may be regarded as onerous by the licensor. The agreement, for instance, may not prohibit the free and unrestricted use of the transferred know-how by the licensee, once the patent has expired; the licensor, in effect, must create his own competitor.

8. Manufacture in Brazil. It will now be clear that exporting offers only the most limited scope, except in the case of industrial products not already manufactured in Brazil (largely industrial plant and high-technology capital goods). Licensing offers more scope, but probably only for a limited period and at a limited rate of return.

For most companies, the Brazilian market, if it is to be considered at all, must be a market for local manufacture on either a joint-venture or an independent basis.

9. Establishing a company in Brazil. A manufacturing company may be the equivalent of a U.K. private limited company or a public company (S.A.). The normally preferred form for a foreign company is the S.A., particularly the S.A. established as an "open company", i.e. with shares widely held among third parties, which offers a number of tax advantages and access to the Brazilian stock market as a source of capital.

10. Joint ventures. There is no limit to the amount of capital a foreign company may invest in Brazil or in any one Brazilian company, except in certain sectors such as banking and communications media.

However, there are advantages in a joint venture, especially a Brazilian-controlled one, apart from the more usual ones of market knowledge and established distribution facilities:

(*a*) Brazilian-controlled companies are eligible for Federal investment incentives not open to foreign-controlled companies;

(*b*) government contracts may normally be awarded only to Brazilian firms; and

(*c*) a licensing agreement becomes more attractive when included in a joint venture.

11. Remittance of profits. Similarly, there is no bar to the remittance of profits. All remittances, however, incur withholding tax, which rises steeply when remittances exceed a certain percentage of capital.

The initial investment of foreign capital must be registered to permit remittance of dividends, and possible eventual repatriation of capital.

12. Investment incentives. Incentives for investment in manufacturing plant are available from a number of organisations at both federal and state levels. Concessions are not exclusive and may be secured from several sources for the same investment. Such incentives must be seriously and carefully considered by any company planning to establish a subsidiary or joint venture in Brazil.

(*a*) *Incentives available.* The various types of incentive cover:
  (*i*) new industrial projects of special significance, e.g. in high-technology industries;
  (*ii*) any manufacturing project to be established in the north-east or Amazonia, i.e. the less-developed regions;
  (*iii*) local developments in the various states;
  (*iv*) export subsidies.

(*b*) *Form of incentives.* The incentives may take the form of:
  (*i*) exemptions from import duty, e.g. on plant, machinery and components;
  (*ii*) exemption from sales taxes and corporation income tax;
  (*iii*) subsidised finance, as equity capital or loans;
  (*iv*) factory rental at subsidised rates.

13. Protection of industry. Brazilian industry is well protected by:

(*a*) import licensing and high customs tariffs (*see* **4**);
(*b*) a Customs Policy Council, which may increase tariffs by up to 30 per cent to protect a local industry threatened by imports;
(*c*) energetic measures to prevent dumping;
(*d*) government purchasing directives (*see* **5**).

14. Price control. Thus the overall picture is one of subsidised investment, subsidised exports and a protected home market in which it should be possible to make satisfactory profits. The Brazilian Government is determined, however, to ensure that excess profits are not made, and a comprehensive price control policy is in operation.

Companies seeking a price increase must seek prior permission from the Interministerial Price Commission (C.I.P.). C.I.P. covers most industrial goods, a large number of pharmaceutical products, and certain essential consumer goods. Companies failing to comply with C.I.P.'s rulings are subjected to sanctions of increasing severity.

15. Conclusion. Exporters to Brazil are now limited in number. More and more foreign enterprises are investing in Brazil, however, and are finding that, with a whole-hearted commitment to the country, those investments are paying off.

PROGRESS TEST 20

1. What is the nature of Brazil's import regulations? **(4)**
2. What special legislation in Brazil applies to commission agents? **(6)**
3. In what ways does the Brazilian Government exercise control over licensing agreements? **(7)**
4. What financial and other incentives are extended by the Brazilian Government to companies investing in manufacturing facilities? **(12)**

CHAPTER XXI

Marketing in Japan

1. Introduction. Japan now has one of the highest gross national products in the world and a per capita income well ahead of that of the U.K. Population is around 116 million.

U.K. exports to Japan have improved over the last few years, but Japan is still only the U.K.'s nineteenth largest export market.

2. Import regulations. Following liberalisation measures over recent years only a few goods remain on quota. Import duties have been unilaterally reduced, but are levied on almost all manufactured goods. Commodity taxes are also payable on some items, but these are applied also to locally produced products.

3. Market research. Japan has received more attention from export-promotion organisations than perhaps almost any other country. There is an immense amount of reliable information available on the market, most of it readily obtainable in the U.K. The B.O.T.B. has established a special Exports to Japan Unit, which has commissioned a number of market studies on product areas offering real potential to the U.K. exporter. The Japan External Trade Organisation, with an office in London, is a valuable source of published information on the Japanese economy and on specific market sectors.

Market research studies can be undertaken by a number of U.K. companies with a subsidiary in Japan and by the Tokyo-based U.K. export-import houses (*see* **8**). There is a wide choice of Japanese research agencies.

4. Department stores. The department store has been described as part of the Japanese way of life. Such stores are leisure, cultural and entertainment centres as well as a most important outlet for quality goods of all kinds. With supermarkets, they account for some 70 per cent of the sales of all *imported* consumer goods. The major stores maintain buying offices in London (*see* **VII, 13**).

5. Self-service stores. Self-service stores, especially the large supermarket groups, represent the most significant change in

Japanese retailing over the last ten years. Their total sales have now overtaken those of the department stores. Food and drink predominate, but most self-service stores sell a wide range of household goods and hardware as well, and some offer clothing and furniture.

Self-service stores offer an important outlet for imported food and drink, though imported goods so far represent only about 1 per cent of total sales.

6. The traditional wholesale–retail distribution system. The Japanese distribution system has simply not developed at the same pace as the rest of the economy. Its outstanding characteristics are still an excessive number of small retail outlets and several intermediate wholesale levels. A typical wholesale–retail pattern for volume products might be as shown in Fig. 12.

Rationalisation is gradually taking place as the Japanese consumer becomes more price-conscious. Voluntary chains are being organised, and the development of self-service stores (*see* **5**) is something of a breakthrough.

Nevertheless, the bulk of Japanese consumer goods passes through the traditional lengthy channels. Even department stores and self-service outlets are heavily dependent on wholesalers, and purchases direct from a manufacturer are still limited.

Exporters content to have their products regarded as low-volume speciality or prestige items need not concern themselves; they can achieve a satisfactory turnover through the department stores and, increasingly, through self-service. Yet it is through the traditional wholesale-retail set-up that the Japanese—almost by accident—retain their dominance over their domestic market: the transition from specialist supplier to high-volume sales is almost impossible of achievement within the system, yet it is difficult to by-pass that system, even with heavy investment in own-distribution arrangements. Some few companies have made that transition successfully.

> EXAMPLE: A few, a very few, succeed. Roger Allen of British B.S.R. is one. He set up the first foreign-owned subsidiary in Japan in 1972. In record changers and turntables, he says, "B.S.R. did a Japanese on the Japanese, collared the biggest volume, sells to them all, and they still cannot compete". . . . B.S.R. is now selling right into the retail outlets with the locals.

7. The trading companies. The trading companies are another

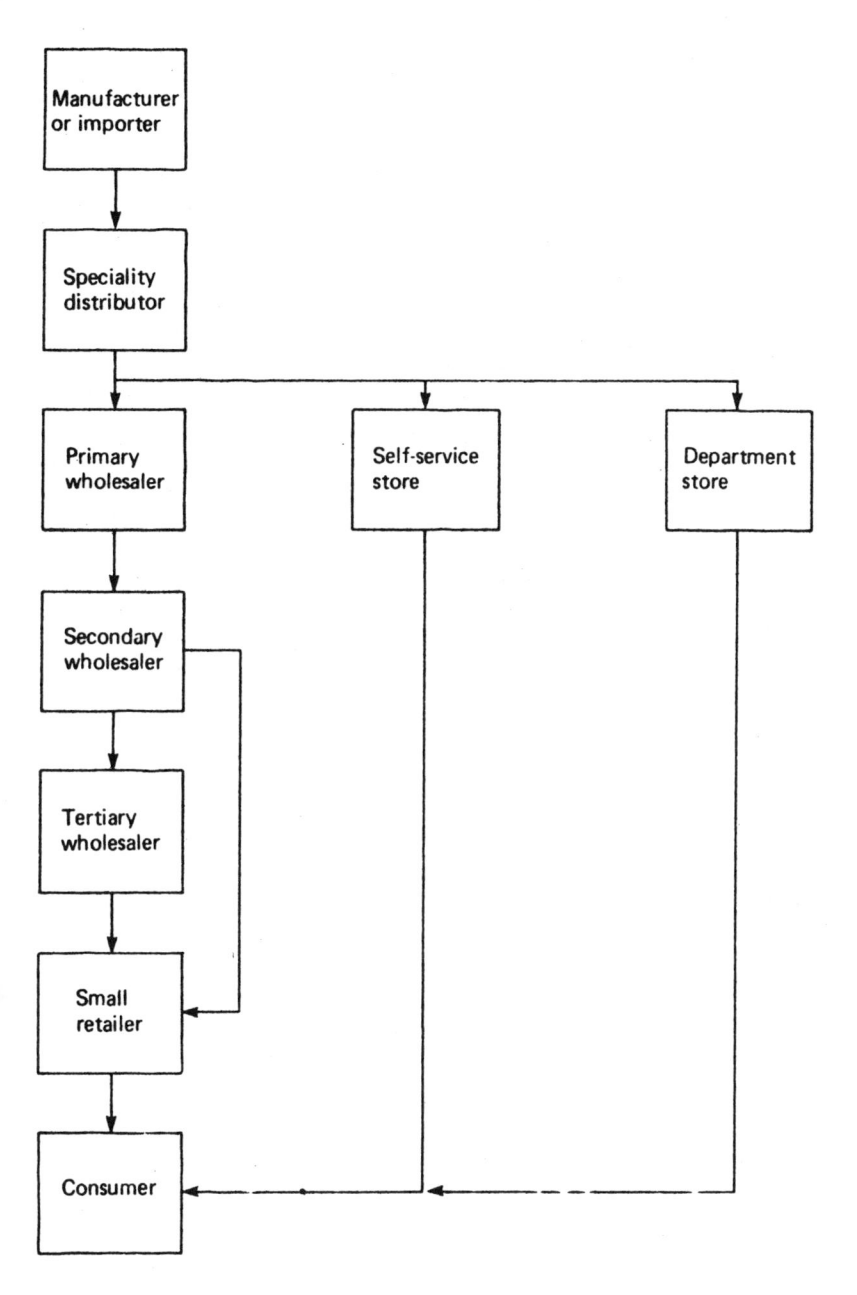

FIG. 12 *Typical wholesale–retail distribution system in Japan*

unique feature of the Japanese commercial scene. In other countries, a manufacturing company will undertake its own marketing, at least for most of its output. In Japan, the vast majority of manufacturing companies concern themselves solely with production. They have virtually no marketing or purchasing organisations, relying entirely on trading companies for these services.

As a result, the Japanese trading companies have developed an unrivalled expertise in all aspects of commerce: marketing, distribution, import and export, banking, insurance and all forms of transportation.

There are now between 5,000 and 6,000 trading companies in Japan, ranging from tiny importing companies specialising in narrow product areas to large and diversified organisations such as Mitsui, Mitsubishi, Sumitomo, C. Itoh, and Marubeni, who may handle as many as 10,000 different product lines, with representation in almost all the major cities of the world, and who are themselves heavily involved in manufacturing.

8. U.K. export–import houses in Japan. There are a number of British export–import houses based in Tokyo, who are in a position to offer agency representation services and who are also involved in other commercial and industrial activities.

9. Agents and distributors. In Japan, the choice of an agent/distributor will usually be between:

(*a*) one of the large general trading companies, most appropriate, perhaps, in high-turnover items;

(*b*) the specialised trading company, appropriate for sophisticated industrial products;

(*c*) the U.K. export–import house;

(*d*) a Japanese producer of complementary products (Japanese manufacturers are showing an increasing interest in taking advantage of their distribution networks in this way).

10. Branch and representative offices. A foreign company which intends to engage in commercial transactions within Japan on a continuous basis must appoint a representative and establish a branch office. Branches are not normally permitted to engage in manufacturing.

Branches are taxed on income from sources in Japan, but assessment is based on the capital of the foreign owning company. It is therefore advantageous to register a head-office company outside Japan with a purely nominal capital.

A representative office may be established as an alternative to a branch, provided the representative does not engage directly in trading activities, i.e. does not actually book orders. The registration procedure is similar, but corporation tax is not payable.

11. Licensing. Japanese industry has entered into a large number of licensing contracts with the full encouragement of the government.

Licensing agreements are subject to government approval, but in most cases such approval is granted automatically.

There are no restrictions on the down payment or the royalty payable, which has ranged from 2 per cent to 8 per cent or more, or on the duration of the licensing contract.

Similarly, there are no exchange control restrictions on the remittance of licensing payments to the licensor, though withholding tax is payable.

12. Local manufacture. Until fairly recently, the establishment of subsidiaries wholly-owned or controlled by foreign companies was not possible. Foreign investment is now almost completely liberalised, however, though the government retains certain controls designed to protect national security, industry, technology and the economy in general.

Nevertheless, because of the very different business environment in Japan (*see* **13**), many foreign companies still prefer the joint venture.

There are no difficulties in the way of remittance of profits abroad from either joint ventures or wholly-owned subsidiaries.

13. The Japanese business environment. It is generally acknowledged that the Japanese business environment presents, for the Western businessman, unusual difficulty. It is impossible to summarise these difficulties in a few short paragraphs, but some brief indications are given below.

(*a*) *Language*. The Japanese language is notorious for its complexities and vaguenesses. Interpretation and translation are vastly difficult and misunderstandings are more than usually probable. The written language suffers from unwieldy and complicated scripts.

(*b*) *Communication*. The Japanese rely heavily on face-to-face contact. Confirmatory letters are not the practice; the gentleman's agreement is. Personal relations are of the highest importance.

(c) *Connections.* Great importance is attached to connections with government, banks, and other companies in Japan.

(d) *Compromise.* The Japanese will seek to avoid disagreement and confrontation. Failure to compromise is seen as a weakness, and litigation is to be avoided. The take-over bid is rare in Japan, and the take-over of an unwilling company would be regarded as reprehensible. Even a change of agent is regarded with disfavour.

(e) *Consensus-style management.* Group decision-making is the norm. Decisions tend to originate at the lower levels, being subsequently co-ordinated and approved in discussion with more senior management; they are not imposed from above. Delays are thus inevitable.

(f) *Personnel policies.* The system of promotion by seniority still dominates the personnel administration of most Japanese companies. The Japanese manager anticipates a job for life, and his unswerving loyalty is expected in return. Japanese companies have been accused of off-loading incompetent executives on to a joint venture, so as to avoid their dismissal.

(g) *Business objectives.* The Japanese company is not regarded as placing the same priority on high profit levels as a Western company. Given its personnel policies, stability and sustained growth come first.

14. Conclusion. The unfamiliarity of the environment, the complex system of distribution, the all-pervading influence of the trading companies: these all combine to make Japan the most difficult of markets. But, above all, the international marketer in Japan is challenging on their own home ground the companies that have proved themselves the world's most efficient exporters. Only the similarly efficient can hope to do more than satisfy the demand for the specialist imported product with its snob appeal.

PROGRESS TEST 21

1. Describe the traditional Japanese wholesale–retail distribution system. **(6)**

2. What alternative agency arrangements are open to an exporter to Japan? **(9)**

3. What special Japanese regulations apply to branches of foreign companies? **(10)**

4. How does the Japanese business environment differ from that familiar to most Western businessmen? **(13)**

CHAPTER XXII

Marketing in Nigeria

1. Introduction. Nigeria is one of the world's major oil-exporting countries. Oil accounts for 93 per cent of its exports and 90 per cent of government revenue. Nevertheless, the pace of its economic development in recent years has outstripped its revenues and the country has had to apply for loans from international agencies to finance essential projects.

Despite this rapid economic growth, Nigeria must still be regarded as a developing country. Much of its expenditure is necessarily devoted to improving the infrastructure of the country, e.g. roads, telecommunications, etc., and to the education of its people.

In 1977, Nigeria was the U.K.'s tenth most important, but fastest-growing, export market.

2. Regional nature of the country. Nigeria is a country of strong local tribal affiliations and four major linguistic groups, i.e. Hausa, Yoruba, Ibo and Fulani.

Paradoxically, economic activity is becoming over-centralised in Lagos, and in 1976 the government emphasised the multi-state structure of the country, dividing it into 19 separate states. (The country was divided into 12 states in 1967, in place of the original four regions.)

3. Market research. Published statistics are limited in scope and may sometimes be of doubtful value (*see* III, 17). Population figures are available as an estimate only, at about 85 million, the results of the 1973 census having been rejected by the government as incorrect.

A number of government ministries and commercial associations can provide useful market information. Several of the advertising agencies in Lagos provide market research services.

4. Import regulations. Almost all imported goods are subject to duty. Nigeria is a member of the Commonwealth, but there is no preferential tariff rate for British goods.

Pursuing its aim of rapid industrialisation, Nigeria is encouraging the import of capital equipment at the expense of consumer goods. A number of consumer goods are now prohibited imports, e.g. many food items, some textiles, beer, wooden furniture, leather goods, etc., while other consumer goods have been placed on licence.

5. Government purchases (Federal Government). The Federal Government sometimes makes use of the purchasing facilities offered by the Crown Agents, but it has established its own purchasing agency in London, the Nigeria National Supply Co., which takes over purchasing for both the government and quasi-government bodies.

Federal Government departments are required by law to purchase goods made in Nigeria, provided such goods are competitive in price, quality and delivery.

6. Government purchases (State Governments). Each of the State Governments is responsible for its own purchasing. They occasionally use the facilities of the Crown Agents, but most are establishing their own purchasing organisations in the State capitals. State Governments offer a huge market, and tend on occasion to issue enquiries through individual local agents who, in effect, must seek appropriate suppliers as principals.

7. Commission agents. Good agents are naturally difficult to find, since they are constantly being approached by would-be principals from all over the world. Nevertheless, the appointment of an agent is usually highly desirable.

Few local agencies are in a position to offer effective coverage of the whole country and it is probably best to appoint a number of regional agents, especially in view of the increased emphasis on decentralisation (*see* **2, 6**).

Nigerian law makes no specific provision for agency agreements or their termination, and the law generally follows closely the English pattern (*see* XVIII, **14**). Nigerian general law, however, gives legal validity to written *or verbal* contracts, and it is therefore advisable to ensure that any agency agreement is put into writing.

8. Trading companies. Trading companies (*see* VII, **12**) are of particular importance in Nigeria. They handle much of the private commerce of the country, over a wide range of imported goods, and their distribution systems, wholesale and retail, cover the whole country.

The policy of the Nigerian Government, however, is to concentrate distribution in the hands of Nigerians and this has already had a considerable effect on the rôle of the trading companies.

9. Confirming and indent houses. Confirming and indent houses (*see* VII, **5** and **6**), again, have traditionally been active in Nigeria.

10. Branches. Branch operations of foreign companies are not normally permitted in Nigeria.

11. Marketing subsidiaries. Establishment of a marketing subsidiary would be subject to the Nigerian Immigration Act of 1963, which precludes foreigners from setting up a business without a permit from the Ministry of Internal Affairs.

12. Local manufacture.

(*a*) *Indigenisation programme.* Like distribution, industry is subject to the indigenisation programme. The Nigerian Enterprises Promotion Decree places industries in three categories, requiring respectively 100 per cent, 60 per cent and 40 per cent Nigerian ownership. The Decree applies to both new and existing industry and has become increasingly stringent over the years, with some industries progressing from the 40 per cent to the 60 per cent category, and others from 60 per cent to 100 per cent.

Effectively, therefore, the foreign company wishing to enter Nigeria is limited to the joint venture.

(*b*) *Investment incentives.* Providing it can ensure Nigerian participation or control, however, the Federal Government is anxious to attract both foreign industry and foreign capital. The Industrial Development (Income Tax) Decree provides for income tax exemptions for new companies engaged in "pioneer industries". Nigerian industry generally is protected by import prohibitions (*see* **4**), which apply particularly to goods produced locally.

Industrial estates, with appropriate infrastructure, e.g. roads, power, water, etc., have been established throughout Nigeria by both Federal and State Governments.

(*c*) *Foreign capital for a joint venture.* New joint ventures must import the necessary foreign exchange either in cash or, in approved cases, in the form of plant and machinery, not so much because of any shortage of local capital but more as a safeguard against ill-conceived or insufficiently considered ventures.

Once established, a joint venture may finance expansion by re-investment of profits or by raising money from local investors.

(*d*) *Procedure for establishing a joint venture.* A foreign company investing in Nigeria must apply for "approved status" for its investment. This gives the official recognition which will permit the possible eventual repatriation of the capital and, more important in the short term, will permit an expatriate quota, allowing foreign managers to work in the country.

(*e*) *Remittance of profits, etc.* "Approved status" certificates specify the profits, royalties, etc., that may be remitted abroad to the foreign partner. Dividends may not exceed 30 per cent of capital.

(*f*) *E.C.O.W.A.S.* Nigeria is a member of the Economic Community of West African States (E.C.O.W.A.S.), which aims at the eventual reduction or elimination of import duties between member states, but the maintenance of tariff barriers against other countries. E.C.O.W.A.S. is a recent development, and effective implementation is years away, but it may be a factor influencing long-term investment plans in relation to Nigeria.

13. Conclusion. The days of large-scale consumer-goods exports to Nigeria are over, probably for good. Joint ventures are the most secure form of long-term involvement in the market and, despite operational difficulties, offer real prospects of success. However, it must be remembered that in Nigeria major changes in both trading and investment conditions can be made by decree, at very short notice.

PROGRESS TEST 22

1. Outline Nigerian national and local government purchasing arrangements. **(5, 6)**
2. What special factors might be considered when appointing a commission agent in Nigeria? **(7)**
3. Outline the Nigerian programme of indigenisation. **(12)**
4. What inducements does the Nigerian Government offer to foreign investors? **(12)**

CHAPTER XXIII

Marketing in the U.S.A.

1. Introduction. The U.K. is the U.S.A.'s fourth largest supplier and third largest customer.

A similar position obtains in relation to international investment. In 1974, American companies invested $12.5 billion in the U.K., while British investment in the U.S.A. amounted to $6 billion (equivalent to 28 per cent of all foreign investment from the U.K.).

2. Size and regional nature of the U.S.A. From a marketing viewpoint a striking feature of the U.S.A. is its sheer size. For some products, e.g. many industrial goods, the market can be regarded as a homogeneous whole, but for others, such as clothing, there will be a distinct regional pattern.

In the U.S.A. the principle of concentration (*see* II, **9**) implies concentration on a particular region rather than on the country as a whole. Very often a regional success can add up to a higher total profit than that available from any one European country.

3. Market research. The U.S.A. is not a market to approach without the most careful preparation and planning. Fortunately, there is a wealth of reliable market data available, much of it free of charge. Whilst the U.K. marketer's first port of call must be the B.O.T.B., he will also take advantage of the services of the U.S. Department of Commerce. The Department has offices in all the major U.S. cities and its information is available to U.K. researchers, not merely to U.S. citizens.

4. Import regulations. There are no foreign exchange restrictions on payments for imports. Further, there is no general licensing of imports and almost all U.K. goods may enter freely.

Special technical regulations, concerning quality, safety, etc., apply to certain goods such as motor vehicles and electrical equipment. The food and drug legislation is widely regarded as a formidable non-tariff barrier (*see* III, 7). It has been estimated, for instance, that pharmaceutical manufacturers may expect to pay around $1 million to steer a new product through the Federal Drug Administration scrutiny.

Classification of goods for duty purposes is complicated in that the U.S.A. has not adopted the Customs Co-operation Council Nomenclature (the Brussels Nomenclature). The valuation rules are in any case complex and the exporter may be well advised to seek a formal ruling from the U.S. Customs Service.

5. Direct selling. American department stores are among those maintaining buying offices or appointing buying agents in London (*see* VII, **13**). Other stores send buyers regularly to London on purchasing missions.

Many industrial products may also, of course, be sold direct, but the U.S.A. is a market where customers demand at the least regular personal contact. If this is impracticable it may prove more satisfactory to employ an agent (*see* **8**).

6. Federal Government purchases. The U.S. Government is itself a major purchaser of goods of all kinds, though the emphasis is on military procurement. Most non-military purchasing is centralised within the General Services Administration.

Non-military purchases are subject to "Buy American" legislation. The Buy American Act of 1933 requires in principle that all Federal organisations should purchase only goods produced within the U.S.A. unless U.S. goods are not available or are "unreasonably" priced. An unreasonable price is generally taken as one which is more than 6 per cent above the foreign price *including duty* (or 12 per cent if the U.S. bidder is in an employment area or is classed as a small business). For certain special products higher percentages may apply before a price becomes unreasonable.

7. State, etc., purchases. Each state, county and municipality has its own independent purchasing organisation, all of which provide a huge and easily identifiable market for a wide range of goods, especially capital goods.

The Buy American legislation applies only to Federal Government purchases, but many states have adopted similar regulations of varying severity. These affect state, county and municipal bodies.

8. Agents and distributors. The size of the market means that very few U.S. agencies or distributors can offer genuine national coverage. Nevertheless, this will not always deter them from seeking nation-wide representation. The granting of an agency on a national basis to a purely regional distributor is the most elementary error that a U.K. exporter can commit, yet such errors are still being made.

Agreements granting an agent an exclusive territory, or confining his sales to the principal's products, may contravene the Federal and State laws prohibiting restraint of trade. Legal advice should always be sought in such circumstances.

U.S. businessmen in general are not noted for their unwillingness to engage in litigation. In the U.S.A., perhaps more than anywhere else, a carefully drawn-up agency agreement (*see* XVIII, **14**), prepared with the benefit of local legal advice, is essential. The agreement should be valid for the shortest acceptable period (perhaps for no more than a year) and should make clear provision for termination. U.S. law (except in Puerto Rico) does not provide any special protection for agents, and the parties are free to agree between themselves on termination arrangements.

9. Branches and sales subsidiaries. Increasingly, U.K. companies have tended to set up branches or sales subsidiaries to undertake local marketing and to maintain stocks in the market place, thus providing a delivery service competitive with that of local manufacturers.

It may prove advantageous to stock goods in the foreign-trade zones (*see* X, **11**) established across the U.S.A. Goods in these zones are not subject to import duty until withdrawn from the zone into the U.S. customs jurisdiction. Assembly is permitted within the zones.

10. Manufacturing subsidiaries. The declared policy of the U.S. Government is "to admit and treat foreign capital on a basis of equality with domestic capital".

In accordance with this policy there are no U.S. exchange controls on inward direct investment, and it is not necessary to register such investment with the U.S. Government for exchange control purposes. Similarly, there are no restrictions on the remittance of dividends from a U.S. subsidiary to its U.K. parent.

Staffing the subsidiary with U.K. management may present difficulties, however, as U.S. immigration laws are stringent.

11. Investment incentives. A factor of particular importance to the intending investor is the financial and other assistance provided to investors in industrial plant, including foreign investors. Investment incentives are organised on State basis, not a Federal basis. All fifty states are interested in promoting foreign manufacturing investment within their borders, and may offer not merely advice but financial assistance, tax allowances, and the provision of land, buildings and equipment at favourable rates.

12. Company taxation. Business corporations are formed under State, not Federal, laws. Company law and taxation regulations vary from one state to another. It is possible to gain certain tax advantages by the careful selection of the state of incorporation.

13. Conclusion. The U.S.A. must be regarded as one of the world's most open markets. It offers few of the restrictions found in so many other markets overseas, while the potential is enormous.

Yet is is not an easy market, and certainly not one for the dilettante or the amateur. Americans are demanding customers, taking first-rate quality and service for granted, while competition, both U.S. and foreign, is intense.

PROGRESS TEST 23

1. Outline briefly any problems that might arise for a U.K. exporter from U.S. import regulations. **(4)**
2. What is the effect of the Buy American Act? **(6)**
3. What special circumstances would you bear in mind when appointing an agent in the U.S.A.? **(8)**
4. What investment incentives are available to the foreign investor in the U.S.A.? **(11)**

CHAPTER XXIV

Marketing in the U.S.S.R.

1. Introduction. The U.S.S.R. is, in area, the largest country in the world. It consists of fifteen republics with a total population of around 262 million. Within these republics 104 different nationalities, each with its own language, are officially recognised, though about half of the population is Russian.

State ownership and centralised planning are the most obvious characteristics of the economy.

2. Comecon. The U.S.S.R. is the dominant member of the Council for Mutual Economic Assistance (Comecon), to which Bulgaria, Cuba, Czechoslovakia, the German Democratic Republic (East Germany), Hungary, Mongolia, Poland, Rumania and Vietnam also belong.

The other Comecon countries have adopted a similar economic system to that of the U.S.S.R., similarly organised in relation to international trade, though usually with much greater concession to market forces and to Western marketing methods.

3. Soviet foreign trade. The U.S.S.R. aims at self-sufficiency within Comecon and will place orders with the West only when its requirements cannot be met from domestic sources, from other Comecon countries, or for soft currency elsewhere. Only the U.S.S.R.'s purchases from Western industrialised countries, therefore, are relevant as an indication of the market open to the U.K. exporter. Even so, those purchases amounted to 12.4 billion roubles (approximately £10 billion) in 1974. U.K. exports to the U.S.S.R. in 1979 amounted to some £419 million pounds.

The U.S.S.R. suffers from a serious and continuing shortage of hard currency. Such hard currency as is available is allocated strictly according to national priorities, and most imports from the West consist of essential raw materials and commodities and high-technology capital goods, or, occasionally, complete production lines or factories. The U.S.S.R. offers no significant market for consumer goods, except for knitwear and footwear, where purchases are in any case declining. The usual motivation for the purchase of consumer goods is that local supply is inadequate in the short term.

4. Foreign trade corporations. Foreign trade (import and export) is a state monopoly conducted only through a number of foreign trade corporations, each of which specialises in a given range of products or commodities. These corporations act as principals in the foreign-trade contract, though they never buy on their own account. The contract between the corporation and the foreign supplier is matched by a parallel contract between the corporation and the eventual user of the goods.

5. Foreign trade corporation contracts. Negotiations with a foreign trade corporation are usually protracted. Because of the constant shortage of foreign currency, extended credit terms or compensation deals (*see* XIII, **15**) will often be sought.

Contracts, when eventually obtained, will be detailed in the extreme and will usually stipulate heavy penalties for late delivery or product failures. Contract terms are strictly enforced.

6. Import regulations. The U.K. exporter need not normally concern himself with import regulations. Foreign trade is conducted in the appropriate foreign currency (the rouble is not convertible) on an f.o.b. basis, and import licences are obtained by the foreign trade corporation.

Commercial samples and goods intended for display at exhibitions may be temporarily imported free of duty.

7. Market research. Market research as practised in market-economy countries is simply not possible in the U.S.S.R. A plethora of generalised information is available, but specific product information is hard to come by. Even when such information can be obtained, and a need for the product is perceived, it cannot, of course, be assumed that hard currency will be made available for purchases from the West.

(*a*) *Desk research.* A general reference source is the *Statistical Yearbook of the Member States of Comecon*, available in English. The *Press Bulletin* of the Moscow Narodny Bank collates all Eastern European economic and trade news on a regular basis. Summaries of the U.S.S.R.'s five-year plan are available.

Several sources may be approached in the U.K. These include the British Overseas Trade Board, the East European Trade Council, the British-Soviet Chamber of Commerce, and the Lon-

XXIV. MARKETING IN THE U.S.S.R.

don Chamber of Commerce and Industry. Companies already trading with the U.S.S.R. can give practical help.

(b) *Original research.* Consumer research is, of course, pointless; industrial research interviews cannot be undertaken in the normal manner—Soviet organisations will normally not reveal any statistical, economic or technical information that is not already available in published form. Research, in fact, tends to be a piecemeal process, often combined with selling efforts. Participation in a trade mission, for instance, can yield valuable information, while exhibitions (*see* **10**) permit face-to-face discussion with the eventual user of the equipment (a rare, if not unheard-of, privilege at any other time).

8. Representation. Agency representation as understood in the West is not possible in the U.S.S.R. Such agency concerns as do exist are foreign-owned.

(a) *U.K. export houses.* Many U.K. export houses can offer special expertise in East–West trade (*see* VII, **3**) and are especially useful for compensation deals.

(b) *Merchant houses in Moscow.* A very limited number of foreign merchant houses have been permitted to establish themselves in Moscow.

(c) *Marketing office.* Western companies may apply to the Ministry of Foreign Trade for permission to open an office in Moscow. This is a privilege rarely granted, except to companies providing essential and continuing services to international commerce, e.g. airlines, etc., or to companies already supplying the Soviet Union on a regular and substantial basis.

Most companies, however, are likely to rely on direct selling from a U.K. base.

9. Licensing. Neither joint ventures with foreign companies, nor, of course, foreign manufacturing subsidiaries, are permitted in the U.S.S.R. Industrial co-operation agreements are possible (*see* IX, **12**), but licensing arrangements play the most important role. The U.S.S.R. subscribes to the International Convention for the Protection of Industrial Property, and the protection available is very similar to that already familiar to the Western businessman (*see* IX, **2–8**).

Licensing agreements are the responsibility of a specialist foreign trade corporation, Litsenzintorg, which is interested in both the sale and purchase of know-how. Purchase of Soviet know-how is acceptable as part of the terms of a compensation deal covering U.K. exports.

10. Exhibitions. Exhibitions in the U.S.S.R. are of two types:

(a) *international exhibitions*, which relate to a particular industry, are on a large scale, and are open to the public;

(b) *specialised exhibitions*, covering a very restricted field of interest and open theoretically only to specially invited firms, though in practice a company whose products are in a relevant product area will have no difficulty in securing an invitation to exhibit.

Independent exhibitions may be staged by individual companies or trade associations, e.g. in hotels.

In all cases, success requires just the same careful preparation, organisation and follow-up as for any other exhibition (*see* XVI, **6–16**).

11. Importance of exhibitions. Exhibitions are more than usually important in the U.S.S.R., since:

(a) few other forms of promotion are available to the foreign firm, apart from limited advertising (*see* **12**);

(b) the international exhibition programme is co-ordinated with the Foreign Trade Plan, and it may therefore be assumed that the U.S.S.R. intends to import the relevant products from the West in the reasonably near future;

(c) exhibitions offer almost the only chance of influencing the end-users of the product;

(d) as mentioned (*see* **7**), useful market information may be obtained in discussion with such end-users.

12. Advertising. Consumer advertising, like consumer research, is not possible and would in any case be pointless. The advertising of industrial goods may, however, be of value in bringing a company's name and technology to the attention of end-users.

(a) *Agency.* In the U.S.S.R. advertising is the monopoly of the state advertising agency, Vneshtorgreklama. Media cannot be approached direct.

(b) *Target audience.* The target audience will be not only the end-user, i.e. the general manager or technical specialist, but also the officials of the foreign trade corporations and the economists and planners in the various ministries.

(c) *Media.* Media selection is usually simple: there is one offi-

XXIV. MARKETING IN THE U.S.S.R.

cial technical journal for each branch of industry and coverage of the relevant industry specialists is believed to be in all cases close to 100 per cent.

A British magazine, *British Industry and Engineering*, is published in Russian and distributed to factories and research institutes in the U.S.S.R.

(*d*) *Theme.* Advertisements should be technical and informative in style, and should relate to products which are technologically advanced or unfamiliar in the Soviet Union. It is probably difficult to give too much technical detail.

Advertisements may also draw attention to a company's participation at a forthcoming exhibition.

(*e*) *Assessment of results.* Assessment of results is more than usually difficult. However, it can be said that there is less competition from other journals, or from other advertisements in the selected journal, than would normally be the case in the West. On the other hand, without the benefit of research, it is difficult to angle the advertisement to the particular competitive factors of interest to the target audience.

13. Direct mail. A very limited amount of direct mail has been permitted.

14. Conclusion. The U.S.S.R. is not everyone's market. Success is likely to go to the company already successful, if not dominant, in its own, often highly technical, field, and large enough to have the financial and other resources to sustain a long and expensive sales campaign in the face of every kind of difficulty, with no guarantee, or even reasonable indication, of a favourable outcome.

But, for the chosen, the rewards can be high: large-scale contracts, no fear of bankruptcies, conservative buyers who are reluctant to change from a proved and reliable supplier, and prompt payment.

PROGRESS TEST 24

1. Which countries are members of Comecon? **(2)**
2. What is a foreign trade corporation? **(4)**
3. What methods of representation are open to a U.K. exporter to the U.S.S.R.? **(8)**
4. Why are exhibitions of special importance to the exporter to the U.S.S.R.? **(11)**
5. What special factors must be borne in mind in relation to advertising in the U.S.S.R.? **(12)**

CHAPTER XXV

Marketing in the Federal Republic of Germany

1. Introduction. The Federal Republic of Germany (West Germany) is Britain's largest export market, and, as a member of the European Community, it offers no real barriers to trade with the U.K.; yet it is widely and officially believed that it has not been fully exploited by U.K. companies, especially in the south of the country.

2. Regional nature of the country. West Germany has a federalist political structure. For historical reasons the various regions of the country are much more distinctive in character than the regions of England, or even of the U.K.

These regional variations must be constantly borne in mind. They may require, for instance, modifications of the product to suit differing regional tastes. Market coverage, e.g. by agency firms, is rarely national, so that several agents may need to be appointed (*see* **6**), or, alternatively, concentration on a particular region is facilitated.

3. Import regulations. Goods imported from the U.K. are subject to an import turnover tax, but this is merely the equivalent of the value-added tax levied on locally-produced goods. Free port facilities (*see* **X, 11**) are available in Hamburg, Bremen and Bremerhaven, and tax is charged only when goods leave the free zone.

4. D.I.N. standards. West German standards and specifications (D.I.N.) apply also to imported goods. They are usually more detailed and sometimes more stringent than the equivalent British standards and are of wider application, covering a broad range of consumer, as well as industrial, goods. There is, however, no reason to believe that most British goods cannot measure up to these standards.

XXV. MARKETING IN THE FEDERAL REPUBLIC OF GERMANY   195

5. Direct selling. Perhaps because of the problems resulting from the regional nature of the country, central and co-operative purchasing in retail distribution is more highly developed than almost anywhere else in the world. Direct selling to store groups, therefore, is an economic proposition, since central buying points are easily identifiable and are capable of placing high-value orders. On the other hand, competition at these central buying points is intense—buyers are inundated with offers from all over the world and it is not easy for a newcomer to break in.

(*a*) *Co-operatives and voluntary chains.* Central purchasing through co-operatives and voluntary chains covers, in West Germany, not merely foodstuffs but hardware, household articles, footwear, textiles and many other goods. Edeka is the largest voluntary foodstuffs co-operative in Europe, buying for around 30,000 retailers.

(*b*) *Hypermarkets.* Hypermarkets have shown a mushroom-like growth in recent years, covering a whole range of goods at competitive prices. They have a share in excess of 10 per cent of the total retail market.

(*c*) *Department stores.* The importance of department stores in West Germany has already been mentioned (*see* VII, **13**).

(*d*) *Mail order.* Mail order accounts for some 5 per cent of the total West German retail market, which is a higher proportion even than in the U.K., and very much higher than in most other countries. Although of the 3,000 or so mail order businesses in West Germany many are small or specialist houses, there are a number of outlets of the utmost significance. Quelle, for instance, in addition to a mail-order turnover of many millions of pounds, covering some 100 countries, controls a number of department stores and is heavily involved in manufacturing.

6. Agencies. A striking feature of domestic business in West Germany is the importance of agents. It has been estimated that 60 per cent of the trade in manufactured goods is effected with the aid of commission agents.

(*a*) *Types of agent.* In West Germany it is usual to distinguish:
   (*i*) commission agents;
   (*ii*) agents who buy on their own account; and
   (*iii*) import agents. The two latter might be more properly described as distributors.

The commission agent is by far the most prevalent, and almost universal in some trades. Agents are usually small firms rather than individuals.

(*b*) *Agency selection.* The regional nature of the country (*see* **2**) will often require the appointment of several agents, perhaps covering only one state or even part of a state.

Because of the problems arising from this situation some agents, especially in the foodstuffs and textiles fields, have established "associations of mutual interest", essentially co-operations of independent agents offering between them national coverage but only one central contact point.

Agents are plentiful, but the good agent is perhaps even more difficult to find than usual. Some companies have given up the quest and have appointed their own local salesmen.

(*c*) *Agency legislation.* West German agency law inclines much more in favour of the agent than British law. Compensation in the event of termination may be substantial, perhaps as much as a year's average commission.

English law will apply if the agreement so stipulates; otherwise German law becomes the law of the contract. In practice, few worthwhile agents are likely to agree to the application of English law.

(*d*) *E.E.C. rules of competition.* Agreements with agents in the strict sense of the word (*see* VIII, **6**) are regarded as outside the scope of Articles 85 and 86 of the Treaty of Rome (*see* XIV, **5**). Exclusive dealing agreements, however, between a supplier and an independent trader *who takes possession of the goods* do come within the scope of Articles 85 and 86. A "block exemption" has been granted for categories of agreement not considered detrimental to the aims of the Community, but in such cases it is desirable to seek legal advice.

7. Branches. West German law makes specific provision for the establishment of a branch, subject to the issue of a licence from the Ministry of Economics (usually a formality).

Registration requirements, however, constitute a lengthy and often expensive legal proceeding, and may take as long as a year.

Further, a branch is taxed on that part of the owning company's profits deemed to have been earned in West Germany through the operation of the branch. Usually this arrangement leads to a less favourable tax situation than might apply to a subsidiary company.

Most foreign firms, therefore, avoid branch operations.

8. Subsidiary companies. Various alternative forms of company organisation are possible but, for a foreign company, the choice lies in practice between a public limited company, A.G., and a private limited company, GmbH.

The A.G. is usually appropriate only to the largest firms. Most U.K. companies have established a GmbH, which is the most convenient form for a small or medium-sized concern and can be simply, quickly and cheaply established.

West German company laws are more liberal than those of many other countries, even for companies outside the E.E.C. For example, there are no restrictions on the extent of the equity held by the foreign parent company, though this may affect tax liability, and directors need not be of German nationality or resident in the country.

9. Investment incentives. Investment incentives are not organised on any central basis. The individual territorial authorities, the Bund (Federation), Länder (Federal States) and the Gemeinden (local authorities), can to a large extent make their own decision as to the use of funds allocated to them. The intending foreign investor will find this situation at first confusing when he is deciding exactly where to locate his plant, but it does give him the opportunity of benefiting from several incentives at one and the same plant.

Investment incentives must clearly be a matter for detailed investigation in every specific case. As a general rule, however, incentives are aimed, as in other countries, at improving the regional economic balance. They therefore favour the "zonal border areas" along the East German frontier and special development areas such as the Saar coal-mining district. It should not be assumed, however, that the richer states will not offer investment incentives. For instance, North-Rhine Westphalia, perhaps the most prosperous of all the West German states, has established an active development agency.

State investment aid is also awarded, regardless of location, for the development of small and medium-size enterprises, but the funds granted are usually too small to interest the foreign investor.

10. Trade fairs. West Germany is one of those countries where exhibitions and trade fairs play a specially important role (*see* XVI, **6**). In many fields, such as textiles, machinery, toys, printing, furniture and food, the world's most important fairs are held in

West Germany. Such fairs are genuinely international, attracting both buyers and exhibitors from all over the world.

It is widely believed that any company that wishes to be taken seriously by a German buyer must exhibit at the appropriate trade fairs.

11. Conclusion. West Germany, like the U.S.A., is one of the world's least restrictive markets, especially to a member country of the European Community. Nevertheless, it is a market for the professional marketer, for the long-term and carefully planned approach. Any other attitude is likely to lead to failure or, at best, to a very short-term success.

PROGRESS TEST 25

1. What factors facilitate direct selling to retail outlets in West Germany? **(5)**

2. What special factors would you consider when contemplating the appointment of a West German agent? **(6)**

3. What alternative forms of subsidiary company might an exporter decide to establish in West Germany? **(8)**

4. What investment incentives are open to the intending investor in manufacturing facilities in West Germany? **(9)**

PART THREE

CASE STUDIES

CHAPTER XXVI

Editôra de Guias (LTB) S.A.: A Brazilian Sales Force

1. Introductory note. This case study gives a brief description of the São Paulo sales force of one of Brazil's most successful companies. The reader may like to compare management's approach with that of any other sales force with which he is familiar.

2. The company. Editôra de Guias are publishers specialising, since 1947, in information transfer, including the publication of directories and information guides. They have a sales operations headquarters in São Paulo, a sales office and printing works in Rio de Janeiro, and branch offices in a number of Brazilian cities.

In 1973 Editôra de Guias were printers and publishers, under contract to the local telephone authorities, of a number of classified telephone directories (the yellow pages) in several Brazilian cities, including São Paulo.

In São Paulo a specialised sales force and a telephone selling organisation concentrated for much of the year on the sales of advertisement space in the yellow pages. It is this sales force that is the subject of this case study.

3. The market. Although advertisements were received from elsewhere in Brazil, the market open to the São Paulo sales force consisted essentially of every commercial or industrial organisation within the São Paulo telephone area—a vast market, despite its relatively small size in geographical terms.

Within this market every business telephone subscriber was entitled to *one* free (one-line) entry under *one* classification. The aim of the sales force was to persuade the subscriber to take additional space in the form of heavy-type entries or display advertisements, or to pay for additional entries under other classifications.

A new issue of the directory was produced every year. Thus, in the case of a renewal of a previous advertisement, at least one sales call per advertiser per annum was required, though renewals often involved call-backs. The aim of the call, of course, was not mere renewal but an increase in total expenditure over the preceding year's entries.

The company's policy was to aim at the complete exploitation of the market through a thoroughly professional and highly motivated personal sales force. Telephone selling concentrated largely on low-potential customers where a personal call was unlikely to prove economic. As a result the total sales force, including field sales supervisors, was over 500 strong.

4. Territory organisation. As a matter of deliberate policy the company rejected the conventional geographical territorial organisation in favour of a customer-allocation system. The main sales force was divided into different teams, according to the level of customer to which they sold, the level of customer being determined by the revenue obtained from the customer in the preceding year.

Within each team the customers were allocated to the salesmen for only brief periods ahead by the team's field-sales supervisor. The supervisor was expected to allocate the more promising accounts to those salesmen who had recently achieved the most successful results, and had the highest productivity in terms of contracts resolved per day (with, therefore, the lowest number of customer accounts outstanding from previous allocations).

In this way the company was able to ensure that the most successful and hard-working salesmen were brought face-to-face with the most promising customers. Nothing would succeed like success.

Again as a matter of policy, the company made it a rule, whenever possible, to avoid assigning an account to a salesman who had handled it in previous years. When sales are made on an annual basis there is perhaps little prospect of establishing a regular and continuing relationship between customer and salesman, but the company deliberately chose to convert every sale into what was, in effect, a speciality sale. (Speciality selling is the approach necessarily adopted with durable products sold to small customers—for instance, with weighing machines sold to small retailers. The speciality salesman must locate his customer, secure an interview, sell himself, his company and his product with as few interviews as possible, preferably only one, and move on to the next prospect to begin the process all over again. He has none of the advantages that result from a continuing and friendly relationship with his customers.)

The company's reasons for this policy were that:

(*a*) in its experience too friendly a relationship led the Brazilian customer to adopt a bargaining posture that might undermine the whole pricing policy;
(*b*) it wished to avoid salesman self-sufficiency, since it felt salesmen had a tendency to believe they were irreplaceable once they had developed strong personal connections with a customer;
(*c*) it felt that salesmen who had made a sale one year believed that that sale could not be improved upon, and aimed, therefore, at mere renewal rather than at an increase, whereas the new salesman regarded his colleague's previous performance in the nature of a challenge;
(*d*) it wished to open up an opportunity for the next salesman to whom the account was assigned to exercise his creativity on behalf of the customer, thus constantly increasing the benefit of the sales calls to the customer.

5. Sales research and planning. The company's aim was to maximise face-to-face selling time with the customer. With this in mind, prior research, e.g. into customer activities, past purchase record and potential, was undertaken by a separate research department, which undertook not merely economic and bibliographical research, but also field research through its own fieldwork team. At the time of customer allocation the salesman received a duplicate of the complete file on each individual customer, fully up to date.

6. Field sales supervision. Supervision was close. A field supervisor was responsible for no more than five or six salesmen, with whom he spent at least four days a week in the field.

In addition, individual discussions were held with each salesman every day, morning and evening. This was a practical proposition, in view of the relatively small geographical area to be covered, especially as salesmen had in any case to bring in advertisement copy to the office in the evenings.

At the morning meeting, customer files were examined and the sales approach planned. In the evening, supervisor and salesman discussed the day's successes and failures, and decided whether or not further calls might prove worthwhile on customers apparently unwilling to place an order.

Under no circumstances were these supervisory meetings allowed to encroach on selling time, which in São Paulo, noted for its devotion to hard work and long hours, might, with the judicious use of early and late appointments, be extended from 9 a.m. until 8 p.m. or even later, when some managers are still at work. As a consequence, salesmen might be seen at Editôra de Guias offices as early as 7.30 a.m. and at late as 10 p.m.

7. Sales training. All salesmen attended an initial three-week induction course. Further follow-up courses were organised, often on Saturday mornings, but in-service training relied heavily on field training by supervisors.

Hitherto, training had concentrated very largely on product knowledge and the techniques of salesmanship. These topics were covered thoroughly and in detail with the aid of impressive sales manuals. The result was a thoroughly professional sales approach in terms of sales techniques, enthusiasm, persistence, and force of character. Discussion at the sales interview, however, usually tended to cover:

(*a*) the advertisements placed by the prospect's competitors;
(*b*) suggestions for the inclusion of the advertiser's entry in additional classifications;
(*c*) the submission of specimen display advertisements or layouts.

Although this approach had always proved outstandingly successful in the past, the company was not satisfied. It now regarded itself as being not in the business of selling advertising space but rather in the business of providing its customers with a vehicle through which they might more effectively reach their target markets. Salesmen in future were to consider their customer's marketing needs and to adapt their offers to those needs.

This market-oriented approach, of course, would involve a radical re-appraisal of training needs. More important, it had wide-ranging implications in terms of sales force organisation and calibre of salesman recruited.

8. Recruitment. As is often the case with speciality selling, labour turnover among salesmen was high, especially within the first few months after recruitment, when many men simply failed to achieve the required results, and after two or three years, when, perhaps, the strain of the unremitting effort so essential to the job was beginning to tell.

In consequence, a good deal of attention was paid to recruitment procedures, and some experimental work on personality tests was being undertaken by company psychologists with the aim of producing the ideal Editôra de Guias salesman profile.

9. Remuneration. Payment of salesman was by commission only, though advances were made against commission earnings. Final commissions were paid only at the end of the campaign year.

Commission payments were based on the increase in revenue obtained from the salesman's accounts over and above the revenue from those same accounts in the preceding year.

For the successful salesman, rewards were high—as much as £20,000 per annum (in 1973).

Prizes awarded on the results of special competitions were also of real significance. The most successful salesman of the year won a holiday for two in Europe or the U.S.A. Cash prizes were on offer at least weekly, and were formally presented to the winners before the day's work, amid the applause of their colleagues. Gifts in kind, e.g. consumer durables, etc., of some value, were often presented at the Friday evening meeting.

10. Motivation. The utmost importance was attached, however, to the non-financial aspects of motivation. The general ethos was openly competitive, and the performance of all salesmen was displayed prominently on a wall in the salesmen's room. Performance figures were brought up to date *daily*. Photographs of the most successful salesmen in each category were pinned on the wall; these photographs increased in size throughout the campaign, in line with total sales revenue, and by the end of the campaign reached life size.

Every Friday evening saw a meeting of managers, supervisors, trainers and salesmen which invariably ended, after the presentation of prizes, as late-night concerts. The salesmen themselves provided the musicians for the samba band, and on occasion provided both words and music for appropriate and topical company songs. Immense enthusiasm was generated, and the Friday meetings provided relief and relaxation after the week's sustained and intensive effort.

11. Conclusion. The overall picture is one of a highly motivated, highly rewarded and intensely hard-working sales force, under close and effective management control, concentrated entirely on its face-to-face selling task, to the exclusion of all ancillary activity.

Perhaps hardly surprisingly, the company was among the most successful in Brazil.

CASE STUDY QUESTIONS

1. Editôra de Guias no longer regarded itself as being in the business of selling advertisement space; it saw itself as providing a vehicle through which its customers could most effectively reach their markets. This would involve far-reaching changes in:

   (a) the present organisation of the sales force;
   (b) the calibre of salesmen recruited;
   (c) the whole basis of salesman training.

Specifically, what changes?

2. In general, the São Paulo sales force sold only one product (directory) at a time, for much of the year this being the classified telephone directory. This single-mindedness of purpose had paid off in the past in terms of sales and profits. Under the new market-oriented approach outlined in Question 1, by which the space salesman would become, to some extent, a marketing adviser, would this approach to the product range still be possible? What might be the ideal product range carried by the salesman?

3. The conventional geographical territory organisation had been rejected by the company in favour of the customer-allocation system. How far would you agree with the company's reasons for adopting this system? What advantages resulted from the system? And what disadvantages?

4. How far would you consider it desirable to establish a separate sales research and planning function to support a field sales force? Why was it desirable in the case of Editôra de Guias?

5. Labour turnover among salesmen was a matter of concern for the company. The true reasons for labour turnover are always difficult to assess, but what likely reasons can you list, judging from the information given in the case study? What other reasons might you suspect?

6. The Friday evening samba sessions were a very real boost to morale, but would be perhaps unlikely to have the same effect in the U.K. Yet any company should endeavour to transform even its regular and routine sales meeting into a morale-raiser. Any suggestions?

CHAPTER XXVII

Letraset in N. America: A Contrast in Distribution Strategies

LETRASET LTD.

1. Introduction. The Letraset success story is by now well-known: an ingenious dry-transfer lettering system brought to technical perfection, some innovative marketing, some highly competent financial management, and—inevitably in a company growing at an explosive rate—some mistakes.

The original product idea on which the fortunes of the company were founded was an easily applied transfer of letters and drawings as a substitute for the tedious and expensive hand-drawing that had hitherto been required.

These original transfers were still based on the use of water when manufacture was begun in 1956. The ultimate aim, however, was the development of the infinitely more convenient *dry* transfer, a technical break-through that was eventually achieved in 1960, after much research and experiment. The simplicity of the product is amply demonstrated in the concise but entirely complete instructions given in Fig. 13.

The company realised at the outset that so revolutionary a product, offering so many cost and other advantages, had a world-wide market and, at an early stage, made a positive decision to promote its product throughout the world, selecting initially a few markets of major potential for thorough exploitation.

LETRASET CANADA LTD.

2. Establishment of the Canadian company. Preoccupied as they were with the need to launch their new product in these major markets, the Letraset directors paid scant attention to Canada, whose potential seemed insignificant in contrast with the vast market offered by its southern neighbour. It was only in response to the urgent and persistent representations of John Soper, a nephew of the then managing director, Bob Chudley, who was

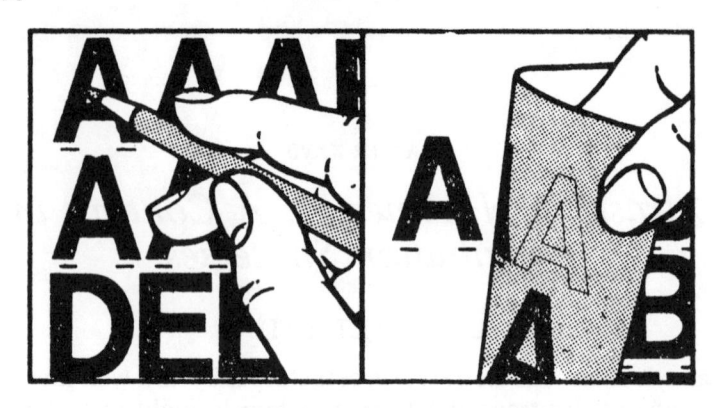

FIG. 13 *The Letraset dry transfer process*

Remove the backing tissue from lettering sheet, and align the guidelines on the sheet with those on the artwork. Rub lightly over the letter with ballpoint pen or blunt pencil, using sweeping strokes. Carefully lift sheet away. Repeat until word is complete. Cover entire word with protective backing tissue and reburnish for added protection and permanence.

already living and working in Toronto, that they agreed to supply the market at all.

Soper headed up, in partnership with Letraset U.K., a new sales company, Letraset Canada Ltd., which imported the product from England. For a short period, when cash was urgently needed, he sold direct to industrial users as opportunities arose.

Soper, however, was well aware of both the potential for the product and the importance of its immediate availability. With the encouragement of Letraset U.K., he determined to establish a nation-wide distribution network that would not only maximise sales and profits but would help to shut out competitors permanently from the market (at that time competitors, too, were concentrating on the U.S.A.).

3. Dealer appointments. Soper's first step was the appointment of official Letraset distributors, usually art dealers, in every major city in Canada. Mindful of the success of Letraset sales in other countries, he foresaw the eventual need to appoint additional dealers and was careful not to offer territorial exclusivity. Logically, therefore, he was in no position to demand that dealers should not stock competing products, though initially, since no such products were on offer in Canada, this presented no problem.

4. Dealer stocks. A condition of dealer appointment was the maintenance of an adequate stock of the Letraset range. With this in mind Letraset Canada provided complete storage systems, persuading dealers to instal them in a prominent position behind the counter, as near as practicable to the store entrance. Each sheet number had its own separate drawer, and a simple reminder card, inserted at an appropriate level in the pile of sheets, ensured automatic re-ordering.

5. Stock-level adjustment. The appropriate re-order level, however, varied from one area to another, according to the nature of local business and the extent to which the market had been developed. Soper was concerned to establish the optimal re-order level for *each individual dealer*, and introduced a system by which the reminder card was date-stamped at each re-order. Over-frequent date stamps meant an upward re-adjustment of the order level; infrequent stamps resulted in a downward adjustment. What could have become a time-consuming stock check, and a burdensome responsibility for Letraset, became a simple and automatic operation for the dealer's staff. To complete the system's reliability, dealers were informed that they could expect a 24-hour delivery service from Letraset in Toronto.

6. The Letraset sales force. Soper's initial sales force consisted of no more than four or five men covering all the major Canadian cities. Significantly, these men were described right from the start as regional managers. Whilst their duties naturally included selling in to dealers, their main tasks were defined as:

(*a*) training the dealer's in-store staff in product knowledge and stock control;

(*b*) assistance to dealers in identifying their major local customers (advertising agencies, art studios, architects, television stations, newspaper offices, publishing houses, large engineering companies with their own design and drawing offices, and similar functions in both government and industry);

(*c*) actively selling to these customers *on behalf of the dealer*;

(*d*) field training of the outside salesmen whom it was hoped the dealer would appoint.

7. Dealer salesmen. Dealers were encouraged to employ—and did employ—at least one, and sometimes two, outside salesmen, who concentrated entirely on selling Letraset products. In addition to the field training provided by Letraset regional managers, these dealer salesmen were trained in both product knowledge and salesmanship at Letraset sales conferences in Toronto.

The partnership between supplier and dealer was complete: the dealers provided a regular sales force, while Letraset provided, in the person of the regional managers, both field sales managers and a commando sales force. Regional managers were soon spending over 60 per cent of their time in helping the dealer to sell out to his major customers.

It was this emphasis on selling out on behalf of dealers that was Soper's major contribution to the Letraset distribution strategy—and perhaps to the art-supply business in general.

8. Additional dealerships. The Canadian operation was an outstanding success, even by Letraset's own high standards. It soon became necessary to appoint additional dealers if the original aims of full development of the market and exclusion of competitors were to be met. Soper, as mentioned, had retained the right to appoint such additional dealers, but nevertheless took great pains to discuss new dealerships with all existing dealers, pointing out that any established art dealer would, on moving into the dry-transfer business, automatically secure a share of the market merely by virtue of his existing customer connections. It was, therefore, in everyone's interests that the newcomer should carry the Letraset range, rather than a competing range which might be the subject of heavy promotional activity from a competing manufacturer anxious to buy his way into any market area where he might gain a foothold.

9. Entry of competition. Inevitably, competitors did attempt to enter the market, and some few dealers began to carry an additional, competitive, line. Letraset's usual answer was to prepare a careful analysis of the effect of that second line on the dealer's return on investment—surprisingly, an accounting concept unfamiliar to many dealers. Usually, it could be shown that a 100 per cent increase in investment costs (the cost of stocking the new range) would result at most in a 5 per cent increase in sales. In the face of this irrefutable logic, competitors scored only isolated successes.

10. The present situation. Few Canadian dealers now carry a competing range, and most have found that Letraset accounts for a major share of their turnover and profits. Many have found the product such a customer attraction that the Letraset storage and display system has deliberately been moved from the once-favoured entrance position to the back of the store, so as to induce customer traffic past all other displays. Letraset Canada responded in typical fashion: far from objecting, they provided illuminated signs, usually 3 to 4 ft. long by 2 ft. 6 in. high, indicating the location of each major product section in the store. One section, of course, is prominently described as the "Letraset" section.

Letraset Canada now have some 150 authorised dealers, most with one or two outside salesmen specialising solely in Letraset products. The original four regional managers have increased to twelve. Despite the unremitting efforts of competitors, some 80 per cent of the market remains in Letraset hands, and the Canadian distribution system has become the model for all Letraset operations world-wide.

LETRASET IN THE U.S.A.

11. Agency appointment. At an early stage in the development of the company, the board of Letraset U.K. recognised the importance of the U.S. market, which is, and is likely to remain, the company's largest single market.

As early as 1961, just two years after the incorporation of Letraset Ltd., a twenty-five-year agency contract was signed with a U.S. agent who distributed art requisites to dealers by means of a nationally syndicated catalogue (dealers bought the catalogue and bound it in their own cover before issue to prospective customers). As might be expected when so novel a product achieved such immediate and extensive distribution, the agency was a real success in that it brought significant and much-needed income to the fledgling Letraset Ltd.

Letraset became, however, one of hundreds of different products in a catalogue. Even at that early stage there was some doubt whether such an arrangement was in the best long-term interests of the company, and the agency agreement, which had been signed by a director without the formal approval of the board, led to a boardroom upset.

12. Licensing agreement. The situation in the U.S.A. was unique in that the company faced serious competition from local manufacturers. One U.S. company, Prestype, had developed independently a product similar to Letraset, though on a paper, rather than a plastic, base. Another company, Chartpak, with an already established distribution network in the art-requisites field, began to manufacture a plastic-base product, which involved Letraset Ltd. in patent litigation.

In 1963, Letraset decided to go public. It was clearly undesirable to have to report, in the prospectus, pending legal actions relating to patents which were vital to the whole future success of the company. The company was forced to consider licensing Chartpak in the U.S.A. Licensing negotiations were initiated, but were so protracted that, in order to reach an early settlement of the patent actions (which Letraset were assured they would eventually have won), the company licensed competition in its major market for what even then appeared a trivial sum, and which today appears derisory.

13. Appointment of distributors. Distribution through the syndicated-catalogue system continued, and, though sales increased, it was clear that the company was rapidly losing market share, largely as a result of the haphazard and patchy distribution inseparable from a catalogue-sale operation. It was decided to appoint a number of authorised distributors as wholesalers, in an endeavour to gain greater control over distribution. This resulted in some improvement in sales, but performance still fell a long way short of that achieved in other, less important, markets.

14. Establishment of a marketing subsidiary and dealer loading. In 1967 Letraset U.S.A. Inc. was formed as a sales and distribution subsidiary with headquarters in California. It was decided to mount a major distribution campaign, loading the Letraset wholesalers so as to provide the "urge of stock on the shelf". Such a policy, of course, could only be successful provided sales *in* to wholesalers were followed by equivalent sales *out* to dealers and thence to end-users. "Selling-out", however, was given scant attention. The agency organisation was not in any way structured to assist with the selling-out function and necessarily depended on the uniqueness of the product to ensure its passage through the distribution chain. Eventually, the agency agreement had to be bought out—at a cost approaching one million dollars.

15. New products and further dealer loading. With the cancellation of the agency agreement, Letraset were in a position to exercise much closer control over their market. Nevertheless, apart from a catalogue issued to known major end-users, there was still no mechanism by which they might assist in the selling-out operation. It was therefore decided to take advantage of the introduction of improved format and designs of the instant-lettering product in order to load the distributors with yet more stock.

These new designs were introduced under the Letraset U.S.A. name at an increased price per sheet, but all distributors, and consequently all their dealers, were offered a complete exchange of stock on a sheet-for-sheet basis—provided they bought, in addition, an equivalent number of sheets at the new price. As the product changes were not readily apparent, the new range was allocated sheet numbers which differed from the hitherto standard international numbering system. A new U.S. catalogue was to include *only* these special numbers. This, rather ingeniously, put pressure on distributors, and their dealers, to accept the exchange offer, since sheets not exchanged would become very largely unsaleable.

Not surprisingly in these circumstances, most distributors and dealers accepted the exchange offer. U.S. sales soared, and it was these sales that largely accounted for the record company profits in 1967–8. Sales *out* to end-users however, fell far short of sales *in* to distributors and their dealers. Further, the length and diffuse nature of the distribution chain meant that this fact was not suspected for many months, and the full extent of distributor and dealer over-stocking was only realised early in 1969.

The new numbering system that had been so effective in persuading distributors to accept the exchange offer brought immediate production problems in its wake. In effect a special product, requiring separate and much shorter production runs, had been created. This in turn gave rise to delivery problems at the U.K. factory (newly built, and still experiencing teething troubles), reduced stock turn, and increased stock control problems. All this occurred at a time when the standard product could have been offered without difficulty—the sheets withdrawn from the U.S.A. were perfectly serviceable.

Worse, in the atmosphere of urgency generated by the sudden upsurge in the U.S. demand a change in product formulation went unnoticed. The supplier of an ingredient of the adhesive used to retain the lettering on the backing sheet altered its composition. The effect of the change was to reduce the satisfactory shelf life of the product, which had up to that point been virtually indefinite—and the high level of stocks forced on distributors resulted inevitably in a longer storage period.

16. Contemplated withdrawal from the market. For all these reasons sales slumped alarmingly and Letraset U.S.A. incurred a swingeing loss. The situation appeared hopeless—it was described by the then managing director, John Chudley, as a shambles—and total withdrawal from the market was seriously considered. Eventually it was decided to combine the Canadian and U.S. operations under the control of John Soper, whose immediate brief was to restore the U.S. operation to profitability and expansion.

17. Replacement of defective stock. Necessarily, Soper's first act was to make a further one-for-one exchange in order to replace the defective sheets still in stock at distributors and dealers (there proved eventually to be about one million defective sheets in all). This apparently straightforward operation proved to be by no means as simple a task as might have been hoped. Although *distributors* were readily identifiable, and although most were only too happy to co-operate, by no means all of them were in a position even to identify their Letraset dealers. Selling a range of perhaps hundreds of products they were quite unable to analyse their sales on a product basis.

18. Introduction of Canadian-style distribution. On completion of this difficult operation, Soper was tempted to continue on the basis of the established wholesaler-dealer-end-user network. The dangers of loss of control over the distribution channel had by now been amply demonstrated, however, and it was clear that the only road to success was the long haul back towards something approaching the Canadian authorised-dealer and regional-manager system. This in turn meant cutting out the wholesaler-distributors and taking back yet more stock from them.

There was, of course, no prospect of achieving the Canadian norm of *exclusive* Letraset dealers. Most U.S. dealers had by now become accustomed to carrying at least two competing lines, and some carried as many as five. Persuading a dealer to drop an already established and successful product is a very different matter from persuading him not to take on a new and untried line. Nevertheless, gradually and painstakingly, Soper achieved some degree of success. Of the 200 or so major U.S. dealers, a few now offer Letraset exclusively and most offer no more than one competing range. Some 150 smaller dealers offer Letraset alone.

19. Success of the new U.S. operation. Now that the competition has established itself, Letraset can never hope to approach in the

U.S.A. the market dominance it enjoys in Canada. Nevertheless, Letraset U.S.A. is now again a market leader, holding over 25 per cent of the market. (Its own licensee, Chartpak, holds another 25 per cent, while the remainder of the market is shared by eight other manufacturers.) The U.S.A. is once again Letraset's major revenue and profit earner, largely as a result of the controlled distribution system established by Soper—an achievement which was hailed by managing director John Chudley as a "resounding success". Since the system was established, American sales (largely accounted for by the Canadian and U.S. operations) have grown consistently each year, from £1,299,000 in 1972 to £11,526,000 in 1977.

CASE STUDY QUESTIONS

1. The Canadian distribution arrangements have proved to be an enduring success. The brief account given in the case study inevitably gives an impression that achieving satisfactory distribution was all plain sailing. What difficulties do you imagine John Soper encountered?

2. The initial appointment of an agent in the U.S.A. was sufficiently controversial to give rise to a boardroom upset. What practical alternatives might reasonably have been considered by the board even at this very early stage of the company's development?

3. Even if the appointment of an agent was the right decision, in what two significant ways might the agency agreement have been improved from the Letraset point of view?

4. Letraset licensed a powerful competitor with an established distribution network in return for an annual payment which it fully realised was quite inadequate. Given the need to present an attractive prospectus, and therefore reach some form of settlement, how best might the problem have been handled?

5. Dealer loading had hitherto proved successful in all Letraset markets. Why in the U.S.A. was it destined to end in failure?

6. What various alternative courses of action might John Soper have considered when he first took over responsibility for the U.S.A.?

CHAPTER XXVIII

CompAir Ltd.: Entry into the West German Market

1. Introductory note. This case study outlines the various steps taken by CompAir Ltd. prior to its succesful entry, in 1972, into the West German market for air compressors and compressed-air road tools and industrial hand tools.

The study may simply be read straight through as an account of one company's market-entry operation. Alternatively, the reader may like to pause at each case problem and prepare his own solution before considering the action taken by CompAir. Purely technical data have been largely omitted and certain market data have necessarily been simplified. Nevertheless, the problems outlined in the case study are those actually faced, and the reader has available all the data necessary to arrive at an independent solution. The CompAir decisions are those actually taken in the light of the inevitable financial constraints on research and other expenditure; they are not put forward as the theoretical ideal.

2. The company. CompAir Ltd. is a major group of companies which resulted mainly from the merger of the two leading U.K. companies in the compressed-air field, Broom and Wade Ltd. and Holman Bros. Both these companies were already heavily engaged in international operations.

The merger gave rise to a global review of the new group's existing marketing activities and to the examination of a number of possible new market opportunities. One such opportunity, it seemed, was West Germany, where it was decided to undertake a detailed market investigation.

3. The products. The products for which it was thought potential existed in West Germany were:

(*a*) *mobile air compressors*, of the type used by construction companies and civil engineering contractors, which can be seen on any major building site and at any road repair operation;

(*b*) *road tools*, known in the trade as road breakers, but more popularly known as pneumatic drills—such tools are, of course, normally powered by compressed air from mobile air compressors;

(c) *high-output stationary air compressors* of the kind installed by major manufacturing companies as a central source of power for compressed-air equipment of all kinds;

(d) *industrial hand tools*, which consist of a compressed-air motor, hand grip, and a tool, usually interchangeable, and often consisting of a simple drill, screwdriver or spanner. Such tools are normally powered from the stationary air compressors already described, and are used in assembly line operations.

The four product lines are illustrated in Fig. 14. All require servicing and repair facilities.

CompAir knew from its experience in other markets that road tools and mobile compressors were frequently sold through distributors, whereas stationary compressors of the size relevant to the survey were bought, as major capital items intended for plant expansion or new factories, direct from manufacturers. Distribution arrangements for hand tools varied from one market to the next. In West Germany, of course, distribution arrangements would not necessarily follow the general pattern.

4. Marketing situation. CompAir had no experience of, or information on, the West German market for these products. The board decided to authorise a market survey, and Norman Burden, Director of Group Marketing, sat down to draft out the terms of reference. Well aware of the extensive and diffuse nature of the markets to be investigated, and of how easy it might be, as a result, to incur heavy and often unnecessary expenditure on research information of only marginal value, he decided:

(a) that no information would be sought that would not influence subsequent marketing action;

(b) that, as regards quantitative estimates, particular care would be taken not to demand an unnecessary degree of precision.

5. Major user industries. It was already known, from previous experience in other markets, that the major user industries included:

(a) for mobile compressors and road tools:
  (i) the construction industry;

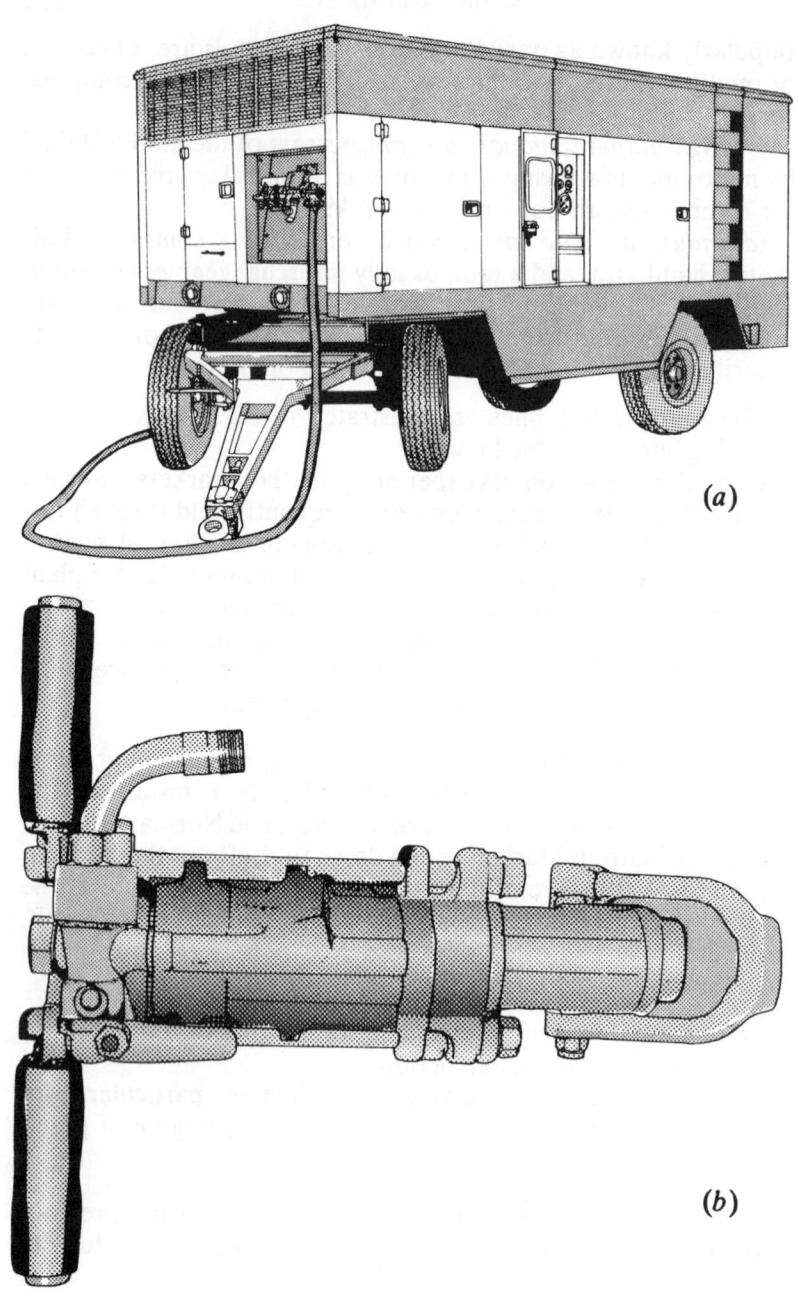

FIG. 14 *CompAir's product lines*

(*a*) Mobile air compressor. (*b*) Road tool. (*c*) Stationary air compressor. (*d*) Industrial hand tool.

(c)

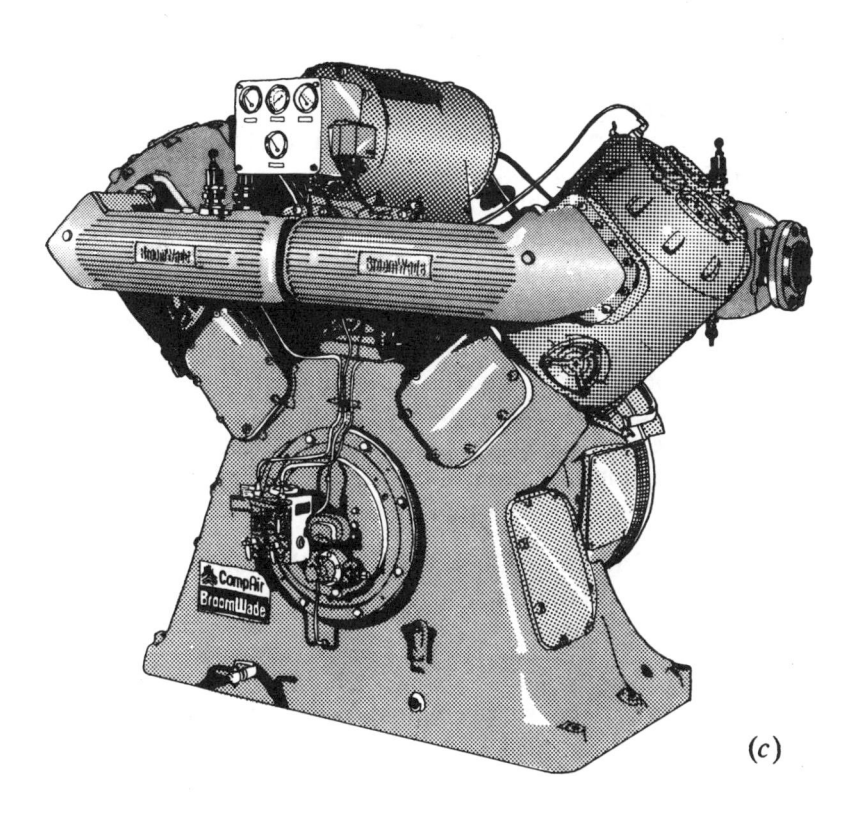

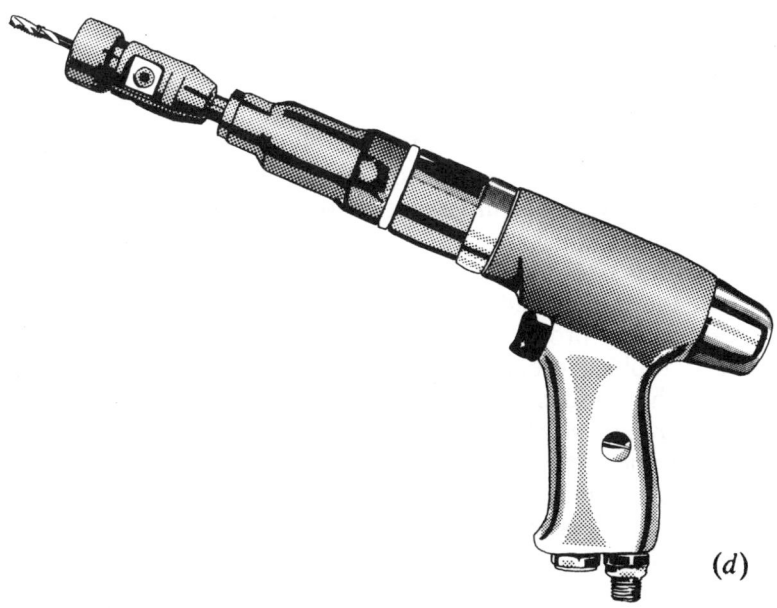

(d)

(*ii*) mining;
(*iii*) quarrying;
(*b*) for stationary compressors and industrial hand tools:
(*i*) car manufacturing;
(*ii*) commercial vehicle manufacturing;
(*c*) for stationary compressors only, food processing.

CASE PROBLEM 1

Prepare summary terms of reference for the market investigation in W. Germany. In the case of quantitative estimates consider the required breakdown by market segment and the required degree of precision. Where you think it appropriate, indicate the reasons for your inclusion (or exclusion) of a particular item of information. The purely technical aspects of the investigation may be ignored.

6. Terms of reference for the market investigation. The terms of reference for the market investigation, as decided by CompAir, are summarised below.

(*a*) *Scope.*
(*i*) *Products.* The survey would cover the four products already discussed.
(*ii*) *Industries.* Initially the survey would cover only the major user industries already known, from experience in other markets, to offer real potential.
(*iii*) *Geographical.* The survey was to cover the whole of West Germany. Initial market entry on a regional basis was not in this case practicable, since some of the products were not only mobile or portable, and, therefore, likely to be moved regularly from one construction site to another, but also required servicing and repair. Servicing facilities at least, therefore, would need to be on a nation-wide basis.
(*b*) *Market size.* Market size estimates would be required for each of the survey industries, with a cross-breakdown by the relevant survey products, as shown in Fig. 15.

A geographical breakdown of market size would not be necessary, for the reasons already indicated.

(*c*) *Degree of precision.* The assessment of market size often presents some difficulty in industrial market research, at least in markets as vast and diffuse as construction and food processing: in such industries it is simply not economically possible to prepare a valid sampling frame, i.e. list of names and addresses of all organisations relevant to the survey, from which a probability sample can be taken. Under these circumstances, insistence on a specific degree of precision can only lead to a vast increase in research expenditure rarely justified by the value of the information obtained.

PRODUCT INDUSTRY	Road tools	Mobile compressors	Hand tools	Stationary compressors
Construction			///	///
Mining and quarrying			///	///
Car and commercial vehicle manufacture	///	///		
Food processing	///	///	///	

☐ REQUIRED /// NOT REQUIRED

FIG. 15 *CompAir Ltd. research terms of reference: market size breakdown required*

Burden reasoned that at this stage all he required was a clear and definite indication of a minimum market size sufficient to enable CompAir to achieve significant turnover and profit without the need to capture an excessively high market share.

(d) *Forecasts.* Forecasts would be required for each major user industry.

(e) *Market shares.* Identification of the leading suppliers, both domestic and foreign, to each major user industry, was essential, together with some indication of their relative importance.

Percentage market-share figures would not be required, as they would be of little value in the preparation of the marketing plan, and would in this market be inordinately expensive to obtain.

(f) *Distribution.* A detailed analysis of the present accepted distribution channels would be essential.

(g) *Prices.* Prices would be required in each product group, related to specific competing products.

Distributor margins, discounts and credit terms would also need to be investigated.

(*h*) *Promotion*. Competitors' promotional activities were to be investigated in as much detail as possible—in particular:

   (*i*) the more usual advertising media;
   (*ii*) the importance of exhibitions;
   (*iii*) the extent to which distributors were relied upon for promotional activity by the manufacturer.

(*i*) *Market entry*. Burden decided that, even at the research stage, mere fact-finding was not enough: the research ought also to generate ideas on the critical subject of market entry. With this in mind he would require the research consultants to report on:

   (*i*) possible areas of user dissatisfaction or market need;
   (*ii*) possible innovation in distribution, e.g. the extent to which plant hire was established in West Germany as an alternative method of distribution;
   (*iii*) the practicability of acquisition of distributors, thus ensuring control of distribution channels;
   (*iv*) possible co-operation with compressor manufacturers, e.g. licensing, or reciprocal distribution of non-competing product ranges;
   (*v*) possible acquisition of compressor manufacturers.

7. Desk research. Burden's next step was to carry out a thorough programme of desk research both in the U.K. and in West Germany. This revealed a published survey giving complete market-size figures, with appropriate breakdowns and forecasts. These figures showed an unexpectedly high market potential and growth rate in all the industries selected as being of interest.

The investigation now became largely qualitative. Designing the research programme, however, still presented a number of problems, which Burden discussed with three different firms of research consultants.

CASE PROBLEM 2

Design the research programme covering the qualitative items of the terms of reference laid down by Burden (items **6** (*e*) to (*i*)). As always, the research design should aim, in its overall strategy, at achieving maximum value (in terms of information of value to the marketing plan) for every pound spent on research. More specifically, it should also consider the composition of the sample, sample size and sampling methods, and the extent of use of the (expensive) personal interview. Bear in mind that a good deal of technical information is to be sought from end-users, even though, for simplicity, the details have been omitted from this case study.

8. Research design.

(a) *Overall strategy.* The research was to cover four different and complex product ranges, in four different industries, two of which have already been described as "vast and diffuse".

Some of the qualitative information could have been analysed on a quantitative basis, as in consumer research, e.g. x per cent of informants in the construction industry were dissatisfied with present servicing and repair arrangements. Burden believed, however, that this would be a facile and over-simplified approach. He regarded it as essential to probe fully the reasons for informants' replies and to obtain full details of their past experiences. Technical problems demanded, in any case, a similar in-depth approach.

In these circumstances, it was clear that a considerable number of personal interviews was required; yet it was difficult to decide *how* many. Burden decided on a two-stage approach:

(i) *an initial stage*, based entirely on personal interviews;

(ii) *a second stage*, perhaps relying principally on telephone interviewing and postal questionnaires designed to cover those points left in doubt on completion of the first stage.

In this way initial research expenditure could be kept within reasonable limits, while subsequent expenditure could be redirected, in the light of the market information then obtained, where it would be most needed.

(b) *Sample.*

(i) *End-user organisations.* End-user organisations, i.e. CompAir's potential customers, would, of course, need to be contacted in all four of the industries relevant to the survey.

(ii) *Other informants.* End-user organisations alone, however, could not provide a complete picture of the market. It would be essential to interview also: component suppliers (principally the manufacturers of petrol and diesel engines supplied to mobile compressor manufacturers); manufacturers of compressors, road tools and industrial hand tools, i.e. competitors; distributors.

In other words, it would be necessary, as with many industrial market research projects, to direct the interviews along the whole chain of demand. The composition of the sample is shown diagrammatically in Fig. 16.

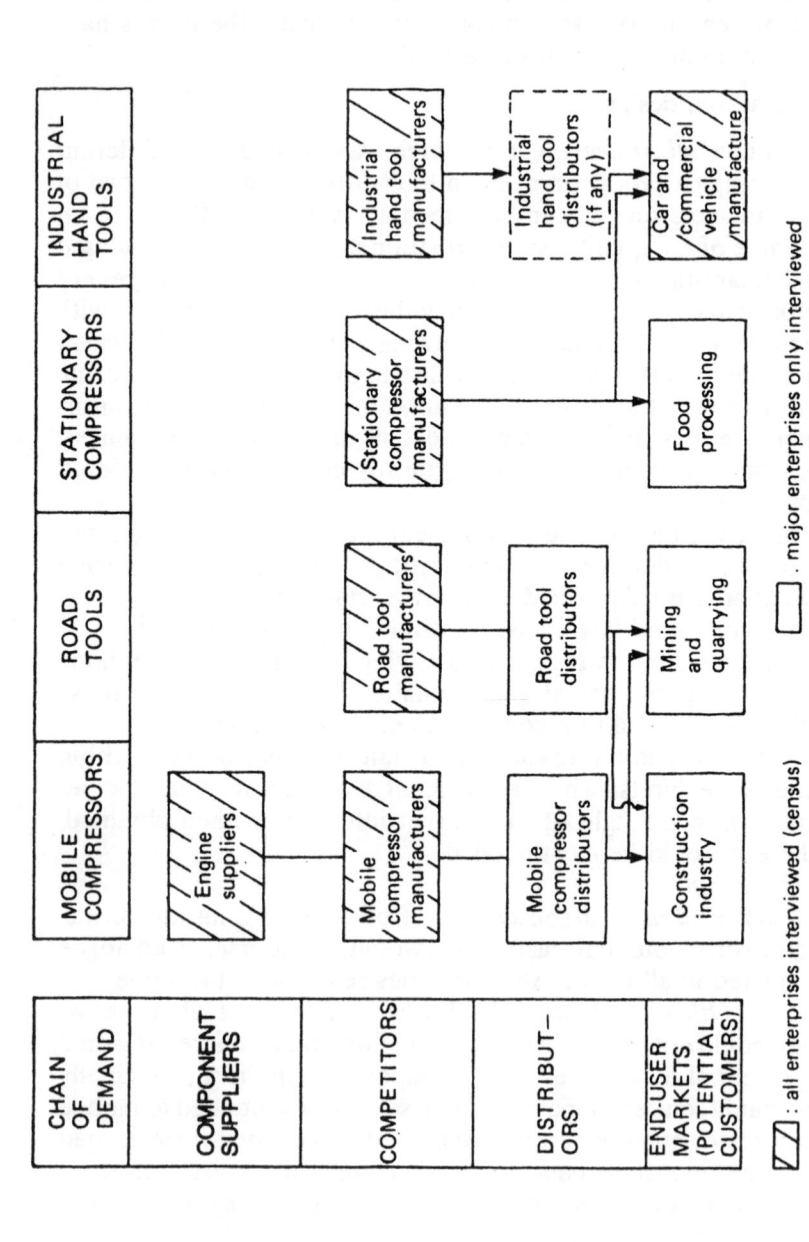

FIG. 16 *CompAir Ltd. research design: composition of the sample*

CHAIN OF DEMAND	MOBILE COMPRESSORS	ROAD TOOLS	STATIONARY COMPRESSORS	INDUSTRIAL HAND TOOLS
COMPONENT SUPPLIERS	Engine suppliers			
COMPETITORS	Mobile compressor manufacturers	Road tool manufacturers	Stationary compressor manufacturers	Industrial hand tool manufacturers
DISTRIBUTORS	Mobile compressor distributors	Road tool distributors		Industrial hand tool distributors (if any)
END-USER MARKETS (POTENTIAL CUSTOMERS)	Construction industry	Mining and quarrying	Food processing	Car and commercial vehicle manufacture

▨ : all enterprises interviewed (census)   ☐ : major enterprises only interviewed

(c) *Sample size and sampling methods.* Certain categories of informant were limited in number and *all* could be interviewed, i.e. a census would be undertaken, not a sampling operation; these included engine manufacturers, competitors, and the car and commercial vehicle industry.

In the case of distributors and the remaining end-user industries, interviewing was to concentrate on the major companies only. (In most industries it will be found that the vast bulk of both purchases and sales are accounted for by a very small number of enterprises.)

The sample size clearly had to cover all major segments of the market adequately, the critical factor being the number of companies of significance in the end-user industries, other than car and commercial vehicle manufacturers. A total of 100 interviews was eventually decided upon. It was recognised that this figure was to some extent arbitrary, but it was certainly a minimum, and it could always be extended at the end of the initial stage.

9. Research findings. Both the planned stages of the assignment were undertaken. The first stage provided most of the required information; the second stage was limited in scope and is not further considered here. The findings of both stages are summarised below.

(a) *All products.* It was found in the case of all products that:

(i) the CompAir range could meet all local technical and legal regulations and was acceptable to all end-users;

(ii) CompAir delivered prices in West Germany would be broadly competitive with other suppliers, but would offer no significant price advantage.

(b) *Mobile compressors.*

(i) *Competition.* Four competitors were found to share 75 per cent of the total market as shown in Table VII.

TABLE VII. COMPAIR'S COMPETITORS

Competitor	Competitor's manufacturing base	Share of market (%)
A	W. German	23
B	multinational	20
C	multinational	17
D	W. German	15
Total		75

(ii) *Distribution.* All competitors except competitor B sold through independent distributors. Competitor B sold mainly through its own network of sales and service branches but was beginning to develop sales through independent distributors as well.

Distributors could be divided into two main categories: the traditional construction industry distributors, dealing in all kinds of construction equipment and plant; and newly developing specialist distributors of compressed air equipment, known as "air-houses". These latter, however, were limited in number and size.

Distributors did not sell on an exclusive-representation basis. Most carried two manufacturers' product lines. They expected, and received, very high discounts from manufacturers on large-quantity purchases.

Plant hire was virtually unknown. There was some feeling among informants that it was alien to the German character.

(iii) *Purchasing influences.* Apart from the obvious factor of price, reliability was of the utmost importance, coupled with the prompt supply of replacement parts when breakdowns did occur. All competitors provided a remarkably efficient service, with the exception of competitor C, which had clearly jeopardised its future prospects in the market.

Purchasers usually endeavoured, though not always with success, to standardise on not more than two makes of compressor, and the products currently available in the market were regarded in all cases as completely satisfactory from a technical viewpoint.

A strong preference was expressed for engines of West German manufacture; about half of the informants felt German-made engines were absolutely essential.

(iv) *Promotion.* Personal selling was heavily relied upon. There was evidence of some direct mail, but little media advertising.

(c) *Road tools.* It was not possible to be confident on the question of market shares. Nevertheless, leading competitors included the four companies already mentioned as suppliers of mobile compressors, plus two specialist manufacturers of road tools only.

Otherwise, as might be expected, the market followed very much the pattern of the mobile-compressor market.

(d) *Stationary compressors.*

(i) *Competition.* Again, it was not possible to establish market shares. Leading manufacturers, however, were competitors A, B, and C (all also involved in the manufacture of mobile compressors) and one other specialist manufacturer of stationary compressors only.

(ii) *Distribution.* Distribution was almost invariably direct from manufacturer to end-user.

(iii) *Purchasing influences.* Cost, reliability and prompt supply of replacement parts were again critical factors.

(e) *Industrial hand tools.*

(i) *Competition.* Leading suppliers were competitors B and C (both also involved in the manufacture of mobile compressors) and three specialist manufacturers.

(ii) *Distribution.* Distribution was both direct and by specialist distributors. These distributors did not operate on an exclusive-dealing basis, but usually concentrated on one or two makes only, so as to take maximum advantage of the very high quantity discounts offered by manufacturers.

CASE PROBLEM 3

In the light of the information given, decide on the most appropriate market-entry strategy for CompAir. Consider the two principal alternatives: independent market entry; or some form of co-operation with, or acquisition of, a competitor. In both cases give particular importance to the problem of distribution. Justify your decisions for or against each course of action considered.

10. Market entry strategy.

(a) *General.* The size and growth rate of the market, coupled with the technical acceptability and price-competitiveness of the whole CompAir range, made West Germany, *prima facie*, a particularly attractive market.

Nevertheless, the overall impression could only be one of a market well catered for. There were some areas of competitor weakness, e.g. in replacement parts, and perhaps some scope for innovation, e.g. in plant hire, but these were not significant. In particular:

(i) although the CompAir products could meet all local technical standards, and compared favourably with competing equipment, they offered no major technical advantage;

(ii) although reasonably competitive on price, there was little scope for major price reductions, and in any case Burden regarded price wars very definitely as an undesirable last resort;

(*iii*) Burden believed that he could improve on the fairly pedestrian promotional methods of his competitors, but to prove this, as he was subsequently to do, it was first essential to secure nation-wide distribution at reasonable cost.

Distribution, it seemed to him, was the key to the market. Even stationary compressors, though necessarily sold direct, would benefit from a local sales force, while local servicing and spares availability, clearly an important factor in the purchasing decision, might almost be regarded as a necessity. For all other products a sales and service network was essential.

(*b*) *Distribution.* Distribution could be obtained by:
—persuading the existing independent distributors to stock and sell the products;
—building up an independent CompAir distribution network, similar to that already established by competitor B;
—acquisition of some of the existing independent distributors;
—some form of co-operation, e.g. licensing, joint-venture assembly or manufacture, with a manufacturer already established in the independent distribution chain.

(*i*) *Sales through independent distributors.* Sales through the existing independent distributors were considered to offer real difficulties, since:
—distributors were known to attempt to standardise on two makes of compressor;
—CompAir could offer the distributor no major product advantage;
—as a newcomer, CompAir could not expect to take, at least initially, large-size orders, yet would need to match the quantity discounts currently offered by competitors;
—although there might be some possibility of capitalising on market disaffection, in an endeavour to replace competitor C in the distribution chain, which, as mentioned, had jeopardised its market position by an inadequate supply of spare parts, this was regarded as a last resort.

(*ii*) *CompAir's own distribution network.* Establishment of an independent distribution network was a possibility, as had been proved by competitor B, but:
—it would involve heavy investment;
—return on investment would be long-term, at best;
—CompAir believed they were likely to achieve a better rate

of return on a manufacturing-based investment.

(*iii*) *Acquisition of distributors.* Acquisition of the traditional construction industry distributors would:

—again involve CompAir in heavy investment in distribution facilities;

—involve them also in the wider aspects of building-materials supply, of which they had no experience;

—require a succession of take-overs if national distribution was to be achieved, since, as mentioned, distributors' influence was limited to specific regions;

—involve CompAir in handling at least one competitive product range and, probably, after several distributor take-overs, in an unsatisfactory mix of competing products which it would be by no means easy to abandon.

The specialist air houses might have offered a more attractive take-over proposition, but at their then early stages of development they clearly shared some of the disadvantages of establishing an independent network.

(*iv*) *Co-operation with a manufacturer.* Under these circumstances, Burden decided that some form of co-operation with a local manufacturer was likely to be the most suitable method of market entry. He preferred a joint venture to an outright acquisition, which would involve a much greater financial outlay, but recognised that much depended on finding a willing partner and on that partner's preferences. Either method would offer both immediate distribution and local assembly facilities for the inclusion of German engines in the CompAir mobile compressors.

Burden set down his criteria for the ideal partner company:

—it must be small enough to enable CompAir to be the dominant partner in the venture, or to acquire it if necessary;

—it must, nevertheless, have a sufficient market share in the mobile compressor and road tool market to have achieved effective distribution on a national basis;

—on the other hand, its mobile compressor and road tool manufacturing facilities should not be too extensive, the aim, after all, being the *export* of CompAir's production to West Germany;

—its product range should otherwise be complementary rather than competitive with CompAir's, and, ideally, it would not manufacture stationary compressors at all;

—it must have an unblemished reputation in the market place.

It will be clear from an examination of even the abridged

market data given that competitor D most nearly approached the ideal, while competitor A offered a reasonable alternative.

11. Market entry. Both competitors D and A were approached and the acquisition route was eventually followed.

Today CompAir (Deutschland) GmbH operates from a newly-completed headquarters strategically located alongside the *autobahn* network on the northern outskirts of Cologne. The premises embrace extensive assembly, repair, and servicing facilities, a central spare parts warehouse, and marketing and administrative support for a national network of company sales and service engineers and independent distributors. With the complete range of equipment now sold under the CompAir name, the company is highly profitable, expanding rapidly, and confident of a good future in this major market.

APPENDIX I

Bibliography (see also list of acknowledgments, pp. vi–ix)

Allen, P., *The Practice of Exporting*, Macdonald and Evans, 1975.
Bolt, Gordon J., *Communicating with E.E.C. Markets*, Kogan Page, 1973.
Brazell, D. E., *Manufacturing under Licence*, Kenneth Mason, 1968.
Brazell, D. E., *Licensing Checklists*, 2nd edition, Kenneth Mason, 1974.
Brooke, Michael Z. and Remmers, H. Lee, *The Strategy of Multinational Enterprise: Organisation and Finance*, Longman, 1970.
Cateora, Philip R. and Hess, John M., *International Marketing*, Richard D. Irwin, 1975.
Day, Arthur J., *Exporting for Profit*, Graham and Trotman, 1976.
Fayerweather, John, *International Marketing*, 2nd edition, Prentice-Hall, 1970.
Ferber, Robert (ed.), *Handbook of Marketing Research*, McGraw Hill, 1974.
International Chamber of Commerce, Paris, *Commercial Agency: Guide for the Drawing up of Contracts between Parties Residing in Different Countries*.
Giles, G. B., *Marketing*, 2nd edition, Macdonald and Evans, 1974.
Kolde, Endel J., *International Business Enterprise*, 2nd edition, Prentice-Hall, 1973.
Kollat, David T., Blackwell, Roger D. and Robeson, James F., *Strategic Marketing*, Holt, Rinehart and Winston, 1972.
Kotler, P., *Marketing Management: Analysis, Planning and Control*, 3rd edition, Prentice-Hall, 1976.
Kramer, Roland L., *International Marketing*, South-Western Publishing, 1970.
McMillan, C. and Paulden, S., *Export Agents: A Complete Guide to their Selection and Control*, 2nd edition, Gower Press, 1974.

Majaro, Simon, *International Marketing: A Strategic Approach to World Markets*, George Allen and Unwin, 1977.

Mason, R. Hal., Miller, Robert R. and Weigel, Dale R., *The Economics of International Business*, John Wiley and Sons, 1975.

Miracle, Gordon E. and Albaum, Gerald S., *International Marketing Management*, Richard D. Irwin, 1970.

Root, Franklin R., *Strategic Planning for Export Marketing*, International Textbook Company, 1966.

Sharman, G. H., *Thinking Managerially—about Exports*, Institute of Export, 1971.

Terpstra, Vern, *International Marketing*, Holt, Rinehart and Winston, 1972.

Tugendhat, Christopher, *The Multinationals*, Penguin, 1973.

APPENDIX II

Addresses of Organisations Mentioned in the Text

Only organisations likely to be of assistance to the student or international marketing executive are included in this list. Where an organisation has offices in several countries the U.K. address only is given.

Betro Trust. c/o Royal Society of Arts, John Adam St., London WC2N 6EZ.
British Export Houses Association. 69 Cannon St., London EC5N 5AB.
British Overseas Trade Board. 1 Victoria St., London SW1H 0ET.
Central Office of Information (C.O.I.). Hercules Rd., Westminster Bridge Rd., London SE1 7DU.
City Business Library. 55 Basinghall St., London EC2V 5BX.
Communications Advertising and Marketing Education Foundation Ltd. (CAM Foundation). Abford House, 15 Wilton Rd., London SW1V 1NJ.
Department of Trade (Export Data Branch, Overseas Tariffs and Regulations Section). Kingsgate House, 66–74 Victoria St., London SW1E 6SH.
Department of Trade (Statistics and Market Intelligence Library). Export House, 50 Ludgate Hill, London EC4M 7HU.
Employment Conditions Abroad Ltd. 13 Devonshire St., London W1N 1FF.
Export Credits Guarantee Department. Aldermanbury House, Aldermanbury, London EC2P 2EL.
Institute of Export. World Trade Centre, London E1 9AA.
Institute of Marketing. Moor Hall, Cookham, Maidenhead, Berks. SL6 9HQ.
Japan External Trade Organisation. 19 Baker St., London W1M 1AE.
London Chamber of Commerce and Industry. 69 Cannon St., London EC4N 5AB.

Market Research Society. 15 Belgrave Sq., London SW1X 8PF.
Technical Help to Exporters (T.H.E.). c/o The British Standards Institution, Maylands Avenue, Hemel Hempstead, Herts. HP2 4SQ.

APPENDIX III
Examination Technique

1. Introduction. This Appendix is concerned not with examination techniques in general but specifically with examinations in international marketing.

2. Syllabus. The first essential is to obtain your own copy of the examination syllabus, to read it carefully as a basis for the initial planning of your study programme, and to refer to it regularly as your studies proceed. You must be sure that you are covering the syllabus laid down by your particular examining body, and *only* that syllabus.

Too many students rely, in this respect, on their tutors: it is, after all, the tutors' duty to adhere to the requirements of the syllabus. Even the most conscientious tutor, however, may have to suit his tuition to the pace of his class, and he may never reach areas of the syllabus in which you have a particular interest. In examinations there is no substitute for self-reliance.

3. Past examination papers and reports. Similarly, you should obtain copies of previous (recent) examination papers and study them with care. At the very least you will gain some idea of what to expect.

Some examining bodies publish examiners' reports. These, too, will give you a very good idea of what the examiners expect of you, and will usually indicate some special pitfalls to be avoided.

4. Factual questions. Most examination papers include some questions which require merely a factual answer or, to put it bluntly, a mere regurgitation of the text-book. If you have learnt the facts, then such questions are a gift. You can usually improve your answers in such cases, however, by including *brief* and *relevant* examples. A recent C.A.M. Foundation examination paper on international advertising and marketing, for instance, stated specifically that extra marks would be awarded for "the use of relevant examples to back views expressed". Ideally these examples would come from your own experience, but they may also be drawn from your own wider reading of newspapers, trade journals and text books.

International Marketing, quite deliberately, has included a large number of examples, a high proportion of them quoted from other text books (see the acknowledgments on p. vii–viii for details of sources).

5. Questions demanding analytical thought. Marketing is a practical subject: the art of the marketing manager is the application of marketing theory to practical business situations. Any marketing examination worth taking will include a number of questions which require the student to apply his knowledge to a specific business problem. In international marketing that problem might typically include references to a particular product, a particular country, or both.

Do not be put off if you are unfamiliar with the product. So many candidates, with widely different business backgrounds, are sitting the examination that no examiner can reasonably expect more than a layman's knowledge of any particular product area. Reference to a specific product will rarely do more than identify the relevant areas of marketing theory, e.g. a reference to research on biscuits would merely indicate consumer, rather than industrial, research techniques.

The position is rather different, however, when specific countries are named. In a paper devoted to international marketing, it is perfectly reasonable to expect candidates to display some familiarity with the special problems associated with at least the countries of major potential. A recent Institute of Marketing paper, for instance, included three questions, out of 10, which required a knowledge of marketing within the E.E.C., Eastern Europe and Latin America; in all three cases the examiners' report deplored the candidates' failure to display any real awareness of the specific problems involved in each area. Again, your own experience can be an invaluable support, but if that experience is limited, then a careful study of Part II of this book is likely to pay off.

But, for questions of this type, the essential knowledge is no more than the start; you still have to prove your ability to *apply* that knowledge. It is here that practice will help. Written answers, assessed and commented on by your tutor, are the ideal, but they are inevitably time-consuming. The progress test questions at the end of each chapter of this book, and Appendix IV, may provide a useful supplement or alternative to written work. You will find that the questions in Appendix IV, whether original to the author or taken from the papers of various examining bodies, do require analytical thought as well as a knowledge of the relevant facts, if they are to be answered fully. To gain the greatest benefit from these questions, learn the chapters first (do not merely read through them) and then frame the answers to each question at least mentally, and perhaps by jotting down the salient points. In this way you can develop your powers of analytical thought and at the same time fix the facts more firmly in your mind.

6. Case studies. Again with the emphasis on the practical application of marketing theory, certain examining bodies, such as the Institute of Marketing and the C.A.M. Foundation, include a compulsory case study in their examination, and the Institute of Export includes a lengthy compulsory question which is, in effect, a small-scale case study. Case-study practice in preparation for examinations of this nature will stand you in good stead. Case studies are inevitably, of course, also a test of your wider knowledge of general marketing theory, even when they are set in an international context.

International Marketing includes three case studies (*see* XXVI–XXVIII). One of these, CompAir Ltd., is in several stages, and is specifically designed to assist the independent student. The others are perhaps best used as a basis for class or syndicate discussion.

7. Conclusion. It goes without saying that you should be certain of your basic facts. Thereafter, it is worthwhile taking some trouble in practising the more thought-provoking or analytical questions and participating in case study work. Preparation of this nature should enable you to prove to the examiner that you are a genuine practical international marketer. And if you can go even half-way towards proving that, he will be only too delighted to award you high marks.

APPENDIX IV

Examination Questions

Chapter I

1. "There is no fundamental difference between international marketing and domestic marketing." Discuss. (*Institute of Marketing, June 1977*)

2. What are the main environmental considerations in international marketing? How do they affect international marketing activity? (*Institute of Marketing, June 1976*)

3. "International marketing is simply the latest O.K. phrase for export marketing, the export manager's latest bid for prestige." Refute this suggestion.

4. It has recently been said that the term multinational is used to describe so many different organisations that it is virtually meaningless. Comment on this proposition. (*Institute of Marketing, June 1977*)

5. "Our justification for a separate treatment (of international marketing) lies not in propounding any new principles. The steps, concepts and techniques for effective marketing management are the same. The justification lies in the fact that differences between nations are typically more striking than regional differences within one country" (Philip Kotler). Expand on this statement, and give specific examples in its support.

6. Discuss the differences you see between "exporting" and "international marketing". (*Institute of Marketing, November 1977*)

Chapter II

1. "Internationally, most companies would do well to adopt a strategy of concentration on a limited number of key markets." Discuss this statement with special reference to any *one* company with which you are familiar.

2. "And finally, a word on what is meant by concentration on key markets. The following question was put to us emphatically by one company which exported to 164 markets, though 90 per cent of its sales went to ten countries: 'Are you suggesting', they asked,

APPENDIXES 237

'that we should stop trading with the other 154 countries?' "
(*Betro report: Concentration on Key Markets*).
In the position of the Betro researcher, how would *you* have answered that question?

Chapter III

1. As the Market Research Manager of a firm making industrial fasteners for use in the building and engineering trades you have been asked by the Export Manager to assist him in selecting new export markets. Describe (*a*) the basis for selecting markets which you would propose and (*b*) how the necessary information could be obtained. (*Institute of Export, May 1977*)

2. "*Secondary* data in many overseas markets suffers from a number of serious shortcomings." What specifically are these shortcomings? And what precautions would you take in using such data?

3. Outline the main problems faced by organisations attempting to conduct consumer market research in an under-developed country. What are the implications of such problems to any organisation? (*Institute of Marketing, November 1977*)

4. Your rapidly expanding Export Department requires increasing amounts of market research to be carried out. This is beyond the scope of existing staff. The alternatives to this are taking on additional qualified staff or using market research consultants. Say what considerations would influence you in this decision and what criteria would be used for the selection of staff or of consultants. (*Institute of Export, May 1977*)

Chapter IV

1. "If it sells in Birmingham, it will sell in Lyon or Dusseldorf or Chicago, for that matter." Comment on this statement.

2. A manufacturer of domestic electrical appliances decides to extend operations from his home market into a number of other countries. What demands is this likely to make on his product development facilities? (*Institute of Marketing, November 1976*)

3. "A multinational company has a real advantage over a domestic company in the generation of new product ideas. But so many fail to capitalise on that advantage." Discuss.

4. "Product elimination procedures are especially difficult, but especially important, in the multinational company." Discuss.

Chapter V

1. You sell confectionery in the form of sweets and chocolates. You find there is a market for them in the main West African markets. What factors would you take into account when repackaging them for these markets? (*Institute of Export, May 1977*)

2. You are the Marketing Manager of a whisky manufacturer selling in some fifty countries. After a recent unfortunate experience in one market you have been asked to establish a clear brand protection policy for the future. Set out that policy in summary form.

Chapter VI

1. Outline the main types of selling arrangement a company can use in its foreign markets. Briefly evaluate them in relation to:
   (*a*) marketing automobiles in developing countries; and
   (*b*) marketing fashion clothing in highly developed countries.
(*Institute of Marketing, June 1977*)

2. You export electronic components used by a wide range of industries. You find your sole distributors are not, in Norway, Sweden and Denmark, obtaining the business you think they should. What other methods of distribution would you consider and why? (*Institute of Export, May 1977*)

3. "The international marketer's interest in a channel of distribution normally ceases when he transfers his title to a buyer." In your experience, is this so? And *should* it be so?

Chapter VII

1. "Export houses offer such a variety of services that their functions can be identified only in the context of their relationship with a given client company." How far is this statement true? What general categories of export houses can you describe?

2. "The real disadvantage to an exporter of using an export house is the loss of control over his market." Discuss.

3. It has been said that you can export without going outside your own country. How can this be done and what advantages has it for small companies? (*Institute of Export, May 1975*)

4. "The best place for a U.K. exporter endeavouring to sell in tropical Africa is London." Discuss.

5. Piggy-back exporting has not proved an unqualified success in the past. Can you suggest why this was so? What advice would you give to a small fabric company contemplating a piggy-back arrangement with a large and successful international company producing sewing machines?

Chapter VIII

1. Some French retail stores have expressed a preference for direct dealing with a U.K. exporter. Others have expressed an equally strong preference for dealing with a local French agent representing the U.K. company. Can you explain the likely motivations of buyers in these stores?

2. "Agencies are a last resort. First you should try selling direct. If that doesn't work you should try every other possibility first." How far would you agree with this statement?

3. How would you define a branch office overseas? Under what circumstances might you feel justified in establishing a branch rather than an overseas sales subsidiary?

4. Nigeria no longer permits branches of foreign firms; France specifically legislates for them. Can you suggest reasons for this difference in attitude?

Chapter IX

1. A patent is not a pre-requisite for a licence. What other forms of saleable expertise can you suggest? And in what alternative ways might payment be made?

2. Discuss the advantages and disadvantages of selecting an agent versus using a licensing agreement for your textile machinery in less developed countries such as those of Latin America. (*Institute of Marketing, June 1976*)

3. Your company is about to license manufacture of a technically advanced photocopying machine in the U.S.A. and you have been asked to prepare the agenda for a meeting at which the draft of the licensing agreement is to be prepared. Jot down the main items for discussion.

4. You have been approached by a large Mexican company who wish to manufacture and sell your specialised chemicals in Mexico, where at present you do no business. Under what circumstances would you agree and how would you negotiate with the Mexican company? (*Institute of Export, May 1977*)

Chapter X

1. Many companies have a policy of retaining control of any manufacturing operation overseas, despite the difficulties involved. Why do you think they take this attitude? In those countries where a foreign majority shareholding is not permitted how might they achieve their objective of effective control?

2. "Financing overseas production is always more expensive than financing home production." Comment.

Chapter XI

1. You are commissioning market research in Brazil covering low-unit-price packaged consumer goods. You are seriously concerned about the distribution channel possibilities. What specific information would you ask the researcher to seek on this aspect?

2. Indicate some special problems the international marketer might encounter in relation to the establishment of marketing channels in a developing country. How might he attempt to overcome them?

3. What difficulties might be encountered specifically in attempting to establish *intensive* distribution in a developing country? What alternatives might be considered if intensive distribution proves impracticable?

4. "In channel management, motivation and control of channel members are the vital factors—but in foreign markets these factors present problems of extreme difficulty." What precisely are these problems and how do you suggest they might be overcome?

Chapter XII

1. "Exporters should charge what the market will bear." Is this invariably true? What factors may make such a policy difficult to achieve?

2. "Export prices should be higher than domestic prices because of the headaches involved." Discuss this statement. (*Institute of Marketing, June 1976*)

3. "Underpricing a product can be a serious mistake. The French earn more than we do and are willing to pay for quality. If the British exporter does not make the profit, the French agent or retailer will do so by putting on a higher mark-up. Exporting must be profitable" (B.O.T.B., *Marketing Consumer Goods in France*). Comment.

4. What considerations would you take into account in arriving at a pricing policy for a range of clothing products to be sold in a wide variety of foreign markets? Choose (but specify) any country of origin. (*Institute of Marketing, November 1976*)

Chapter XIII

1. "The more permanently held view is that on the whole exports are less profitable than home sales" (Betro report). How far do you feel this view might be the result of incorrect calculations of the profitability of export sales by the exporters themselves? What factors might lead even experienced exporters to reach incorrect conclusions?

2. At a time when the pound sterling has been falling in value relative to many other currencies, many British exporters would have gained by quoting prices in a foreign currency. Yet they have often been reluctant to do this. Suggest reasons for this reluctance and outline the arguments which indicate that they are not valid in such circumstances. (*Institute of Marketing, June 1977*)

3. "The trouble with our export department is that their minds never rise above marginal-cost prices. Now we have to keep them out of the accounts department altogether." Comment on this attitude, and indicate the circumstances in which marginal-cost pricing might be justifiable.

4. What is dumping? Why is it difficult to prove? How far should an exporter bear in mind anti-dumping legislation when setting his price levels?

5. You are an export manager selling knitwear, principally, and with considerable success, into the U.S.A. The pound sterling is devalued by about 15 per cent against the U.S. dollar, and you decide you must reconsider your price levels. What alternative courses of action are open to you?

6. What is barter trading? Why do countries engage in it? Why should the individual company be interested in it? And what precautions should that company take before entering into the deal?

Chapter XIV

1. Discuss the various ways in which governments attempt to influence prices. Give examples from one or two markets other than the U.K.

2. In setting prices for intra-company sales across national boundaries, it is possible to minimise tax or import-duty liability. Explain exactly how this can be achieved.

3. It has been suggested that manipulation of international transfer prices with the aim of reducing tax or import-duty liability is, though legal, unethical. How far would you agree with this view?

Chapter XV

1. Outline the circumstances favouring a standardised as opposed to a non-standardised advertising approach when marketing the same products in a number of different countries. (*Institute of Marketing, November 1976*)

2. Advertising methods and practices are different in different countries. Why should this be so, even where habits and living conditions have much in common? (*Institute of Marketing, June 1976*)

3. "The advantages of creating a Pan-European 'Tiger in the Tank' campaign were nevertheless too promising to be ignored" (Brian Ash, *Tiger in your Tank*). What would you say those advantages were for this product (petrol)?

4. As export marketing manager for an aerosols manufacturer, you have just returned from your first tour. Several of your more successful local agents say they do not think the centrally conceived advertising campaign is right for their market and one of them has even shown you a presentation from a local advertising agency for his market.

On your return you find a memo from your chairman exhorting you to implement the new U.K. campaign in all overseas markets at once. Write a letter either:

(*a*) to your chairman; or
(*b*) to one of your local agents,

stating your views of this problem and recommending a course of action. (*C.A.M. Foundation, May 1976*)

5. "A good advertisement is impossible to translate." Discuss. (*C.A.M. Foundation, May 1977*)

6. You need to have one of your sales leaflets put into German for distribution in Germany. State how you would get this done and what precautions you would take to ensure that the final result was both accurate and acceptable to the people locally. (*Institute of Export, May 1975*)

7. You export a range of frozen foods to Belgium and, as the market is rapidly expanding, decide to spend £500,000 on an advertising campaign there. How would you handle this and what factors would you take into account for this market? (*Institute of Export, May 1977*)

Chapter XVI

1. "Occasional participation in trade fairs on an *ad hoc* basis is usually a recipe for failure." Why should this be so? What steps would you take to ensure that an exhibition is fully integrated within the marketing plan?

2. Your company has agreed to exhibit at the next Hannover Trade Fair. You have been made responsible for your firm's stand. What action would you take at each stage of the operation? (*Institute of Export, May 1973*)

3. Your company manufactures high-quality leather goods. It has been suggested that you should take part in a store promotion organised in conjunction with a major New York department

store group. What factors would you consider in arriving at your decision?

4. In what way can the Central Office of Information be of help to you with your publicity overseas? (*Institute of Export, May 1976*)

5. "An expatriate subsidiary should be careful to be, and to be seen to be, a good corporate citizen of the host country." What do you understand by the phrase "good corporate citizen"?

Chapter XVII

1. As a manufacturer of optical instruments such as microscopes you decide to have a company representative to work with your distributors in:
   (*a*) the Caribbean markets, based in Jamaica;
   (*b*) the Far East markets, based in Hong Kong.

What kind of persons would you appoint; what special qualities should they possess? (*Institute of Export, May 1977*)

2. "There are many companies where almost the entire export effort revolves around one man (including a number exporting from 50 per cent to 80 per cent of their production)." How would you decide on the number of export salesmen you needed?

3. "Companies organise their selling operations for exports in an entirely different manner from that in the home market. Thus one export sales specialist can 'look after' ten or more countries. This approach would be regarded as monstrously inefficient in the home market." How would you deploy an existing force of export salesmen? In what ways, if any, would your approach differ from that adopted in the home market?

4. "Some companies are trying to find a satisfactory alternative (to agents) by engaging salesmen from among the nationals of the country in which they plan further expansion. This system seems to be working well" (Betro report). Under what circumstances would you consider this alternative?

Chapter XVIII

1. Market research indicates a good potential for your products (dyestuffs and chemicals for industrial use) in West Germany, and you decide to appoint an agent. How would you set about seeking a suitable agency? Bearing in mind that West Germany is one of the world's leading suppliers of the products in question, you anticipate some initial difficulty in convincing prospective agents that the market research findings are not over-optimistic. Apart

from justifying the research project itself, how would you set about interesting local agencies in your company?

2. "The only way to select an agent is to talk to his customers and then to him. Everything else is a waste of time." Discuss.

3. "Agency agreements are legal gobbledygook. They serve no practical marketing purpose whatever. Few people read them, and fewer still understand them." Refute this statement, indicating the value of a well-thought-out agency agreement from a *marketing* viewpoint.

4. You are about to meet a prospective agent, whose services you are most interested in securing, in order to discuss the outline of the agency agreement. Note down the major headings you would wish to discuss. (The product is special steels of high quality and value, and there is no question of holding stocks in the market.)

5. A company marketing a range of electric welding equipment uses agents to sell its products in various countries in Asia, Africa and South America. Results have been disappointing and the new international marketing manager believes it is because the agents all sell other products.

How could he confirm whether this view is correct and, if it proves to be so, how might he be able to motivate the agents to be more effective? (*Institute of Marketing, November 1977*)

6. "Finally, what of the future? Is the agent still the best solution for most exporting companies? The practical answer must be a qualified 'yes' (the theoretical answer might well be an emphatic 'no')" (Betro report, *Concentration on Key Markets*). Why do you think the writer is tempted to give an emphatic "no"? And what practical considerations might have led him to suggest instead a qualified "yes"?

Chapter XIX

1. "However the export department is organised, it must be a marketing, not merely a sales, organisation." What do you understand by this statement? What characteristics, in terms of organisation structure, would distinguish the marketing organisation from the sales organisation?

2. "The functionally organised international division is probably the best organisational approach for a company that has just moved into limited manufacturing overseas." Discuss.

3. "Organisation is only a means to an end, it does not constitute an end in itself." What do you consider are the ends that

APPENDIXES

should be furthered in the organisation of a multinational company?

4. The organisation structure of many industrial-goods companies shows international decentralisation primarily on a product basis, while consumer-goods companies tend to decentralise primarily on a regional basis. Why should this be so?

5. A company with many products and many overseas markets has the options of organising its overseas marketing division by geographical area or by product groups. Discuss the pros and cons of each method. (*C.A.M. Foundation, May 1974*)

Chapter XX

1. "Brazil is not a market for the consumer goods exporter, and is not likely to become one in the near future." Why not?

2. "Half-hearted entry into Brazil is doomed to failure. Quick killings are a thing of the past and success is a medium to long-term haul." Discuss.

3. "Nine out of ten of *Fortune's* top 50 companies have invested in Brazil." What do you think induced them to do so?

Chapter XXI

1. Some companies appear to have special difficulty in marketing their products in Japan. Suggest reasons for this problem. (*Institute of Marketing, June 1977*)

2. "Although a variety of importing methods exist side by side in Japan, overshadowing all others is the pervasive influence of the ubiquitous Japanese trading company."

(*a*) Outline the activities of these trading companies.

(*b*) Describe briefly the alternative "importing methods" available.

3. The Japanese retail distribution system has been described as "complex, somewhat archaic in foreigners' eyes, but showing signs of adapting to modern trends". Give a brief account of this system and say how far you would agree with the description quoted.

Chapter XXII

1. What would you expect to be the main special features involved in marketing capital equipment to fast-developing oil-rich countries, such as Iran and Nigeria, from a base in Europe or N. America? (*Institute of Marketing, November 1976*)

2. You have agreed to appoint I. Yoruba as your sole distributor in Nigeria. What essential points would you include in the

agency agreement you draw up for him to sign? (*Institute of Export, May 1975*)

3. Your products, previously exported in quantity to Nigeria, have just been placed on the list of prohibited imports. Your agent, a small local company, has written to your board to suggest a joint manufacturing venture. Advise the board as to the special problems and opportunities for joint ventures in Nigeria in this particular marketing situation.

Chapter XXIII

1. "Too often selling into the U.S. market is centred on one person, without even an office in the market place. U.S. customers don't like that . . . they like to see some sort of operation." What sort of distribution operations might be practicable in the U.S.A.?

2. What special local considerations would you take into account in establishing an assembly or manufacturing operation in the U.S.A.?

3. "The U.S.A. must be regarded as one of the world's most open markets. It offers few of the restrictions found in so many other markets overseas." Justify this statement, comparing the U.S.A. with one other more restrictive market with which you are acquainted. Can you think of any exceptions to the statement?

Chapter XXIV

1. What are the trading policies of the Soviet Union? How do these influence British trade with that country? At the practical level, what obstacles exist and how can they be overcome? (*Institute of Export, May 1975*)

2. Explain what is meant by selling "know-how" and show how you would attempt to do this in one of the Eastern European countries. (*Institute of Export, May 1975*)

3. What are the key factors involved in trading with the "Eastern bloc" countries in Europe? (*Institute of Marketing, November 1976*)

Chapter XXV

1. The West German market has one of the world's highest per capita incomes, no tariff problems for the U.K. exporter, and very few restrictions of any kind. Yet it has been officially described as "a very difficult market". Why is it difficult?

2. What are the most important features of retail distribution in West Germany? How might they affect an exporter's marketing approach?

3. You have decided to set up a manufacturing subsidiary in West Germany. What factors would you take into account in relation to the legal formation of the company and the location of the plant?

Index

Advertising, 1, 2, 32, 47, 92, 94, 102, 109, 120, 129, 133, 147, 149, 152, 158–9
  agent, 120, 122, 127, 149, 192
  media, 120, 122–3, 126, 129, 134, 192
  international, 46, 123, 125
  spillover, 46, 123
  message, 120, 123–5
  standardisation, 121–2
  U.S.S.R., 192–3
Advertising Publications Inc., 22
Africa, 30, 59, 64, 112
Agency, agent, 49, 50, 52, 54, 66, 74, 91, 103, 138–9, 140, 160, 162
  agreement, 150–4
  Brazil, 171
  commission, 64, 195
  del credere, 65
  Japan, 178, 180
  Nigeria, 182
  motivation, 154–5
  search, 131, 146–9
  selection, 149–50
  stocking, 64
  U.S.A., 186–7
  U.S.S.R., 191
  W. Germany, 195–6
  (*See also* stockist, distributor)
American Marketing Association, 30
Anglo-Venezuelan Chamber of Commerce, 148
Asia, 30, 63
Assembly (of components) abroad, 17, 51, 70, 79, 85
Atlas Copco, 61
Au Printemps, 63
Australasia, 167
Australia, 30, 64, 84, 135
Austria, 75, 76
Avis Rent-a-Car, 122
Ayer, N. W., 22

Bahamas, 84
Bangladesh, 110
Bank of Brazil, 170
Barter trading, 3, 56, 110–13
Betro, 12, 99, 140
B.I.C.C., 61
Boeing, 112
Branch office, 50, 54, 66, 67–9, 138, 144
  Japan, 178
  Nigeria, 183
  U.S.A., 187
  W. Germany, 196
Brand name, 33, 44–6, 72 (*See also* trade mark)
Brazil, 2, 84, 169–74, 199–204
Brazilian Central Bank, 171
British Export Marketing Centre, 131

British Overseas Trade Board, 22, 30–1, 134, 147, 151, 180, 185–90
British Soviet Chamber of Commerce, 190
Broom and Wade, 214
Brussels Nomenclature, 186
B.S.R., 176
Bulgaria, 110, 189
Bureau of the Budget, 22
Bureau of the Census, 22
Buy American Act, 186
Buy-back contract, 110–11, 113
Buying/indent house, 54–5, 57, 183
Buying offices (in U.K.), 50, 59, 62, 175, 186

Cadbury-Schweppes, 110
Canada, 125, 135–6, 205–13
Central Office of Information, 134–5
Channels of distribution, 47, 54, 56, 146, 159, 164, 176
  between nations, 48–52
  design, 48, 52–3, 90–4
  management, 48, 52–3, 67, 94–5
  within nations, 48, 52–3
Chile, 2
City Business Library, 20
Clearing arrangements, 110, 111
Coca-Cola, 12
Colombia, 45, 125
Combination export manager, 57
Comecon, 56, 194
Commonwealth, 181
Communications (linguistic), 26–8, 179
Communications (marketing), 34, 37, 120–55
(*See also* advertising personal selling, promotion, public relations, publicity, sales promotion)
Communications (organisational), 87, 94, 106, 154–5, 165
Compagnie Française de l'Afrique Occidentale, 63
CompAir Ltd., 214–28
Compensation trading, 110, 190, 192
Competitor-oriented pricing, 97
Complementary marketing, 60
Concentrated marketing, 11–13, 16
Confirming house, 54–5, 57, 183
Congressional Information Service, 22
Consignment stocks, 150, 152–3
Consortia, 60–1
Contract manufacture, 40, 51, 70, 76–7, 85
Contra-trading, 110
Co-operative exporting, 50, 60
Cost-oriented pricing, 97
Crown Agents, 182
Cuba, 189
Customs Co-operation Council Nomenclature, 186
Customs Policy Council, 173

249

INDEX

Czechoslovakia, 75, 189

DATAR, 83
Demand-oriented pricing, 97
Denmark, 63
Department of Industry, 20, 21
Department of Trade, 17, 20, 21, 42, 131
Department stores, 59, 62, 175–77, 186, 195
Devaluation, 73, 80, 108–9, 118, 141
Differential pricing, 100
Differentiated marketing, 11–13, 16
Direct export, 48–9, 50, 58, 62–9
Direct mail, 62, 132, 193
Direct sales to customer, 50, 62–3
Distribution, 1, 8, 47–95, 158, 169, 176–7, 180, 205–13
(*See also* channels of distribution)
Distributor, 43, 49, 50, 60, 64, 66–7, 68, 92, 103, 109, 123, 127, 131, 178, 186–7, 195
Dumping, 106, 107–8
Duty, 10, 71, 85, 102, 103, 118, 119, 169, 182

Early cash recovery pricing, 99
East Asiatic Company, 63–4
East European Trade Council, 190
East Germany, 111, 189
Economic Community of West African States, 184
Ecuador, 21
Editôra de Guias, 199–204
Egypt, 91
Emcol International, 38
Employment Conditions Abroad Ltd., 142
England, 194
Ernest Bradford, 30
Esso (Exxon), 35, 121, 124
Europe (East), 23, 107, 110, 112, 113, 130
Europe (West), 27, 63, 122, 167, 169
European Community, 84, 116, 117, 138, 165, 194, 196, 197, 198
Exchange,
 control, 94, 141
 forward cover, 104–5
 rate of, 10, 94, 108, 112
 risk, 80
Exhibition, 129, 130–3
 U.S.S.R., 191–2
 W. Germany, 197–8
Export Credits Guarantee Department, 80, 82, 83, 104, 105, 113
Export department, 157–9, 161
Export house, 50, 54–9, 151, 175, 178, 191
(*See also* confirming house, buying/indent house, manufacturer's agent, merchant, specialist export manager)
Export Intelligence Service, 60
Exports to Japan Unit, 175

Far East, 41, 167
Federal Republic of Germany, *see* West Germany
Forecasting, 7, 9
Foreign currency pricing, 104–5
Foreign Investment Review Agency, 135
Foreign Trade Corporations, 130, 190, 192
France, 63, 84, 123, 125, 126, 149
Franchising, 40, 51, 70, 74–5

Free trade area, port, zone, 84, 85, 171, 187, 194

Gallup International, 19
General Agreement on Tariffs and Trade, 107–8
General Electric Company Switchgear, 61
General Motors, 111
German Democratic Republic, *see* East Germany
Ghana, 115
Government Printing Office, 22
Greece, 111
Groupement d'Achats des Grands Magasins Indépendants, 63

Herbert Morris, 61
Hertie, 59
Hilton Hotels, 36, 77
Holman Bros., 214
Hugh Smith, 61
Hungary, 75, 189

Ikarus, 75
Indent house, *see* buying/indent house
India, 24, 25, 45, 91
Indirect export, 4, 11, 48–9, 50, 54–61
Indonesia, 124
Industrial co-operation agreement, 51, 70, 75–6, 191
Industrial Development (Income Tax) Decree, 183
Institute of Marketing, 1
Interministerial Price Commission, 173–4
International Convention for the Protection of Industrial Property, 191
International division, 157, 159–61, 163
International marketing,
 concept, 1–6
 decision, 7–11
 definition, 3
 principles, 1–167
International trading companies, 50, 58, 63–4, 176, 178, 180, 182
International Union of Commercial Agents and Brokers, 148–9
Investment incentives, 81, 84, 88
 Brazil, 172, 173
 France, 83
 Nigeria, 183
 U.S.A., 188
 W. Germany, 197
Italy, 92, 124
Itoh, C., 178

Japan, 30, 56, 59, 92, 175–80
Japan External Trade Organisation, 175
Johnnie Walker, 45
Joint ventures, 3, 27, 63, 79, 86, 127, 161
 Brazil, 172
 Japan, 179
 Nigeria, 183–4
 U.S.S.R., 191
(*See also* assembly abroad, contract manufacture, franchising, industrial co-operation agreement, licensing, management contract, manufacture abroad)

INDEX

Karstadt, 59
Kline, C. H., 22
Kodak, 36, 42

Labelling, 33, 34, 42
Letraset, 53, 65, 205–13
Licence, licensing, 3, 17, 32, 40, 49, 51, 52, 70–4, 75, 86, 123, 159, 160, 162–3
  Brazil, 171–2
  Japan, 179
  royalties, 72, 73, 172, 179
  U.S.S.R., 191
Litsenzintorg, 191
London Chamber of Commerce and Industry, 148, 190

Madrid Convention, 45
Mail order, 62, 195
Management contract(ing), 40, 51, 70, 77, 87
Manufacture (manufacturing investment) abroad, 3, 4, 10, 17, 49, 51, 52, 67, 70, 72, 76
  acquisition, 79, 88
  Brazil, 172
  investment decision, 79–84
  Japan, 179
  joint venture manufacture, 79, 86–88
  Nigeria, 183
  plant location, 79
  third-country, 5, 51, 83
  U.S.A., 187
  U.S.S.R., 191
  W. Germany, 197
(*See also* assembly abroad)
Manufacturers' agent, 54, 55, 57
Manufrance, 63
Marginal-cost pricing, 10, 105–7
Market entry decision, 8, 18
Market Entry Guarantee Scheme, 31
Market penetration pricing, 98
Market research, 7, 8, 9, 14, 15–32, 139, 154, 158, 175, 181, 185, 190, 193
  agencies, 26–30, 175
  bibliographical, 15
  consumer, 15, 19, 24, 26, 28, 191, 196
  desk, 15–18, 20–3, 190
  field, 15–16, 18, 19, 20, 23–6
  industrial, 15, 21, 24–5, 28, 192
  interviewing, 24–6
  motivation, 26
  omnibus, 18, 19
  original, 15, 17
  primary, 15
  questionnaire, 24
  sampling, 24, 25
  secondary, 15, 23
  telephone, 24
Market Research Society, 19, 30
Market selection, 7–8, 11–14
Market size assessment, 17
Market-skimming pricing, 98
Marketing, definition, 1
Marketing channel, *see* channels of distribution
Marketing mix, 1, 2, 12, 33
  decision, 7–8, 33–155
Marketing office, *see* representative office
Martinique, 84
Marubeni, 178

Matrix organisation, 166
McGraw-Hill, 22
Media, *see* advertising
Merchant, 31, 49, 54–7, 58, 60, 65, 111, 113, 196
Mexico, 135
Middle East, 25, 61, 123, 143
Middle East Market Research Bureau, 19
Ministry of Economics, 196
Ministry of Internal Affairs, 183
Mitsubishi, 178
Mitsui, 178
Mongolia, 189
Monopoly, 10, 115–16
Monoprix, 63
Moscow Narodny Bank, 190
Multinational company, 4, 5–6, 36, 38, 40, 115
  organisation structures, 157, 161–7

National Institute for Industrial Property, 171
Nestlé, 36
Netherlands, 63
Nigeria, 39, 86, 181–4
Nigeria National Supply Company, 182
Nigerian Immigration Act, 183
North America, 27, 64, 205–13
Norway, 92, 115
Nouvelles Galéries, 63

Organisation decision, 8
Organisation of Petroleum Exporting Countries, 61, 112
Organisation structures, 156–67
Österreichische Stickstoffwerke, 75

P.A. International Management Consultants Ltd., 143
Packaging, 1, 33, 34, 41–2
Pakistan, 110
Paris France, 63
Parunis, 63
Patent, 32, 70, 72, 73, 76, 81, 87, 172
Patent Office, 171
Pechiney, 45
Pechiney Ugine Kuhlmann, 45
Pepsi-Cola, 75
Personal selling, 1, 47, 92, 120, 129, 138
(*See also* sales force)
Piggy-back exporting, 60
Poland, 111, 189
Potomac Books, 22
Predicasts, 22
Pricing policy, 1, 2, 8, 47, 136
  control, 3, 81, 115–17, 173
  export pricing, 102–13
  foreign-market decisions, 115–19
  objectives, 98–9
  orientation, 97
Prisunic, 63
Product life cycle, 9, 10, 40
Product policy, 1, 2, 8, 33–4, 121
  elimination, 33, 34, 39–40
  modification, 33, 34–7, 38, 43, 85
  new-product development, 33, 34, 38–9, 71
(*See also* labelling, packaging, servicing, trade mark)

INDEX

Promotion, 1, 2, 8, 33, 164, 192
(*See also* advertising, public relations, publicity, personal selling, sales promotion)
Prototype advertising campaign, 123
Public relations, 1, 120, 129, 133, 134–6
Publicity, 32, 94, 102, 131, 132, 133, 159, 160
(*See also* advertising, public relations)
Puerto Rico, 84, 187

Quelle, 200

Radio Luxembourg, 125
Reciprocal trading, 110
Representative office, 183–4, 196
(*See also* branch office, subsidiary company abroad)
Research Services Ltd., 19
Restrictive trade practices, 81, 115
Royal Dutch Shell, 6
Rumania, 111, 189

Sales force, 48, 74, 102, 138–40, 144–5, 199–204
(*See also* personal selling)
Sales management, 138–45
Sales promotion, 1, 32, 47, 120, 129–34
Satisfactory rate of return pricing, 99
Saurer, 75
Segmentation, 11–12, 13
Selling, *see* personal selling
Service, servicing, 33, 42–4, 65, 67, 68, 92, 104, 146, 149, 151, 152
Singer Sewing Machine Company, 60
Slovnaft, 75
South America, 64, 169
Specialist export manager, 54, 55, 57–8
Standard Rate and Data Service, 22
Standardisation,
  communications, 34, 46, 121–3, 124, 164
  media, 125
  packaging, 41
  price, 99
  product, 34, 36, 40
State trading organisation, *see* Foreign Trade Corporations
Statistics and Market Intelligence Library, 20
Stockist, 54, 64, 66
(*See also* distributor, agent)
Store promotion, 129, 133–4
Subsidiary company abroad, 50, 68–9, 123, 127, 135, 138, 144
  Brazil, 172
  Japan, 179
  Nigeria, 183
  U.S.A., 187
  U.S.S.R., 191
  W. Germany, 197
Sumitomo, 178
Survey Research Group, 19
Switch dealing, 111
Switzerland, 63, 127

Tax, taxation, 10, 37, 82, 83, 84, 103, 118, 119
  agency agreement, 151, 153, 171
  branches and subsidiaries, 67, 68, 69, 178, 188, 196
  Brazil, 171, 172, 173
  double, 81
  Japan, 178–9
  media, 126
  turnover, sales, value-added, 10, 23, 103, 126, 194
  U.S.A., 188
  W. Germany, 194, 196
  withholding, 73, 172, 173, 179
Technical Help to Exporters, 17
Télé Monte Carlo, 125
Thailand, 124
Trade fair, *see* exhibition
Trade mark, 32, 33, 70, 72, 73, 87
  definition, 44
  imitation, 44, 45
  piracy, 44, 45
  protection, 44, 73, 81
  registration, 44, 45, 46
(*See also* brand name)
Trading companies, *see* international trading companies
Transfer pricing, 87, 117–19
Translation, 24, 123–5, 152
Transnational company, 6
Treaty of Rome, 100, 117, 196
Tupperware Home Products, 92
Turkey, 91

U.A.C. International, 59
Ugine Kuhlmann, 45
Undifferentiated marketing, 11–13, 16
Unilever, 6
Uniprix, 63
Union of Soviet Socialist Republics, 3, 111, 169, 189–90
United Kingdom, 3, 4, 17, 20–1, 23, 25, 27–31, 54–5, 57, 59–60, 63, 64, 65, 67, 82, 84, 87, 99, 107, 108, 109, 113, 125, 126, 130, 134, 135, 140–3, 147, 148, 151, 154, 171–2, 175, 181, 185, 187, 189–92, 194, 197
United Nations, 21
United States of America, 3, 21, 22, 23, 24, 35, 45, 57, 60, 84, 92, 99, 107, 116, 122, 124, 125, 167, 185–88, 205–13
U.S. Department of Commerce, 20, 60, 185
U.S. Embassy, 20

Venezuela, 42, 91, 125
Vneshtorgreklama, 192

Weir, 61
West Germany, 35, 59, 63, 95, 123, 129, 194–8, 214–28
Whole-channel concept, 52–3
Wilkinson Sword, 111

Yugoslavia, 189

M&E Handbooks

Law

'A' Level Law/B Jones
Basic Law/L B Curzon
Company Law/M C Oliver, E Marshall
Constitutional and Administrative Law/I N Stevens
Consumer Law/M J Leder
Conveyancing Law/P H Kenny, C Bevan
Criminal Law/L B Curzon
Employment Law/C J Carr, P J Kay
Family Law/P J Pace
General Principles of English Law/P W D Redmond,
    I N Stevens, P Shears
Introduction to Business Law/P W D Redmond, R G Lawson
Jurisprudence/L B Curzon
Land Law/L B Curzon
Landlord and Tenant/J M Male, J Cotter
Law of Banking/D Palfreman
Law of Contract/W T Major
Law of Evidence/L B Curzon
Law of Torts/G M Tyas, A Pannett, C Willett
Meetings: Their Law and Practice/L Hall, P Lawton, E Rigby

Business and Management

Advertising/F Jefkins
Basic Economics/G L Thirkettle
Basic of Business/D Lewis
Business and Financial Management/B K R Watts
Business Mathematics/L W T Stafford
Business Systems/R G Anderson
Data Processing Vol 1: Principles and Practice/R G Anderson
Data Processing Vol 2: Information Systems and Technology/R G Anderson
Human Resources Management/H T Graham, R Bennett
International Marketing/L S Walsh
Managerial Economics/J R Davies, S Hughes
Marketing/G B Giles
Marketing Overseas/A West
Modern Commercial Knowledge/L W T Stafford
Modern Marketing/F Jefkins
Office Administration/J C Denyer, A L Mugridge
Operational Research/W M Harper, H C Lim
Production Management/H A Harding
Public Administration/M Barber, R Stacey
Public Relations/F Jefkins
Purchasing/C K Lysons
Retail Management/R Cox, P Brittain
Selling: Management and Practice/P Allen
Statistics/W M Harper
Stores Management/R J Carter

Accounting and Finance

Auditing/L R Howard
Basic Accounting/J O Magee
Basic Book-keeping/J O Magee
Company Accounts/J O Magee
Company Secretarial Practice/L Hall, G M Thom
Cost Accounting/W M Harper
Elements of Banking/D P Whiting
Elements of Insurance/D S Hansell
Finance of Foreign Trade/D P Whiting
Investment: A Practical Approach/D Kerridge
Investment Appraisal/G Mott
Management Accounting/W M Harper
Practice of Banking/E P Doyle, J E Kelly
Principles of Accounts/E F Castle, N P Owens

Humanities and Science

European History 1789–1914/C A Leeds
Land Surveying/R J P Wilson
World History: 1900 to the Present Day/C A Leeds